Cosmic

Lovers

10% of Authors' Royalties goes to The Living Tree Educational
Foundation for its Tree Planting Programme.

Our soul mate is our friend, student and teacher,
our day-to-day partner who dances us
deeper into our essence

– Gabrielle Roth, *Maps to Ecstasy*

Readers' Comments

♥

"Love permeates throughout this story. It celebrates its very
existence. The reader will be absorbed by the sensuality and
openness of these lovers and possibly quite turned on! And yet ... it
goes beyond our base human desire and takes the reader into the
spiritual realm of sexual bliss."   – *Paula McLinchey, Ireland.*

"Cosmic Lovers provides clear signposts to a happy and fulfilling
relationship."   – *Bernard Bossonet, Ireland.*

"I was reading Cosmic Lovers 'out loud' to my partner this
weekend – not all of it in one go, mind. We both found it so
reflective, honest, erotic, meditative, inspirational, colourful and so
many more things ..."   – *Sheila Crowley, London.*

"Cosmic Lovers is an absolute winner ... by two special beings, Elly
and Roderic, kindred souls who will do much to effect beautiful
change in the world."   – *Signe Quinn Taff, Arizona, USA.*

"You get a lot of wisdom in a very entertaining way."
                                            – *Sheila Kern, Paris, France.*

"A uniquely inspiring and refreshing book which provides
privileged insights into the workings of an extraordinary love and
companionship. I enjoyed every word of it and never wanted it to
end.   – *Charlotte Cargin, Ireland.*

"For us, Elly and Roderic have become a symbol of the spirituality
of Ireland."   – *Aourana Peretrutova, Moscow, Russia.*

"I was entranced, entertained and educated on every page. What an honour to be 'a fly on the wall' witnessing this utterly unique dance of intimacy, freedom, creativity, honesty, pain, joy and much more besides, spiral into a sensuous blending of the ordinary with the extraordinary, the mundane with the mystical, the irreverent with the sacred! … This is a 'must read' for anyone aspiring to a higher, more meaningful relationship. A bound-to-be modern classic."
– Ann Clare McCarthy, Ireland.

"Thank you Elly and Roderic for being such great conduits of the bounty of Creation." *– Omalara Ewuosho, Nigeria.*

"Could this be the idea that your heart and soul have been awaiting? Roderic and Elly bravely reveal through their own lives and creative spiritual endeavour a revival of the ancient Celtic Marriage tradition, balancing near-perfectly the individual needs of freedom, commitment, permanence and flexibility …
A thrilling and uplifting example and alternative for us all."
– Roger Foxall, Spain.

"Thank you Elly and Roderic for introducing us to a wonderful way of living together. A Celtic marriage is a wonderful recipe for a successful relationship in the 21st Century. Everyone should know about it!" *– Anke & Stewart, Australia.*

"If ever there was a pair to show the world that true love exists, that pair is Elly and Roderic." *– Harper Stone, Colorado, USA*

A CIP catalogue for this book is available from the National Library, Ireland, and the British Library.

ISBN: 978-0-9561042-0-5
1. Love Story. 2. Soul Mates. 3. Celtic Marriage. 4. Spiritual Partnership.

Cover design by Harper Stone.

Published by:
Earth Cosmos Press, Ireland.
www.EarthCosmosPress.org

Contacting the Authors:
ellyandroderic@cosmic-lovers.org

Invitations to Readers:
See page 267

Cosmic Lovers

A Woman's Quest
for the Ideal Relationship

ELLY VAN VEEN &
RODERIC KNOWLES

Earth Cosmos Press

Dedicated to all Lovers

Contents

Chapter 1

Cosmic
Dating Service

Elly

One sunny afternoon, I was sitting under a tree in my favourite wood in Warmond, Holland, reading a book on soul mates and how to meet one.

"All one has to do is ask the Universe," it said.

"Amazing!" I thought.

I lay back against the tree, an old sequoia, and gazed out across the canal and meadows. Ducks, swans and waterfowl glided by. Swans, they had found *their* life-long mates and seemed to be happy. Cows grazed. They shared one randy bull. Not for me!

The sails of a windmill turned gently on the horizon.

Ask the Universe? Could it really be that simple? I wondered. The only way to find out was to try.

I yearned for a companion, a lover with whom I could share intimately and deeply, and lay there dreaming of the ideal man walking into my life.

I dreamed and yes the dream could be real; but who was the ideal man for me?

The day was changing into evening. All was becoming still.

I stretched my body like the trees around me, breathing in the sweet smell of pine. I heard the tapping of a woodpecker and followed the flight of a bumblebee. I felt refreshed and elated. Nature is so healing and inspiring. I sat, visualizing my lover, picked up my diary and drew a picture of him.

He was tall, agile, with wild jumping hair. He had sensual lips and beautiful eyes, blue-grey. I drew big feet, symbolising his thorough down-to-earthness. I didn't want a wishy-washy!

1

I imagined him soft to touch, as someone who likes to cuddle and be cuddled. He loves dancing, freely, intuitively; and enjoys sex, desiring like me to reach new peaks of ecstasy in the tantric and transcendental. Mmmh! I was really beginning to get into this.

As the author suggested, I made a list of my requirements, doing so on four levels, physical, emotional, mental and spiritual, for a relationship must work on all of these. Having visualized his physical attributes, I lay back and imagined the other aspects:

Emotionally, he is able to show and share his feelings openly and honestly, willing to be vulnerable rather than defensive. I don't want someone who claims ownership of me or is emotionally dependent or manipulative. While I'm open to supporting him lovingly, I'm not willing to be the object of projections, and certainly not a mother substitute. He's light-hearted, warm and loving, someone with whom I'd feel safe to share my innermost self.

What about his mind? Intelligent, lively, open, flexible, one of life's explorers. Not always talking on the purely mental level, which I find boring, he communicates from his heart and soul, focused on the essence and truth of life.

Chapel bells rang, chanting through the wood. Perhaps they were agreeing with me?

On the spiritual level? He must be awake on this, in touch with his higher self, living with it as an everyday reality. I'm tired of dragging my boyfriends into their spiritual awakening. He's beyond all religions, not locked into the dogmas of any, with a broad view of existence, accepting the immortality of the soul and therefore the reality of past and future lives. He's a seeker of truth, committed to his inner growth while supporting me in mine. Ideally he's more enlightened than I, so I can learn from him. He inspires and challenges me. He takes me deeper into understandings of the mysteries of life. Yes, that's what I really want, a lover wisdom-teacher. I see us meditating together, surrounded by Beings of Light.

What else? This is fun!

He is serious but has a good sense of humour. He's able to go with the flow and walks his talk. As a Reiki Master*, kinesiologist**, and working with flower essences, I would love to share life with

2

someone who is also interested in vibrational healing. And maybe we'll have a child together. But as I am in my late thirties, that might be asking too much.

These were my specifications. In putting out my request to the Universe, I was serious but also laughing at myself for dreaming of my White Prince to appear. Perhaps I was being ridiculous?

* Reiki is a hands-on healing art originating in Japan, which involves the channelling of life-force energy.

** A kinesiologist tests muscles for weaknesses that indicate energy blockages in the body, and uses techniques that clear these, relieve tensions, and otherwise permit life-force energies to flow in their natural manner.

Roderic

Based in the wilds of the west coast of Ireland with many a worldly adventure behind me, I lived a primitive but blissful life close to Nature, cultivating my garden, metaphorically and literally.

I had been celibate for close to four years. Being far from the main streams of human civilisation, the possibility of an intimate relationship had not presented itself, at least not one meeting my requirements. With many interests I was passionately absorbed, so this hadn't bothered me. I was also writing and my rhythms in this were not at all relationship-friendly, since I often rose at three in the morning or worked into the night. I treasured my freedom and these hours of uninterrupted flow and creativity, which I doubted another would be willing to accept. So, I'd been closed to the idea of an intimate relationship, which was one good reason why one hadn't happened.

There were others. Over the years, I had been carrying in my depths an unresolved yearning which, while largely unconscious, had been moving me beyond more obvious desires, colouring them greatly. It was for no less than the ultimate: Union with the Divine and Eternal Feminine. I had been projecting this outwards onto various earthly females, thus heaping great expectations upon them in search of the essentially unachievable. On rapturously aspiring flights of love, fantasy creations of my own imagination, I had become like Icarus, believing he could reach the sun, failing of course, ever singeing his homemade wings and landing on the rocks. Evidently, there was something fundamental I had been failing to grasp. I had resolved to fathom what this impulse was and, thereby, what I was really seeking.

Deep down I knew it was nothing on the outside, not even the most beautiful goddess on earth. Rather it was this: My 'I' at the level of ordinary consciousness, being but an aspect of my larger Self, yearned for union with its heavenly counterpart, the feminine *anima*, my own soul, a sleeping princess who was beginning to awaken. It is union with the Eternal Feminine *within* that represents man's deepest longing, the mystical union, the alchemical marriage, subliminal subject of all Grail quests. So I had cut myself off from seeking in the world the one great love that would substitute for this, no longer looking for another to complete me or fill emptiness. I needed more time to integrate these realizations before entering another relationship, I felt.

Elly

Yes, I declared, lying under my sequoia, I feel ready for my next lover.

I also feel ready for a new way of relating. Relationships todate have got me nowhere, bringing me neither the love nor fulfilment I've been seeking, though I've learned a lot along the way.

Previous lovers flashed through my mind. I remembered when 'the man of my dreams' had walked into my life. His brown eyes, curly hair and soft southern accent had melted me every time I'd thought of him. I had never fallen so much in love, nor been so hurt and angry, particularly as he'd been playing a game of 'push and pull' for which I had no answer. Not only had he broken my heart, but shattered my dreams and illusions. "What is a relationship all about," I'd wondered, "if it doesn't work with the man of your dreams?"

Later, much later, I was grateful for the separation, for I would have given my life trying to please him, rather than honouring my own. It had been a wake-up call. I had to learn to set my boundaries, speak my truth, and be the centre of my life.

I thought of Jonathan whom I'd met in Australia, with his sensual body and way of laughing, his sense of freedom and the beauty of his face. He'd recently sent me a package of jasmine tea, fresh honeysuckle and a CD of Nat King Cole, which gave me butterflies in my stomach. Was he just a holiday romance or could he be more? He had kindled in me a thirst for adventure. But would he ever want to make a commitment, being the free spirit he was?

Aside from the occasional part-time relationship, I had been living on my own for almost ten years, spending my time exploring, healing and strengthening my inner life, so I'd never lose myself in one again. What I want now is a relationship that honours, nourishes and supports me, which liberates and empowers me; above all, one that includes the spiritual dimension, acknowledging soul not only as a concept but an everyday reality.

Now that I'm clear what I really want, I am ready to fly with the lover of my dreams into the magic of love and life. But shall I ever get what I desire? Or do I need to compromise?

Roderic

Even in my most ascetic moments, I have never ceased to be intrigued by Woman. I'm easily seduced by her beauty and mysteries. I'm in love with love, have dreams of love, and was born to be a lover. Mystic, fool, or whatever else I may be, I'll never be other than a sensual animal and incurably romantic. A being of many parts am "I", with body, mind, spirit, soul, each with needs and pleasures of their own, living a life of unresolved paradoxes.

Which brings me to the sexual! Even in my most ascetic moments, I have always been conscious of this dimension as an integral aspect of life's wholeness. One of life's primary energies, no other is so potent. What I find amazing is how little it's understood, almost not at all in religious circles, nor even in a purely evolutionary context. What *is* its nature? Why the surplus way beyond what is required for procreation? What are its purposes? I had been pondering on its mysteries for years. Clearly we cannot deny any aspect of our wholeness without serious repercussions. Our churches' views and teachings on the subject, resulting in ludicrous self-denial, have impacted disastrously on our civilization, "restricting the entire psycho-emotional system of the human being," to quote Jean Markale in his *Women of the Celts*.

Yet, if the energy of sex is not to be condemned and suppressed, how, ideally, is it to be expressed? Not outwardly, say the wise, but inwardly, for not only is it the energy of ecstasy but of transformation and creativity. Rather than being released wastefully, it can be retained and consciously directed within one's system. I had been studying the teachings and methods of the Taoist masters, Mantak and Maneewan Chia. Writing on the flow and control of sexual energy within an individual and between couples, they show how two may come together, love and share more consciously and pleasurably in their unions with the maximum of physiological and spiritual advantages. But theoretical study was not enough. I felt the growing desire for a partner with whom to practise. A teacher was what I needed. A lover-teacher she would need to be. The very best! I dreamed the ideal, a tantric priestess!

I was, I realized, ready for a relationship.

Elly

I returned to the thought: Am I being ridiculous in expecting the Universe to fulfil my dreams? To be my Cosmic Dating Service? By what magic?

While travelling in Australia the previous summer, in 1996, I had discovered a clear connection between my thoughts and the fulfilment of them. I had observed that if I simply asked for a bar of soap, a lift to a certain place, or to be invited to a party, my needs were met almost immediately. That's how Jonathan came into my life. I had arrived in Broom on a Thursday night and had to wait until Monday morning before starting a ten-day camping tour through the Kimberley to Darwin. Meanwile I had wanted a fun weekend and to meet someone special, in fact a lover. So, I'd asked the Universe. The following morning, I walked into town wearing the only skirt I'd brought, which flowed in the breeze, making me feel sensual. Wandering around, I turned up an alley drawn by the sound of Egyptian music and almost stumbled into a sun-bronzed Apollo seated by a market stall. I could hardly breathe as every cell of my body ignited and waves ran up and down my spine. Our eyes met, but I turned away, though I lingered there a while, looking at the handcrafts, beads and jewellery, feeling the penetration of his gaze. "Is that lapis lazuli you're wearing around your neck?" he asked, approaching me. One thing led to another. We drew song-lines to the stars. I had the most erotic days ever.

So, yes, I expected the Universe to respond. Having discovered that it did so in small and inexplicable ways, I could now be more ambitious. No, I wouldn't compromise, but go for my ultimate. I removed all doubt, this being crucial, as it would only be an obstacle; and released my request, as you're supposed to do, trusting it would be met one day. After a few months, I had forgotten all about it.

Roderic

But what kind of a relationship? I wondered. I still had reservations. Conventional ideas of a couple didn't interest me. Boy meets girl, falls in love and settles down? To what? A life of mutual dependency and systematized mundaneness, with mortgages and bank loans? While ideal for some, for me a form of slavery and slow way of dying. After one marriage I had become wiser. After two, more so!

Life is for play, exploration, learning and growth. I'll share it with someone in freedom, not in shackles. But how is this to be achieved? Love can neither be bound by contract nor perpetuated by decree. Nor can it be conditional. Beyond possessing or being possessed, it thrives in freedom or ceases to be. Perhaps a relationship, open and flowing, without any form of commitment? But, without one, what can be achieved?

I'm open to a relationship which, like life itself, is a creative adventure, in which the separate paths of each are honoured, in which freedom and togetherness find harmony and balance, which is growth-based rather than need-based, and whose common purposes include mutual support in the unfolding of the unique potentials of each.

Now fully open, I dreamed of the ideal lover to draw into my life.

Looking for one was a waste of time. It was easier and more effective simply to put out a request to the Universe. "Ask and you shall receive," the Master had said. I took this literally and had had many experiences over the years doing just this, with some quite phenomenal results, which had thoroughly convinced me. Like ordering anything, it's advisable to be specific. Even the colour of the elephant is important or one may get a pink one! The Universe responds to one's clarity or lack of it. So, I specified my requirements, not simply listing but feeling into them:

Closing my eyes, I visualized *her* in the living moment, seated beside me. She sparkles with life, serenely radiating her love and light. There's a smile on her face. She's warm, sensual, playful and responsive. I can feel her energy.

Sex is one of her primary passions. In this, she is uninhibited. While she revels in the sensuality and ecstasies of it, it is also a yoga, a spiritual practice. She has studied this aspect as much as I. Indeed, more so, experientially.

Our energies mingle, interpenetrating in a dance; and merge. I am aroused in every cell of my body. It's as if energetically she is already present.

Kindred spirits, we resonate at the deepest levels. Though, while I am more active mentally, she is more in her feelings, as I need to be. Alive in her body, she loves to dance. We dance, chant and trance. She's a lover of truth, with an exploring and receptive mind. She practises meditation, works with her higher self and is open in principle to realms of the invisible, to other dimensions of reality, as integral aspects of the wholeness of life. Committed to her healing and personal growth, she's familiar with many disciplines. In fact, she's a healer. We complement each other perfectly.

I consider other details. She's a lover of nature, of trees, flowers, herbs, and wild places. Aware and sensitive, she is open to working with angels and devas*. She is also interested in education. She's allowing and non-judgemental, particularly of my foolishness which, she appreciates, is my path to wisdom. Essentially, while loving our togetherness, we respect each other's freedom and need for separateness. Clearly we're on our own individual paths, for which we each take full and sole responsibility, though we support each other. We are souls, each on an ongoing adventure through Time, with many a coming and going on this planet, this one life being but a passing phase. All in all, it's a lively, joyful, creative, healing, abundant and harmonious relationship. I feel all this in the depths of my being and thank the Universe for being so blessed, knowing my request has already been met; and that she is on her way.

Nature spirits.

Chapter 2

How the Universe Responds

Elly
The following summer, I had a call from Jonathan in Bali, who was on his way to England and desired to see me. I was greatly excited. Remembering our erotic weekend in Australia, I longed to be with him again. As I had already decided on a visit to Ireland, I suggested that we meet there. "Okay," he replied, "let's spend a whole month together."

I had been as celibate as a nun lately and was looking forward to a passionate reunion. After booking my flight to Dublin, I went on further flights of imagination: Maybe, if we fell in love, I would join him in Bali and we'd go to other exotic places.

A few days later, he left a message on my answering machine: "I've made a mistake: I only have two weeks to spare." This made me angry. Once again someone had made a promise and was withdrawing. So we had a fight even before we'd met, which almost resulted in his cancelling the trip.

On my arrival in Ireland, everything turned out differently to what I'd expected, disastrously so. While he talked about beautiful women on tropical beaches, we were huddled in a tent in which neither of us could move, pelted by wind and rain, on top of which, he declared himself to be sexually incapacitated, which left me frustrated beyond belief. What's more, the only subject in which he appeared to be interested was his business – in particular, where to find locations for his stall so he could sell his jewellery. With this mission in mind, we traipsed across Ireland from Dublin to Donegal, Galway to Cork, from one city to another, confined in buses. I wondered why we weren't doing what I had imagined, being free, out in the open, in the wild and breathtaking spaces of the Irish countryside. And yet, despite the misery, I still thought him wonderful, was proud to be with him and gazed at him lustily. But I felt terribly alone, lying awake every night, hoping he would touch me. As he never did, I hardly slept a wink. Once again, I'd repeated a pattern, losing my centredness, power and goals, simply in order to make a man happy. That's what I had concluded. The truth was otherwise. This was no unconditional loving on my part, but my way of acquiring what I sought, attention, love and affection at any price – a life strategy not destined to succeed! I learned a good lesson. It made me realize there's nothing in the world for which it's worth giving away your power or freedom, not even to be with the most beautiful man on Earth. I also had to learn to speak and act my truth. Not being interested in big cities, I should have said so. My dreams were shattered.

After the two weeks, which left me exhausted, I retreated to Ballycotton, a picturesque fisherman's haven, where I camped on the cliffs. After days of torrential rain, the sun began to shine. This was the Ireland I was looking for. I now had two weeks on my own with all the freedom I needed.

I decided to call Kristin, a Reiki master from Wales whom I'd met in Germany a few months earlier, who was living close by. She had invited me to stay. We linked up in Cork the following day at a poetry recital where she'd arranged to meet a friend, Roderic.

I had never seen anyone like him. He had an unusual face and looked as if he'd just stepped out of a fairy-tale wood, with wild flowing hair, sparkling eyes, and wrinkled lines criss-crossing mischievously from brow to chin. He had an air of independence, seemed sympathetic and understanding, and radiated warmth. There was something special about his energy.

He had brought two friends with him, a couple from Hawaii on their way around the world, who were madly in love. The flow between them touched me. I had a longing to be in such a relationship. Would it ever happen?

We sat in silence as a female vocalist and a brave stuttering poet gave their performances. During a pause, Roderic asked me what my plans were, looking at me intensely, yet open and relaxed. I wasn't sure. Other than spending the night with Kristin, I wanted to go west. After the recitals – and he'd told me how much he liked my boots! – we parted company. That was it as far as I was concerned, two strangers passing, never really to meet.

Roderic

"What's this?" I wondered, seated beside Elly. Her feet were dancing, with one leg crossing the other, swinging gently to and fro. While a foot rolled in its ankle socket, invisible toes weaved spirals through the air. In fact, her whole body seemed engaged in a dance, constant as in the humming of a chant.

Her hair was short and blonde with a fringe. She had large blue eyes that spoke of openness, radiating both the innocence of a child and wisdom of a woman. When she laughed it was like a naughty monkey. Mmmh! – I liked her pouting lips. What I would like to have done was communicate my delight in her corporeal exquisiteness inch by inch in a tactile appreciation from her boots up; or, if I were not the primitively sensual animal that I am, a more refined version of this in visuals and verbals, less invasive and more socially acceptable. However, I refrained from any such expressions and let the meeting pass to its inevitable conclusion. With her travelling onwards and I being busy, where could it go? After saying goodbye, I thought no more of her.

Back at home, after a walk on the beach, I resumed my work. Unexpectedly, while sipping a cup of hawthorn blossom tea, I had what could be described as an intuitive flash, though that would not be sufficiently accurate. What I felt in the most vivid way was a line of energy, a living but invisible thread, extending from my being like an umbilical chord out across the countryside at the speed of light, connecting me with this woman I'd only just met. I'd had similar experiences before, linking me to people or places, which I took as the promptings of unseen hands guiding my destiny, since they usually turned out to be of significance; and I always acted on them. But why her? I was surprised. Okay, she was attractive and had aroused me, but my inner guides were hardly concerned with my primal urges, more usefully transformed into creativity. But I'd got the hint and had to make contact.

I'd had a vague plan to drive to Sneem in County Kerry and visit my sister, Coral. Since Elly had mentioned she was heading west, I called her at Kristin's to ask her if she'd like a lift in that direction. She was out, so I left a message.

Elly

When I heard that Roderic had called and offered me a lift, I became quite excited, not because I was so interested in seeing him again, but I had wanted to visit a stone circle and now had transport with a chauffeur and guide. Then Kristin told me he'd be taking me to a lovely place and knew a lot about the healing aspects of trees, plants and flowers. She too was excited for me: "This is perfect," she enthused. "He's your man." I assumed she meant simply for the trip.

When he arrived to collect me, Kristin suggested we each draw from a pack of Insight Cards as a means of acquiring feedback from the Universe, our guides or angels. Remarkably, from a pack of fifty or more, we each picked the same one, signifying 'Relationship'.

On this oracle-note, our journey began. I trembled as I stepped into his little Suzuki, as he had an incense stick burning, and there was a book on my seat, which I had to move, *Trance Dance* by Frank Natale, which had a special significance for me. I had been told recently that one of my purposes in life was to be a trance-dance teacher. Dance was in my bones and yearned for expression. Amazing, I thought, that Roderic was reading this. Another coincidence!

"Bye," said Kristin. "Have a great adventure. You've got the right person for it."

"Yes," he replied with an intriguing smile, "if you like living dangerously."

What he meant, I had no idea, though Kristin had mentioned he had once robbed banks. Could he really have done so? I wondered. While he looked a bit mischievous, he also seemed honest. In any event, I felt I could trust him.

On the way, we stopped at the cottage where he was living, from which I could hear the roaring of waves on nearby rocks and beach. I was enchanted. Inside, it was erotic. His nature artworks hung on the walls. Perfumed candles, arrays of white feathers, tiny shells in miniature glass cases, stones and crystals, holy powder from an ashram in India and other exquisite or sacred items, along with curios such as a glass jar of Sahara sand with a camel-dung dropping, lay displayed on recesses and shelves. In cabinets were books on healing, nature, flower essences, working with angels and devas, and a range of other subjects in which I was interested. Soon, he had the magic flute of Tim Wheater playing, my favourite music for relaxation. Yet another coincidence! What was going on? I wondered.

Handing me a pair of Afghan slipper-socks, he suggested I take off my boots. Had he in mind a creeping, cosy, romantic build-up? I wondered. What would I be asked to remove next? After two weeks of nightmare, the last thing I felt like was being involved again in any kind of an affair. Better to cut any approaches in the bud. "No thank you," I replied.

"Like some lunch before we leave?"

As he cooked, I looked around, examining his artworks. They had titles such as *Tree Oracle* and *Letters from My Earth Mother*. There was also a series of calligraphic works, *Sea Scrolls*, made with fragments of coral arranged to look like the characters of an alphabet, with a Chinese or Japanese flavour – one, the imaginary script of a lost civilization. I noticed a large illustrated coffee-table book he'd compiled and written on contemporary Irish art, and flicked through this, while the sizzling sound and smell of garlic frying issued from the kitchen.

Roderic

I was wondering: What was this woman doing in my space? The first I'd ever entertained in this cottage. Of course I had invited her, but not as the result of an ordinary pick-up, merely responding to a Cosmic prompting. Perhaps she was *the* woman. The signs were positive, though it was too early to tell. In any event, warming to her company and playful, I sensed a lively day ahead.

Elly

We had a delicious meal of mushrooms, eggs and spinach, sipping red wine, which, ironically, happened to be Australian.

"Why don't you go for a stroll on the beach," he suggested, "while I pack some things. I'll join you there."

The beach was small, private and empty. Waves, driven by a warm west wind, rolled, raced and crashed to the shore. The rocks lining each side of the bay were awesome in their shapes and colours – brown, black, yellow, pink, white and green. What a place! So beautiful! I was excited being here and having met this man. I waited on the rocks in a dreamy ecstasy, gazing into a pool, a miniature Universe, oceanic music playing in the background. I marvelled at how life could change so much in a couple of days, as I waited for my new companion. I observed him as he approached, relaxed and self-confident over the dunes.

We headed off towards Sneem, deciding to take the long route around the coast so I could see the scenery and visit the stone circle. As we drove, I hardly dared look at him. I couldn't believe I was sitting beside this unusual stranger. But I peeped occasionally, happy his Suzuki made so much noise that I didn't feel uncomfortable whenever there was silence. Yet I loved his voice and wanted him to speak, particularly about himself, as I'd heard from Kristin he'd had an adventurous life. Not daring to ask him about it directly, I simply invited him to talk about his interests. "Tell me what you know about nature," I suggested. He was passionately into trees, he said, which he'd been studying for the past ten years, culturally more than horticulturally. "I'm in the middle of writing a book on the subject, *Gospel of The Living Tree*, a guide to the mysteries of trees. Subtitled *For Mystics, Lovers, Poets & Warriors*."

He had set up a centre for nature research and education. *KOAD*, it was called, meaning 'sacred grove' or 'meeting place' in ancient Celtic; and had won a national award for this the previous year. "We had students from around the world," he informed me. "But I closed it down to concentrate on writing." Well, I had come to Ireland to explore nature, so I couldn't have been with a better person.

Roderic

"Where are you going in the west?" I asked as we wound our way down a narrow, twisting lane, towards the stone circle.

"Wherever," she replied, "but eventually to the Burren in County Clare, to Kilfenora, to a healing centre called Boghill, where I'm going to stay in a few days time. Do you know it?"

I didn't, but the name sounded very familiar.

Elly

"What an extraordinary coincidence!" Roderic exclaimed almost an hour later as we sat sipping beer overlooking the picturesque harbour of Glandore. "Boghill, the place where you're going, was the name of my mother's house. She used to live there with her hundred donkeys and sold it ten or fifteen years ago."

This gave me goose pimples.

Roderic

How bizarre to pick up a woman who has just arrived from overseas in a country with a population of five million people and discover that she's going to stay in one's mother's house.

In my understanding, there is no such thing as 'coincidences', not in the sense of being without significance. So, what are they? When they defy mathematical probability, as they often do, then there must be an element of intention. But intention implies intelligence, which humankind appears to have difficulty in ascribing to anything beyond itself, though it's clearly at work in life all around us. In my understanding, these 'coincidental' patterns of events are part of a language spoken by the Universe, including one's guides or guardian angels. With evident intention, they convey a message that can be either guidance or a confirmation, or even a warning. Thousands of years ago at the time of King Solomon, such patterns observable in everyday life were taken as signs or symbols in what was known as *The Language of the Birds*. The king himself was a master at reading it. It provided him with insights and was one of the keys of his proverbial wisdom, as it has been for shamans and sages throughout the ages – even Socrates, acclaimed as the wisest. Today, with the emphasis on information and knowledge of a purely intellectual kind, we have lost many of the arts of wisdom.

So, what did this unusual 'coincidence' mean? That destiny was at work, that Elly and I were being linked 'Cosmically'? With our

16

souls as conscious participants, no doubt! Why did I think so? Firstly, there was the 'flash of intuition' by which I had been connected with her energetically; secondly, the 'coincidence' in picking the same Insight Card signifying 'Relationship'; and thirdly, this latest improbable fact that she was planning to stay at my mother's former house. In *The Language of the Birds*, or otherwise, could the indications have been more explicit? They told me I was on the right path; that mystery was in the air. All would unfold magically, I knew. All I had to do was go with the flow, trusting it.

Elly

I enjoyed the wild open spaces as we travelled.

"Wait till we get to Bantry, Glengariff, and beyond. Then it becomes really awesome," said Roderic.

It was indeed. And the feeling of space and freedom were overwhelming. Particularly after two weeks of being cooped up with Jonathan.

Approaching the end of our journey, we turned off the main road, hardly more than a country lane, onto a stony and bumpy track that led us through a forest with a primeval flavour of twisted tree-roots, swamps and mosses. One mile later, weaving our way through overhanging branches, we emerged into the open, to another panorama of mountains, sea, bays, islands and creeks.

When Kristin had told me he was taking me to his nature research centre, I had imagined a modern complex of buildings with people milling around. But I saw neither. As we turned a corner and got out of the car, "This is it," he indicated; and, pointing to an expanse of bog and rocks: "You'll be staying over there."

Seeing nothing but gorse, grass and heather, I was a little shocked. Looking more carefully as we walked down a narrow gravelled path, I began to see some kind of a construction emerging, rising out of the landscape almost as a natural extension of it. I was amazed. It was a two-storey wooden round house, strapped with log poles, tilting slightly to one side, and had a grass roof with flowers. Was this really where I was going to be sleeping?

As we approached, it looked more and more charming. What a creation! It seemed to belong to a fairy-tale Hansel and Gretel world. Or was it meant for goblins and dwarfs? Flowers grew everywhere.

When I opened the door, I couldn't believe my eyes. While rough and rickety on the outside, inside it was so beautiful, colourful and unique. As in his seaside cottage in County Cork, there were artworks, books, feathers, stones and crystals neatly arranged around the place. But my attention was drawn out to nature, to an incredible view down the mountainside, over bogland and woodlands, across bays and islands, with a range of mountains to the left and right extending into the horizon far out to sea.

After my initial sighs of wonderment, my eyes returned to the dwelling itself, which was built around a massive tapering pole, evidently once the trunk of a tree. "Bog chestnut," said Roderic as I put my arms around it, "a few thousand years old. Extremely rare. Found buried in the earth not far from here."

Against a wall of the dwelling was a spherical stove on legs. "A relic from World War II," he informed me, "an anti-submarine buoy, which I had converted. The whole building is made of natural or re-cycled materials."

I loved being in this space. It was so warm and cosy. Surprisingly, it had electricity and running water. "Come and have a look at the bathroom," he suggested, just as I was wondering if it had a toilet or whether I was expected to go outside. The room was enchanting, with walls of twisted branches of silver birch. Plants, umbrella palms, were dotted on the floor. There was an elegant wash area with a round handpainted pottery sink, sunk into a shelf of polished beech, on which shells and bottles of essential oils were arranged. Around a corner, hidden behind a tree-trunk, was the bath. "You can lie in it and gaze out to sea," he said. "And if you want a taste of the ultimate in bath-experience," he added smiling, "I can fill it up with seaweed or twigs of rosemary for you." I relished his attention to the little joys of life and smiled back appreciatively.

He pointed to a large wooden box. "That's the toilet. It's a compost one." As he lifted the lid, I wondered if there would be a smell. It was a pleasant one of fresh pine sawdust. There was a sack of it alongside. "After a year of composting on a heap outside, the contents get returned to the earth," he explained. "A great fertiliser!"

For a city woman these were cultural surprises. Well, I had wanted to be in nature, now I was; but I hadn't imagined going to this extreme, nothing so primitive.

Returning to the main room, I noticed a ladder and realized there was a platform above the kitchen. "You sleep up there," he said. Yes, I had been wondering about the sleeping arrangements. "There are seven steps up, like those to heaven! Have a look!" So I climbed. Stunning! I could lie on a large double mattress and gaze out to sea. Yes, indeed, seventh heaven.

"I'll be staying with my sister," he said to my relief. "Her house is just behind those trees."

I was exhausted and ready to be on my own. Two weeks with Jonathan had depleted me. Happily, after a light meal, Roderic left. At last, for the first time in Ireland, I could relax in solitude and comfort. I had a great night.

Roderic
With bird in cage, I was looking forward to the morning chase!

Elly
I enjoyed lying lazily in bed on awaking and was hoping for a relaxing day. But I was a little nervous about meeting Roderic again, not knowing what to expect. Was I going to be staying in this extraordinary place? Would he return to Cork and leave me here? Or expect me to continue on my journey? Or come into my bed? I wasn't ready to leave, nor for intimacy, though to spend more time in his company would be great.

As he arrived, I was sitting outside, breathing in the peace and beauty.
The second he appeared, my nervousness vanished. Why had it ever existed? He was so wonderful to be with, so open, relaxed, and accepting; and he took such an interest in me. All the things I'd missed with Jonathan, he was giving me. He didn't seem to have any plans, in fact to have all the time in the world.

19

"If you go down to the woods today, you're in for a big surpise," he sung, as we gazed down the mountainside, over treetops and across the ocean. "Fancy a walk?" So down through the woods we went, until we reached the first of many creeks. We crossed over bridges from island to island and along paths hollowed out of jungles of rhododendrons, journeying, it seemed, through the veins and arteries of Mother Earth. When we finally emerged at the end of the furthest island, we came upon a colony of seals. Finding rocks to sit on, we watched them as they basked in the sun or fished, popping their heads up and down in the water. What delight!

I felt like lingering alone for a while, so Roderic walked on. I was still brooding over my anger with Jonathan and busy processing. Why should I have been so affected by his attitudes? We'd had such an intensely erotic relationship in Australia: So why his sudden sexual incapacity? Why hadn't he told me about this earlier? His not wanting to touch me had knocked my confidence. I seriously doubted my beauty and sensuality.

Linking up with Roderic further along the shore, I shared my thoughts and feelings with him.

"When you're in your centre, you don't need the attentions or support of anyone," he commented.

"Well that's true. The last two weeks, I haven't felt centred at all, trying to make Jonathan happy instead of myself." And how I had disempowered myself, yet again!

I looked at Roderic, towards whom sexual feelings had begun to arise. Strangely, I was both attracted to him and not at all. While young in spirit, he was older than I, much older, as I knew by his wrinkles.

Later in the afternoon, I gave him a hands-on Reiki treatment, by way of thanking him, which enabled me to be physically near him without being too close. It was an unusual experience. While I was aware of the energy flowing through me, it seemed to bounce off him as if he were wearing a metal suit. In my many treatments, I had never encountered such a block on receiving.

We picked chanterelles for dinner, drove into the village for a pint in a pub, and spent the rest of the evening alone again, which gave me more time to reflect.

Maybe I need to change my life? It's at a critical point, I feel. My job as a physiotherapist no longer fulfils me. While it's served me well, providing me with valuable learning experiences, it no longer permits me, with its limited concepts, to give as I wish, therefore to express my full potential. How can I honour what is in my heart, my own truth, my own uniqueness? I need to find another way of being, another life-style. Perhaps I should leave the city and go somewhere in nature? Do more travelling before putting down a root? I don't feel ready to settle down or even start the healing centre of which I've been dreaming. What is my next step?

There was also the question of a relationship. Maybe, rather than being locked in a marriage box, I should live in a community? But I long for the ideal soul mate coming into my life.

The next day, I shared my thoughts with Roderic. "What kind of a relationship do you want to manifest?" he asked, which surprised me greatly, implying that you can consciously create or draw into your life whatever you choose. For me, it was a new idea I was exploring: For Roderic it was a matter of fact.

Roderic

Drawing into one's life what one requires? Wasn't this what I had just done? Wasn't this her?

In any event, it seemed to me we were on our way to being lovers, even though this may not have dawned on her yet. There was an easy flow of energy between us, which could easily move from a stream to a torrent; and an air of inevitability in our encounter, as when an arrow has been fired and there is no stopping it. I found great delight in the fragrance of her being. She oozed sensuality and was, I imagined, deliciously erotic.

Underlying whatever else, there was a dynamic of seduction in which I was inclined to be more passive than active, to wait, to go with the flow and simply allow events to unfold. In fact, I resolved, I'd let *her* seduce *me*, if that was to be, at least let *her* make the first moves. I'd pave the way of course.

Elly

We spent most of the following day in and around the Round House sharing experiences, during which time I learned a great

21

deal more about my new companion. He had travelled the world, working and adventuring, or 'playing', as he put it, in over forty countries. New York based, he had been an international business consultant, negotiating projects with foreign governments. Light years away from being a man of the woods! How had he got from one point to the other? Too long a story. It seemed to have begun in India in the *ashram* of a holy man, Swami Muktananda. "He was a close confidant of the Prime Minister, Mrs Indira Gandhi, whose approval I needed on a project; and my direct line to her whenever I needed it," he informed me. "So I stayed in his *ashram* for several months, not like others as a seeker, disciple or pilgrim, but for business purposes." While there, he had had various enlightening experiences, wholly unexpected, which he shared. "That's when I had my first pre-this-lifetime remembrance. One day in a sudden explosive vision, as I was sitting in the temple, I remembered moments before I came into this world, even before I was conceived, when I was *choosing* my parents and early life circumstances. Imagine my shock. I had never heard of such a thing. It was ten years later when I learned that such a thing was possible."

I was excited hearing someone talking from his experiences on such a topic, particularly on such a rare and significant event. While I accepted the concept that one chooses one's parents and circumstances, I had never thought it through, never considered the practical implications. Maybe I could do so now with him?

"Imagine the shock," he continued, "of discovering that one has never been a victim, but has chosen everything. Almost all of one's life perspectives change."

"Yes, I can imagine," I sighed, shuddering at the thought of such a possibility.

"In that moment, I realized that I had neither begun at 'birth' nor will end at 'death', but that I have always existed, coming and going on this planet for aeons."

The subject of past lives interested me greatly and I had never met anyone who remembered theirs so vividly. "How does one start remembering?" I asked.

"For me it was spontaneous, at least initially. But one can trigger the process simply by asking, as I did a decade or so later."

"Tell me."

"It began for me in earnest, in an accelerated fashion, after I had stood on top of Montségur, a fortress-pinnacle in the South of France, and put out a passionate plea to the Universe, "Who am I? Who was I? I want to remember, *now*." I was demanding, even commanding! "Almost immediately, the magic started. As if a veil had been removed from my eyes, I began remembering one life after another. I was led to places where I had once resided; and recognised them.

"In matters of healing, growth or awakening, you only have to ask the Universe and you'll receive whatever assistance you need. The more passionate your plea, the more it comes to you," he assured me.

Illustrating how unresolved issues in previous lives are carried through to future ones until they're resolved, he shared some riveting personal stories. "In my early twenties, I fell in love with an Austrian Baroness. We had a tragic affair in Vienna, which ended in a murder-cum-suicide attempt in which I almost killed her."

"What!" I shuddered. Almost killed her? Could he really have done so? Questions began whizzing around my mind. Robbed banks? Almost killed his lover? Been in prison twice? What kind of a guy am I with? What next? While I wasn't alarmed, I was greatly perplexed.

"I had been introduced to her by our common closest friend, the Countess Hoyos," he continued in a matter-of-fact way as if these were normal daily occurrences. "Later, I discovered that I had re-enacted a celebrated crime which had taken place nearly a century earlier, also in Vienna, when the Crown Prince Rudolf of Habsburg died in a believed suicide pact with *his* great love, also a young Austrian Baroness – to whom, 'coincidentally', *he* had been introduced by *his* closest friend, the Count Hoyos. The same family! Isn't that incredible?"

"Yes!" I murmured, struggling to digest.

"Later still, I remembered being Rudolf."

Was he testing my limits? I wondered.

From past lives, the subject led to higher self. "It's not simply a concept," he insisted. "It is an aspect of one's being which functions dynamically, presiding over all aspects of one's life." I agreed. "It's the real 'I', the living soul, the ongoing reincarnating entity. The challenge today is to learn how it works and then work with it." That's what I wanted to learn more about. In practice. In everyday life. Illustrating this, he shared more intriguing stories which, though some would consider them unbelievable, seemed more and more credible to me.

Thus we continued into the night.

Roderic

I seldom shared details of my life. Elly, whom I felt to be a special case, was a rare exception. We had started, I believed, on a long journey. Reflecting on her in the context of what I'd put out to the Universe, she seemed the perfect response in every way. The more I got to know her, the more amazed I became by how precisely my specifications were being met. She was warm and sensual. Sex, I had gathered, was of primary interest. She was versed in tantra, as I had requested, having attended weeklong workshops on the subject, the only woman I had ever met who'd done so. She was fully into her body, had cycled around Europe and across America from the west coast to east, and loved to dance, reading my book on Trance Dance as if it were a thriller. Since I'd specified to the Universe 'dance, trance and chant', I wondered about the latter: In Muktananda's *ashram*, I had spent seven hours a day chanting, a more earthy form of meditation, which I had found powerful. While she'd done no chanting, she was interested in doing so, and had been attending voice workshops in recent months. She was consciously on her spiritual path, actively engaged in her own growth and healing; and was also a healer. In this, too, we had much in common: While she was a Reiki Master, I had done the first two degrees. We had both been initiated twelve years earlier. While she used kinesiology professionally, I had attended courses on the subject. While I studied vibrational healing, purely theoretically, she practised it. While I'd run teaching centres that included the healing arts, one of her dreams was to start a healing centre. She loved to be in nature. While I'd worked with herbs, she worked with flower essences. She was sensitive, aware, and open to other dimensions. She knew her soul to be on a journey through Time, accepting that she'd had other earthly lives. She practised

24

meditation, attuned to her higher self, and was open to exploring ways of working with it. Clearly a truth-seeker. As kindred spirits, we complemented each other perfectly.

So I had no reservations in sharing with her openly and truthfully, perhaps a little to impress, a little to entertain, but always to illustrate points I viewed as essential to an understanding of life, aware that I was laying the foundations of our relationship … though I had yet to tell her of my wilder adventures, as a result of which I had been banned from nine countries around the world or they'd become too hot for me to re-enter … though, foolish in my daring, I had often done so!

Chapter 3

Approaching Intimacy

Elly

After breakfast, we returned to the woods, intending to climb the mountain. Once again, it was like entering a fairy-tale. I expected to see elves and dwarfs peeping from behind trees. We followed a slippery trail on the rocky bank of a steeply rising stream, which flowed past us in waterfalls; and came to a plateau with a grove of oaks. Leaving these behind, we began our ascent through a waist-deep entanglement of heather, gorse, bog myrtle and tall grasses.

"It could be dangerous here," said Roderic. "One can't always tell what's underneath. Watch you don't fall into a hole."

Thirty minutes later, we stood on the summit, absorbing yet another panorama. I could walk like this for days amidst such wildness and power of emptiness.

On our way down, we took slightly different routes. Half way, I leant back against a rocky outcrop and felt a growing connection with the Earth; then became aware of a flow of energy circulating between my sexual, heart and crown chakras. I felt my oneness with the Earth as Mother, who welcomed my beauty and femininity. It made me realize I'd always been involved in relationships in which the man had never really appreciated me fully, making me feel I was never good enough, beautiful or sensual enough, that something essential was missing, that my essence and truth were not understood. This moment was a turning point. I'm not going to accept this anymore, I decided. I want to flower as a woman and celebrate my uniqueness, independent of any man's wish. What a freedom! I thanked the Earth for this deep connection and for giving me the clarity.

Descending the mountain, I reached the wood, where I stayed a while, bathing in its energy and hugging a tree. "I'm here for you," it seemed to say. I was surprised to discover that I found as much comfort in holding it as in holding a man. I could feel support and safely surrender. After a few minutes of embracing its mossy-barked trunk, soft, sensual and mushy, I exploded in orgasm.

Later it dawned on me that it's *my* openness and surrendering rather than anything on the outside which brings me into ecstasy. What a discovery! Thank you tree.

Returning to the Round House, I swam naked in the ice-cold rocky pool in front of it, in a kind of ritual, to wash away my negative memories. Then I returned to the loft and slept until Roderic woke me. "I'm off to the village to do some shopping," he called up from the floor beneath. I liked his voice, a mixture of certitude, authority and tenderness.

Lying in bed, I listened to the pouring rain, in a cosy reverie.

I was soaking in a bath, to which I had added ylang ylang, when I heard him return. He put on music by Peter Gabriel and lit a fire which I could hear crackling. What bliss to lie like this, luxuriating in steamy perfumed waters in a magical environment to the strains of *Passion*.

I emerged feeling not only refreshed but re-birthed. Drying myself, I wondered whether he could see me in my nakedness through a crack between the planks. I pretended he could. As *Passion* played, I moved my body rhythmically, exploring it sensually as I oiled it with jasmine. That should bring him to his erotic senses! It certainly brought me to mine!

I put on my sarong and was ready for anything. Yet, I felt shy as I entered the room. Maybe he could read my thoughts and feelings, emanating through every pore of my skin.

Roderic

"Ah, you're wearing a sarong!" I exclaimed, noting the obvious. "I used to wear them in Sri Lanka and still have a collection." So I put one on as well.

We reclined on sofas opposite each other, close to the fire, as wind and rain pelted against the windows with increasing force. Nestled cosily in the Round House, surrounded and bombarded by the storm brewing, we could enjoy its ravings while feeling protected.

"Whiskey?" I suggested.

"Wonderful," she sighed, beaming her delight.

We sipped and relaxed.

"Tell me about your tantric experiences," I asked out of the blue, provocatively.

Responding with a sheepish giggle and wriggling of her body, no words were uttered. Of course, I had presented her with a very personal and penetrating question, suggesting she tell me not simply about her love life but her sex life with its intimate details. Pretending that this was not my intention, I rephrased it: "Tell me about your tantric workshop."

She was not quick at replying, I'd observed, preferring to connect with her feelings first. "What do you want to know?" she asked with a teasing smile.

"What did it consist of? Why did you attend?"

Fingers twirled around a lock of hair as she pondered. "I wanted to explore sex in a different way."

"Why?" I asked, though it was easy to guess.

"I wasn't satisfied with regular sex the way I'd experienced it."

"*We* could have great explorations," I was tempted to suggest, but the evening was young, certain to be fun, and I had only just taken the top off the bottle. "Why?" I asked instead.

"I always had the feeling it could be much more enjoyable, ecstatic, and shared more deeply. It was always too quick, ruled by the drive of the man to get his orgasm. Often I've felt so unfulfilled and lonely after an orgasm – whenever I had one, that is. Usually exhausted rather than elated, I knew I was missing something essential." She paused between sentences, probing what she felt. "What I was yearning for was a full body, heart and soul experience, rather than a purely physical one. I was aware of the tremendous amount of sexual energy you can generate, but I didn't know what to do with it. Rather than release it, I wanted to use it spiritually, at least more wholesomely. Also, what's the fun in having an orgasm that lasts but seconds? I wanted to extend the possibilities of remaining in a state of ecstasy."

I put wood on the fire, while my own was beginning to blaze furiously.

"One classic experience," she related, "finally triggered me into saying, 'I've had enough of this. I want something more.' It was sex in seconds, followed by a snore. I couldn't believe it! And laughed at finding myself in such an absurd situation. I'd read a little about tantra and practised some of the exercises, then heard about the workshop and wanted to explore."

I found her refreshingly open on the subject. Indeed, one of the great delights in being with her was her openness. Even bodily she expressed this quality. Rather provocatively sometimes, I observed. As she lounged in her chair, her legs, bare from the tips of her toes to well above her knees, were spread out casually in an arousing pose, revealing more than is the usual drawing-room custom, the tender flesh of inner thighs. Was this intentional? A signal of her availability? No, she assured me afterwards. Nevertheless, her body spoke, seeming to possess a longing of its own.

"So, how was it?" I asked, wondering how she had occupied her eight days, in what intimacies with what strangers.

"It was the most wonderful workshop I've ever done," she replied with effusive jubilance. "Profoundly serious yet full of play, and so creative. Everything was prepared and conducted with such perfection."

"What took place exactly?"

"First and foremost, we focused on awareness, which we began realizing is the key to everything. So the emphasis throughout was on quality of being rather than on performing."

Tantra, I knew, was not about positions. Whilst an erotic art, rather than one of gymnastics, its fundamental premise is that the energies of sex and spirituality are one and the same – those of creativity, transformation and ecstasy. Not being opposites, they cannot be split. Therefore, one cannot deny sex in order to be more spiritual. In the futile attempt to do so, one blocks the flow of the very energy one is seeking. The primary intention in this ancient art, as I knew in theory, is in the control and direction of this energy, in raising the level of awareness and consciousness, to become more spiritual, alive and creative, while achieving self-mastery.

"We started each day with a meditation," she continued, exposing her thighs a little more carelessly, "giving attention to our bodies, thoughts and emotions – not judging, not attempting to change anything, just being aware, just observing. We also danced a lot, to warm and free us up, running, jumping, hopping, firstly with clothes, later in the nude, weaving coloured scarves in twirls, ridding ourselves of our inhibitions, enjoying our nakedness shamelessly, celebrating with the abandonment of children. It was so much fun."

"How many people were doing all this?" I asked.

"Thirty, fifteen men and fifteen women. Plus five teachers, who were brilliant."

"What else did you do?"

"We explored archetypes, different aspects of our being, such as the whore and the goddess."

"That must have been exciting! What did you discover?"

"How much I enjoyed being a whore ..."

How I loved this woman! I smiled, enchanted.

"We spent hours dressing up for a whore party. I had one naked breast with a flower, which someone painted around my nipple. I wore a short black skirt with one side raised up to a hip. I plastered my face with make-up and put on huge vulgar earrings. At the party, we danced wildly. It was a challenge to let go of your inhibitions and stretch your limits, go beyond being the nice little girl and explore yourself outrageously, not only privately but also publicly – in particular, your seductiveness. The great thing about it was that we were given permission to act like this and encouraged to do so. 'The conditioning of society,' they said, 'has resulted in a massive blocking of the natural flow of life's energies within our beings. So, we've got to get it going again.'"

"Yes," I murmured.

"One of the primary intentions of the workshop was to encourage people to speak their truth openly and honestly. Daring to do so, to share your normally hidden thoughts and desires in such intimate surroundings, was challenging. Speaking your truth fully in the now moment was a central part of the teaching. At the same time, we were encouraged to express ourselves lovingly from the heart. 'Honesty with love creates space for healing, honesty without love destroys,' they said. We did many provocative exercises, practising these with various partners, all of which involved constant eye-to-eye contact. Sometimes we stood naked in front of each other; at other times we touched. We also did breathing exercises, alone or in pairs, linked with drawing energy from the sexual centre up into other energy-centres of the body."

We paused for snacks, smoked oysters on toast, and listened to the sounds of a howling wind and torrential rain.

"Okay," I resumed, "you had both males and females present, dancing naked and exploring sexual issues. What was the interaction on a physical level?"

"Well, we had all kinds of interactive sessions: In one, all the men lined up in a circle, holding hands, naked, blind-folded and facing outwards. We, the women, were invited to move around and touch them where we wished. We were also naked. The men were allowed to say 'no' or 'stop'. The idea of this, explained in advance, brought up so much fear in the men that we discussed it for over two hours before we could begin."

"So, what actually happened?" I asked.

"I was impressed seeing the openness and vulnerability of the men holding hands. We touched them lovingly, kissed and hugged. Sometimes, with three women, we touched one guy. Also, we had our favourites, sometimes queuing," she chuckled.

"I'd have become very excited with three pairs of lips and six hands exploring *my* body," I confessed. "Didn't any of them become aroused by your tactile attentions?"

This caused more chuckles. "Well, one had said before we started how easily he got an erection. This was his biggest fear."

"Did he get one?"

"Sort of. But it was accepted. However, while there was a little playing by the women and passionate kisses, nobody went to the extent of arousing them over the top. As far as I know. And, remember, they were allowed to say 'stop'."

"What was the point of all this?"

"They explained it as follows: In a society in which male sexuality predominates, casting both males and females into stereotyped roles, the intention was to reverse these so men could experience being receptive, passive, defenceless and vulnerable, while women could be in control and take initiatives."

"What about the women? Did they stand in a circle?"

"Yes."

"So, what was *your* experience?"

31

She twirled another strand of hair, changed her position on the sofa, and declared: "I need another whiskey."

After attending to the fire, I invited her to continue.

"I discovered how much I loved to be touched, particularly by more than one guy, in a context that was safe. My feeling was: I want more and more arms and bodies around me, more hugs, more warmth."

"Did anyone go too far?" I asked. "And what was too far?"

"At one moment I was sandwiched between two guys, one from the front, one from the back. It was a great feeling. I didn't say 'no' to anyone or anything."

Well, I was here, alive and fully present, and so was she. Perhaps she wouldn't say 'no' to me either? If her body was her voice, open and welcoming in its gestures, she had already spoken. I had been visually drinking in its sensual voluptuousness, finding her bared limbs arousing. One glance and my loins stirred. Mentally and vibrationally, we attuned wonderfully. What setting could be more romantic? As ready as I was, I would await her advances.

While what she had described might be seen as an excuse for a Bacchanalian orgy, an abandonment into lustful sensuality, I felt it perfectly appropriate. If one were to be exclusively on the sensual and erotic level, one would miss the whole point. But one cannot exclude it. Since so much pertaining to the body has been denied from the wholeness of life and repressed in the psycho-emotional make-up of man with distorted and crippling effects, it is time to include it. At the same time, I was still curious to know how far anyone had gone during the workshops in their explorations on the purely physical level.

"Well," she said. "This was merely an introduction to tantra, so physical lovemaking was not part of the course, as it is on advanced ones, I think. However, moans and groans of passion could be heard breaking the silence of the night."

"What about the god and goddess aspect?"

"This was about recognising and honouring the divinity in each of us, knowing that sexual energy is a part of this. Sex is a communion between souls, also with the Divine, not just a physical act."

"I agree."

"So, what did you get out of the workshop finally?"

"It took me a long time to integrate fully what had happened during the week."

"How was your sex life afterwards?" I asked audaciously.

"I didn't find out. I realised how sacred my *yoni** was, and didn't want to let anyone near it. During the week, we had a woman's day, which included a long conversation with one's *yoni*; and I made a commitment that I'd always ask its permission before anyone could enter this holy space."

"Have you ever asked?" I enquired, seeking to extract the last drop of detail. "Yes. But it keeps saying 'no'."

A colourful sarong, easily removed, was draped across its entrance.

*A Sanskrit word denoting the sacredness of the vagina.

Elly

I was happy to go on talking about tantra for hours, but we'd drunk half a bottle of whiskey and I was hungry. I decided to cook a meal of quinoa and wokked vegetables.

I was also wondering whether we'd be going to the Burren together or whether our paths would separate. While I wanted to go, Roderic hesitated. So, do I seduce him? It's now or never. Yet, I was ambivalent. He wasn't like Jonathan, my dream Apollo. On the other hand, the idea of him touching me, of feeling his hands on my naked body, aroused me. While my mind prevaricated, my *yoni* roared 'yes'. So, when I started cooking, dropping things all over the place, all of a sudden I heard myself asking him to give me a hug. This was like opening the cage of a wild animal. Responding in what seemed like a flash, he nailed me against the trunk of the chestnut tree, the central pole holding up the house. A few seconds later, in the heat of a feverishly caressing embrace, my sarong slipped down my body.

This was the wildest, most unexpected, tempestuous hug I'd ever had. Good. It was decided. We'd go to the Burren.

Chapter 4

Opening to the Magic

Elly

I awoke at six, raised my head from the pillow and breathed in the vista, with an eagle's eye view over the top of the woodlands descending to the shore. Islands shimmered in a sparkling sea between a range of mountains stretching out on either side, extending themselves in diminishing shades of blue before disappearing in the mists of the horizon. This is paradise. But where is Adam?

My body was filled with the memories of his touchings. I stroked it lovingly. It feels so warm and soft in the mornings.

Shortly I heard footsteps along the gravel path and a door creaking open. It was Roderic, I assumed. I heard him tiptoe to the foot of the ladder and pretended to be asleep, wondering whether he'd climb it and enter my bed. I was ready. But he didn't. Stopping half-way, he popped his head over the ledge and simply said: "Let's go! We leave in a couple of hours."

I was surprised. But while a part of me was disappointed, another felt okay. We didn't have to plunge into each other's arms straight away. He had honoured me by not assuming an automatic right to enter my space. I liked that.

"Let's tune in," he suggested as we sat in the car ready to drive off. "Let's ask the angels for a fun adventure," he added as I closed my eyes and entered the silence, my own inner silence, for birds were twittering busily in the trees and a wind rustled.

"Do you really think that angels exist?" I asked as we weaved our way through fuchsia hedges, overhanging branches of rhododendron and birch.

"It's one of humankind's illusions, an ignorance if not also an arrogance, that man's is the only intelligence in the Universe," he replied. "In one form or another, it exists all around us. In fact, it is actively and dynamically engaged in all aspects of life. Further, we can communicate with this intelligence on whatever levels it exists. Further still, we can consciously work with it. Anyone can do so. It's knowledge we once had, which we are re-learning."

"Tell me about it."

"First we must free ourselves of the limited concepts we're holding, by which we've been conditioned. In denying the existence of something, we keep our minds closed. Even our perceptive faculties go into a state of numbness. So we begin by declaring ourselves open. After this, we may have to wait a little."

Leaving the bumpy woodland lane, we reached the main road and headed towards the mountains and lakes of Killarney.

Energy flowed easily between us. Occasionally, as we sat in silence, he put his hand on my knee and stroked my leg. As it moved along my inner thigh, softly and slowly towards my *yoni*, my whole body responded with a shiver. Closing my eyes, I savoured the moments, yielding to his caressing touch. Not long enough, unfortunately, as both hands were needed for the winding roads.

"Have you ever seen an angel?" I asked some time later, wondering how serious he'd been with his invocation.

"I had many conversations with them, purely imaginary, before I actually saw one. When I did, over fifteen years ago in England, it was wholly unexpected and stunned my mind momentarily, for, while I'd accepted their existence, I didn't seriously believe they had wings. But that's what I saw. As I looked out of my window one morning, one was hovering above my car, wearing a robe of blue with golden stars. And it had wings! Yes, wings!"

"As the vision lasted no more than a few seconds, I wasn't absolutely convinced of its reality. Was this an objective perception or merely a subjective projection? I assumed the former, temporarily, in order to explore the question further. Since it had appeared above my car, or seemed to have done, I took this as a signal, an invitation to get into it and drive off, sensing it would lead me somewhere. It did. I found myself approaching what turned out to be an arts centre on the edge of a village, where there was a fair going on. Inside the building, an eight-sided converted chapel, I met the owner and his wife, who invited me back to their house for tea. There, to my astonishment, I saw a replica of the angel, a large four-foot-high cardboard cutout representation of it, in the same blue robe with golden stars, displayed on their mantlepiece. Even the ceiling of their drawing room was the same blue with golden stars. This being far too improbable to be a meaningless coincidence, it proved to me that I had actually seen one. Taking it as a sign, I moved into this house, believing it was my next step. This was the first of a series of angel-guided journeys which I have experienced over the years."

As we drove, he related story after story of his encounters with them, each more improbable than the one he'd just told. I was keen to hear more, to grasp the reality of these 'Beings of Light'.

"Their appearances followed a step-by-step sequence. First, an angel appeared, saying in effect: *"Yes, we exist, here I am."* Then, suggestively, with its appearance above my car: *"Follow me, I can guide you."* So I followed on numerous occasions, once across France."

He shared details of these adventures. He lived in a world of magic, it seemed.

"Later, the angels said: *"You can communicate with us."* I met others who communicated with them on a regular basis. Later still, they let it be known: *"We can work together. We can help you."* I had heard of individuals, even groups, who had been working with angels for years, successfully in practical worldly projects. I visited them, lived with some, and learned much.

"Having declared myself open to working with angels, I tested them, even by asking the seemingly impossible. One day, in a communication with the Archangel Michael, it was suggested that I open a centre for "higher learning" in Glastonbury. But I had no money at the time. Arriving in the town, I went to the top of the Tor and simply asked the Archangel. "If this is really what I am supposed to be doing, then I need your assistance. A million dollars, at least. The response was immediate. Within a week, I was appointed managing director of the largest centre in the town, a spiritual-cultural-commercial complex; and, within six months, I was gifted all of the buildings and businesses by the owners, worth well over a million and a half dollars at the time – five or more today, perhaps. I still have the Deed of Gift and related documents."

The way he spoke, with a racy fluency, conviction and clarity, left no room for doubts.

"I learned that working with angels is not only possible but highly effective, as well as magical and fun. They are fun-loving beings."

Listening to him kindled in me a deep desire for my own experiences. Would I ever be able to see, hear or feel their presence myself? I had never thought of them featuring in my life, though I could imagine them being present at birth, death and Christmas.

We lingered at various beauty spots in Killarney's National Park, punctuating our journey as well as Roderic's stories.

"Do things come so easily simply by asking?" I wondered, perched on a rock, gazing out across a dark lake, as waves rippled across my feet. "Is anyone able to communicate with angels? Do you need to be highly sensitive?"

I breathed in the crisp, fresh morning air and stretched. I heard his footsteps approaching. His arms enfolded me, while his lips caressed the nape of my neck.

Warmed, loved and refreshed, we drove on.

"Asking," he said, serious once more, "is one of the divine gifts we've all been given, but which few use."

"When was the first time you discovered it worked?"

"When I was living in Geneva in my late thirties."

Another story! I felt so cosy in our little Suzuki, winding noisily along mountain roads, being both entertained and enlightened. This was fun.

"I'd been there a year," he began, "painting, wandering meadows and snowy slopes, after giving up business in the Far East; and it was time to leave. But where to go and what to do, I had no idea. I was at a crossroads. Should I return to London or New York? Go back to India or even Ireland? No, not Ireland! That was the last place I wanted to be, for personal reasons. Anyway, I asked the Universe for clarity."

I observed myself sliding into my usual pattern in which I became a passive listener, absorbing new concepts and information while putting my own knowledge and experience on hold, open to evaluation later.

"After breakfast one day, I lay down on my bed, lazily meditating, and, unexpectedly, had a vision, which flashed into my head: Much to my surprise, I was in Ireland, driving around the countryside in a white Volkswagen van. I could see its number-plate: DIU 94." He spelt it out slowly. "The vision was so vivid and explicit and so evidently a response to my question that I had to act on it; otherwise I would never know whether there was any truth in it. Also, I had to know incontrovertibly whether the asking and receiving process worked. My previous experiences, as much as they'd astounded me, might simply have been fortuitous coincidences, even though I didn't believe so. Therefore, acting on this vision, I packed up my belongings and arrived in Ireland within twenty-four hours."

I found this extraordinary, to alter your life's direction so immediately, simply on a vision.

"Three weeks later, driving through Ennistymon, a town in County Clare, I saw a white Volkswagen van parked outside a warehouse ahead of me. I knew in that instant that this was the vehicle. Driving past, I saw its registration: DIU 94, of course."

Of course! I was getting used to the improbable.

"I was determined to buy it, but the owner refused to part with it. So I told him of my vision in Geneva. And concluded by saying, "I don't mind how many "no's" you give me, I *know* this vehicle is already mine." He thought I was crazy, but ended by selling it."

"Incredible! You must have been really convincing." I was really impressed.

"So my vision had been real. I hadn't been to Ireland for fifteen years, when the vehicle had not been manufactured. And I was wholly unfamiliar with Irish registration codes. So my vision could not have been based on information already possessed by me, nor be the product of wishful thinking since I didn't even want to be in the country. I had simply asked the Universe, not for a vehicle, but for clarity on my next steps; and this was its answer. While the vision had pointed me in the right direction, Ireland, the discovery of the vehicle in actuality confirmed that in coming here I was on my right path."

"Amazing!" My fascination had been rising in leaps and bounds. What a life he lived! Finally, after two and a half weeks, I was where I wanted to be, with a wild yet wise man in the Irish Wild West.

"Since the DIU 94 experience, I have been asking and receiving ever since," he continued. "On and off," he confessed, "as I don't always remember to do it. I've also been studying the process, for while it seems easy, there's also a great deal to understand."

I agreed, for I knew of many who had asked or prayed quite fervently and received no replies whatsoever.

"Mostly, it's we ourselves who block this magical but natural process," he explained. "While there's an art in asking, there is also one in listening. There is also one in 'reading' – that is, in recognising and interpreting the responses. Sometimes, these are merely clues, not always so explicit as Ireland, a white VW van, and a clearly numbered plate. Sometimes they are riddles, challenging to decypher."

We drove through the town of Listowel on our way to Tarbert, the ferry-port on the Shannon Estuary, which we had to cross to get to County Clare. "Ah, Tarbert!" he exclaimed. "That brings back memories! The last time I was heading in this direction was also the result of a vision, and another experiment in asking the Universe for guidance, this time with three sceptics – a Polish professor, his Brazilian fiancée, and an American writer. Want to hear about it?"

Of course! Roderic was the first person I'd met who didn't simply talk about higher self, angels and the guidance of Spirit, but actually worked with them in everyday life; and I loved hearing of actual experiences. While many speak theoretically, few dare to trust, so the experience is missed. I, too, ask and notice the signs but continue living my ordinary life, preferring to rely on the logic of my mind. Yet, while some might think a man like Roderic crazy, his way of working seemed thoroughly practical, down to earth, and it produced results. This is what I wished to learn: practical magic!

I had been living with a sense of isolation, as if alone in a hostile world, still trying to please the God outside. Roderic showed me another way of looking and acting. We're not alone. Life may be testing but it's essentially supportive. We're surrounded by all kinds of Beings of Light ready to assist us simply through our asking. If I could really believe, trust and act on this, it would change my life entirely. How much easier it would become as well as much more exciting! Even as Roderic's, so magical.

But how to open to that magic?

"Here again," he explained, "once we've got rid of our limited and self-limiting concepts which tell us we have no soul or higher self or can't possibly have any dialogue with it ... that intelligence doesn't exist in life all around us, in Nature and the Cosmos, or that if it does we can't possibly communicate with it ... that there are no such things as beings of Light, angels or devas ... that we have no inner guides ... that Spirit doesn't exist ... that the One Supreme Being that caused this Universe isn't living and breathing throughout Its Creation ... that God effectively is dead ... that this or that is not possible, etcetera ... then it's simply a question of cultivating awareness! In a state of openness, we begin by noticing."

I thought of Jonathan who had insisted there was no such thing as a soul or higher self. "Spirituality in any form," he'd said, "is a drug for people who want to escape reality. The only thing one can trust to reach one's goals is oneself and one's own efforts." He had denied my spirituality completely, wasn't interested in my experiences, and was only willing to talk about the healing energy in Reiki from the business point of view. I was convinced now that no relationship like that could work for me anymore – in fact, no relationship that was not spiritually based – as one's spiritual perspectives touch every little aspect of life.

Seated on the sundeck of the ferry, I enjoyed being blasted by the salt-laden wind, feeling excited about the next phase of our journey. The boat was full of tourists, families on holidays with their children and cameras. Why wasn't I having just an ordinary holiday? Instead, I seemed to have enrolled on a workshop! Then I looked at Roderic beside his little Suzuki and thought about the stories he'd told me and wondered what the people in their cars would think if they heard them. When I returned to sit beside him, it felt so good. I lay my head on his shoulder in silent pleasure and gratitude.

As we meandered through the countryside of Clare, I had a tingling feeling of familiarity. I had a sense I'd once been a part of its life, the cottages, the views of the ocean, the windswept environment, the clear blue sky and crispness of air with its salty flavour.

We drove along the coast and passed a pink house with a painting of the Mona Lisa and my name, *elly*, written on it. We laughed and reversed to have a look. Once it had been beautiful, clearly, but it was now desolate and for sale. At the rear was a sign, *Nelly's Restaurant, A Little Bit of Heaven*. Though it had once been Nelly's place, it felt like Elly's. We thought it amusing the "N" had dropped off.

We stopped at the Cliffs of Moher, which rise spectacularly above the Atlantic, but moved swiftly on as they were crawling with tourists and found refuge in a quiet fisherman's pub where we ordered creamy black Guinness.

Throughout our journey, Roderic had been carrying a shoulder bag, which he seemed to be guarding with his life. Suddenly I became suspicious. Did it hold a gun? After all, he'd been a bank robber, as Kristin had mentioned; and I remembered his words, "if you like to live dangerously." Maybe, after all, he was not to be trusted? While I'd had a taste of a nature man and mystic teacher and knew he'd had a career in art and been a business consultant, where did robbing banks fit in?

"What's in your bag?" I asked, no longer able to resist.

"Computer discs."

"Oh!" I was relieved.

"Yes, of half a dozen books I've written or am writing."

It was a good moment to ask him about other aspects of his colourful his past.

"Is it true you once robbed banks?"

"A long time ago, in my late twenties."

I visualized him wearing a black mask and holding revolvers.

"Not in a Bonnie and Clyde style. Strictly without violence," he emphasized.

How then? "I used codes, top secret international money-transfer codes which had never been broken. And, considered unbreakable, banks paid out immediately, on instruction, no questions asked."

"How did you get them? Through a vision lying in bed? Or did the angels whisper in your ears?"

"No," he laughed. "I obtained them from a senior bank official while running gold into South Korea," he chuckled, knowing he was adding fuel to my fire.

I almost choked in my Guinness. Nothing seemed beyond his possibilities. How could these vastly different life experiences come together in a single person?

"I used to run a gold-smuggling organisation. In fact, I set it up. I bought gold in Europe and sold it throughout the Far East, using around forty carriers. After changes in the gold market, which drastically affected business, I used some of them, young gentlemen adventurers, to milk money from banks: While one sent coded instructions from Hong Kong, others drew out the cash in Zurich and Amsterdam."

"Did you get caught?"

"Not gold smuggling. But my man in Holland, an aspiring actor with excellent credentials, overplayed his part, caused suspicion at the bank, got arrested, broke down and shopped me. I was detained in Amsterdam. I could have been sent to half a dozen countries and served ten to fifteen years in prison. The Swiss, for example, don't take too kindly to those who steal from their holy of holies, treating this on a par with murder. But thanks to the intelligence of your Dutch police, particularly Gijs Toorenaar, head of Amsterdam's C.I.D., who thought it better to give me a chance to get back into everyday life, I served only twelve months. I have written about this in a book, *How to Rob Banks Without Violence*, which is about to be made into a feature film. Well, I've told you enough," he finished abruptly. "You're keeping company with a notorious villain. I can see you need another beer!"

I could hardly believe what I'd heard, though I didn't doubt a word of it. I thought of my father who was on the board of a bank. What would he think about all of this?

"What was motivating you?" I asked, licking malty cream from my lips.

"Dreaming, scheming, adventuring, love of play, challenges and risks."

"Isn't life more serious?"

"You asked me what *was* motivating me, so I answered in the past. I lived then existentially with a *carte blanche* freedom based on my philosophical conclusions at the time, after years of searching for a meaning to life."

"What were your conclusions?"

"In a nutshell: All of creation emerges from a Void and returns to it. Speed up this process of billions of years, Universes coming into existence and dissolving, so that all takes place in a few seconds, and all you have is a giant firework display, here one moment and gone the next."

Sounded absurd. Was it really like this? If it was, I didn't want to know about it. Life must have a deeper meaning.

"In that context," he continued, "there are no ultimate meanings, no ultimate purposes, therefore, also, no ultimate imperatives, since all returns to the Void from whence it came. So there's nothing *ultimately* to be lost or gained."

Sounded reasonable, but I was unlikely to be convinced.

"However," he concluded, looking into my eyes with a mischievous smile, as one about to reveal a naughty secret: "Since there are no ultimate meanings, one has the freedom while one lives to create whatever meaning one chooses. So I chose to live and create as I wished, with the world as my arena. This was my freedom, but also everyone's, as I saw it, if they dared to claim it. I did. I've not simply dreamed but dared to live my dreams, to act them out, make them real – sometimes, by the standards of others, quite outrageously. Fools, as you know, jump over cliffs."

I too loved freedom, though mine was within conventional limits. I wasn't into jumping over cliffs!

Once started, there was no stopping him. My simple questions had triggered a flow. "In point of fact, I'd come close to discovering a profound truth. All life *is* play; but, as mystics and teachers of the Mysteries proclaim, it's the Divine Play of the One Supreme Being, the One Great Spirit."

"Surely it has a more serious purpose?" I insisted.

"Only within this One Play. Otherwise none."

"What do you mean?"

"When you're playing Hamlet, for example, it's all deadly serious; and the play has serious themes. But this is only so because you've chosen to identify with the role and live it. Afterwards you can have a good laugh. Nobody really got killed. Your father wasn't murdered. Nor did Ophelia float down the river in a watery grave. After her thoroughly convincing performance, she left the stage, went out to dinner, and spent the night in the arms of her lover. When you're the audience, it's also serious, but only because you've decided to give it the 'stamp of reality', identifying yourself with the drama. You wept, were outraged, it moved you greatly, you got a great thrill out of it. Otherwise, it had no reality. It was simply a play, which can, like life, have whatever intentions, themes, meanings, serious or otherwise, its authors choose to give it."

"So, we're just players in God's game? Is that what you're saying?"

"Not at all. We are neither puppets nor victims. Far from it."

"How is that?" I asked, puzzled and eager to understand his picture.

"Just as the actor, before reaching the stage, chooses his roles and plays, so we, as souls, choose ours before coming into life. Our stage! Our souls being immortal, don't get killed either. We take on earthly roles, one after the other, in one life after another, putting on and discarding bodies like actors their costumes. That we have many lives has been proved beyond doubt by university professors with scientific methodology, using the data of hypnotic regression. Also, the fact that we choose them has been established," he proceded unstoppably, clearly the subject being one of his passions. "In the ongoing theatre of life, we can choose to be and experience whatever we like, for whatever reasons we like. Such is our freedom. It's one we have before we incarnate, primarily, which we exercise – let us be clear – at the level of our souls. It's then, like the actor before appearing on the stage, that we choose our roles and the themes, issues and circumstances of our lives, and our goals. We choose our own plays."

"Who is the author?" I asked again. "Is it not God?"

"Yes, but also no. But then again, always yes. I know this sounds strange, but it's really quite simple. You see, we're living in a play within a play within a play, so the question can be answered on many levels from many perspectives."

It didn't sound simple to me.

"From one point of view," he attempted to explain, "leaving God out of the picture for the moment, it's *we* who are the creators of our selves and our lives. We cause, create and/or choose our circumstances. We determine our futures. We do so, drawing things into our lives by every thought, feeling and deed, every intention, desire and attitude, according to the powers we have and the rules of the game – the Laws of Life, such as the Laws of Attraction, Karma, and so forth – having been given the power and the freedom – created, as we've been, in God's image. So, no, it's not God but *we* who are the authors of our plays."

I definitely needed time to reflect.

"However," he continued, "the answer to your question is also always yes, for in truth there *is* only One Player, the One Supreme Being, the Player behind all players. That's the Great Mystery. It's also the Great Cosmic Joke," he laughed, "for, the Divine is not only *within* each one of us, but *is* each one of us. There is only the Divine and nothing else. We are the Divine in disguise, who sprang out of Oneness and took on many forms – all in order to play with Itself, to explore all possibilities of Life and Beingness …"

I was overwhelmed. I had never imagined sitting in an Irish pub, munching crisps and sipping Guinness, listening to a bank-robber speaking of cosmology.

"So, what is the purpose of Creation?" I asked again, unable to digest what he'd just said, being in such contrast to my own beliefs.

"Joy," he replied, "the only motive. Creation proceeds out of Joy, as an expression of Divinity whose nature is Joy. We, in the essence of our Beings, as aspects of Divinity, are also Joy. It's the fundamental reality beyond all appearances."

I didn't know what he was talking about. I'd been living with the idea of a loving but serious God, a demanding, even judging one. All was Joy? Impossible! I looked around the pub: The barman didn't look so happy. Was he, too, God in disguise? Besides: The fact of suffering in the world was obvious. What about the ravages of war and disease and the loss of loved ones? I had many questions. He had many answers! All of them invited me to see a larger picture:

"We cannot understand much about human life in the framework of just one earthly existence. Within that limited perspective, it makes no sense at all. Nor can we understand very much if we insist on looking at man primarily as a creature of this

Earth, when, in reality, he is a Cosmic Being. Indeed, we are primarily Cosmic Beings, souls, come from afar, merely inhabiting the Earth temporarily. The underlying context of our earthly existence is the ongoing journey of our souls through Time, through many earthly and other lives. Our births and deaths are merely transitions, points of arrival and departure. All is governed by Cosmic Laws which, while regulating our lives, ensure that there is perfect justice for all – which, of course, we are unable to appreciate without the larger picture."

"And joy?" I asked, feeling my question had not been answered.

"We need even more of a cosmic overview," he replied, "for joy, being the reason for all that exists, has a cosmological foundation. To appreciate this, one needs to go back to the beginning of Time. Even before that. To answer your question, if you're really interested, I'll lead you through a step-by-step explanation of why and how the Universe came into existence."

"Okay," I agreed, "but let's eat something first. I'm starving and the beer is going to my head."

"We could go to Doolin," he suggested.

The weather had changed. Once again, it was pouring with rain. We wound down a narrow corkscrew lane, passing the converted ruin of a castle, and came to the seaside village of Doolin, once a quiet haven for fishermen, now an international mecca for musicians, so my lover-chauffeur told me.

I wanted traditional Irish food and music. We weren't in the mood for wandering around, so entered the first restaurant we came to, which flaunted the sign: 'LIVE MUSIC TONIGHT'.

"Well, what's it going to be?" Roderic asked, as we seated ourselves in a cosy corner by a peat fire. "Poached wild salmon? Irish stew? Lamb chops with mint sauce? Or bacon and cabbage? Maybe you'd like to start with oysters?" We chose the salmon.

"Okay. Are you ready," he asked, as we waited for it to arrive, "to hear the story of Creation and what it's really all about?"

I replied with a mixture of curiosity and reluctance. Part of me really didn't want to know. I felt resistant to the possibility I might have to review my lifelong convictions. On the other hand, maybe I'd be enlightened and enriched. At least entertained!

"*You* are going to do the creative imagining," he declared to my surprise, "and discover all the answers yourself. Are you ready?"

"Give me some wine; then I may be."

"Imagine that *you* are the One Supreme Being," he began.

I giggled and looked around, feeling a bit embarrassed. Could anyone hear us?

"Nothing else exists. Only you! *You* are the One Supreme Being out of which all Creation sprang. Go into the Void, into the nothingness, and allow yourself to imagine from this perspective."

I closed my eyes, attempting to do just that.

"Go back to that moment *before* anything existed and ask Your Self, *as the One Supreme Being*, why You have any need for Creation in the first place. For one who is All That Is, what could possibly motivate You to create anything?"

I needed time to think.

"Erudite philosophers may not give you the answers, but children know instinctively," he proclaimed, giving me a clue, I guessed.

"I'd say it's pretty boring being on one's own," I suggested.

"Exactly."

"I'd want someone to be with, to love, share, play, and interact with."

"Precisely. It comes down to this: All life *is* play, all life *is* joy, at least from the perspective of the Creator. Playing for the *joy* of playing, loving for the *joy* of loving, creating for the *joy* of creating – that is all. Life exists for no other reasons. Can you, as the One Supreme Being, give me any other?"

I couldn't. Not in a few seconds, maybe not in a few minutes.

"The cosmologists of the ancient Vedas knew this over five thousand years ago," he said, "and they haven't been surpassed in the vastness and all-inclusiveness of their cosmic view since."

"So what did *You*, the One Creator, do?" he asked, not waiting for an answer. "In order to play, It, *You*, needed another. As you've stated, it's boring on one's own. So It, *You*, divided Its Self. Thus, the One became Two. This was the Beginning, the creation of duality – of opposites, polarity, dark and light, negative and positive, *yin* and *yang*, feminine and masculine principles, matter and spirit. Then the Two gave birth to the Three. The Trinity we call it, the Three in One and One in Three. And this process of division continued, the Three becoming 'the Ten Thousand Things' as the Taoists say, the zillion things which comprise All That Is."

This I could follow.

"But this was not enough. There was a major problem. At least, there would have been, had it not been so perfectly resolved before the whole process began. While the One Supreme divided Itself for the purpose of play, there could only be minimal interaction – indeed, there could be no authentic interaction – so long as each aspect of Itself remained fully empowered and fully conscious of Its Divine Nature. It's obvious, isn't it, that no game is possible when each party knows precisely what the other is thinking, when each is all-knowing and all-powerful. So another process coincided:

"The One Supreme Being continued not only dividing Itself *ad infinitum* but 'fell' into increasing limitation and, above all, into forgetfulness of Its own true nature. This, in what the Church calls the 'Fall', was not due to any sins of man, as you can see, but an enactment of Divine Intent."

I didn't know whether I could see it or not. Partially, yes, but not fully.

"In the entirety of existence," he continued, "there is nothing but the One Supreme Self. You, I, and all that exists, are but manifested aspects of that Divinity which has *chosen* to fall into forgetfulness of Itself. We are, thus, Divinity in disguise, as the wisest have known and taught throughout the ages – including, let me add, many a Christian saint. This One Self hides Itself playfully in Its creation in order, ultimately, to find Itself. A game which children call 'Hide and Seek'!"

An amazing view! I had never heard anything like it. Could it be true? This notion of the 'Fall' sounded much nicer and more wholesome than the Christian Church picture of sin and damnation; and turned all I'd been taught on the subject on its head.

"The process overall is this," he declared as our fish arrived: "In the Great Cosmic Out-breath when the One becomes Two, becomes the Ten Thousand Things, the One Supreme Being 'loses' Itself in Its creation. Then, billions of years later, in the Great Cosmic In-breath, It begins Its return, ultimately to the Void from whence It came, gradually collecting Itself unto Itself, as It re-awakens and re-members, on Its path back to Oneness."

"What about us? I like to see things personally."

"This, too, is *our* Path of Return, as *we* awaken and remember who and what *we* truly are, expanding in an ever-greater awareness until finally, as fully Self-realized Beings, *we* become one with that Oneness."

"It's all but a play," he concluded, "'the Great Cosmic Play' I call it. Its reasons? Simply for the joys of creativity and play, hiding and finding One's Self, imagining and exploring all the possibilities of Beingness, inventing and playing every conceivable game in every conceivable role, like an actor on a stage, simply for the pleasure … of going to sleep, dreaming, and finally awaking! All for the joy!

"One of my favourite quotations is by the great teacher, Ramtha: "To have understood and become joy is the only destiny that God has given to all mankind, whatever plane they're on. For when you have returned to a state of joy, you have returned to a state of God. For joy *is* what the Father is, an isness that is in joy at all times. To know and become joy, this is the Father's only desire for you." Don't you think that's lovely?"

His discourse complete, we sat in silence.

It's too big to be 'lovely', I thought. In fact, as I reflected, I began to feel upset. No one had ever told me that joy is my God-approved destiny. For a long time, it had felt so 'right' choosing a path of suffering. I had been doing my best to please Him, ignoring my feelings and desires while serving others. Indeed, the more I suffered on Earth, the more I'd be rewarded in Heaven. This was the thought I'd had as a member of my Church. I didn't dare to be joyful, which seemed too selfish. God was serious, so was life. This seemed to work until I had a complete burnout, several years ago, with nothing left to give, either to others or myself. Then I'd realized that my approach to life couldn't possibly be God's will.

It was through Reiki that I learned to care about myself and listen within to my own higher self, which I came to understand as part of my wholeness with its link to the One Great Spirit. It was a shift from seeing 'God' exclusively on the outside to acknowledging His/Her accessability and presence within my own Being. This gave me the opportunity to build a new, personal and more intimate relationship with the Divine, without any mediators. It was then I'd left the Church. Hearing Roderic talk about joy and 'God' with such clarity and conviction triggered painful memories of my past denials, highlighting my limited and negative concepts. I longed to fully release the image of a serious, demanding 'God', which had been paralysing my existence for a long time; and replace it with a loving and joyful one within my own Being. I loved the idea of the Cosmic Out-breath and In-breath. I could see more and more people starting to wake up, connecting with their True Essence, on their way back to Oneness.

There was also the fact, I was beginning to realize, that if you *believe* life is hard, then it will be – not because it is, but because you have declared it so, thereby creating or drawing yourself into situations which prove that you're right. Conversely, as I'd observed with Roderic, if you believe it to be magical, with the Universe supporting you, then this becomes your life experience. At the profoundest level, the choice is ours.

Yet, as for joy being 'the fundamental reality beyond all appearances', I still had difficulties with this. I couldn't imagine that the death of a loved one could be joyful in any way.

"Joy is wholly independent of external circumstances," he insisted, as we resumed our conversation later. "May I tell you a story to illustrate this?"

"Yes, but shall we order some tea first?"

"There's an amazing account by a Hungarian woman who survived a concentration camp and wrote of her experiences in a book called *Talking With Angels*. Do you know it?" I didn't. "Before the war, she'd been meeting weekly for meditation with three companions, all of whom were taken to the camp with her and died in gas chambers. One day, during their meditations, an angel appeared, and most of her book consists of their dialogues with it. Of course, at first, she asked it the obvious question: "Why am I in this horrendous place?"

"'Because you chose to be here,' the angel replied to her astonishment.

"Clearly she hadn't done so consciously. On the contrary, she experienced herself as a powerless victim. Having asked for an explanation, she received this reply: 'Your own soul chose this experience.'

"'Why would it possibly do that?' she asked, finding this response outrageously unbelievable, for what an absurd idea that any soul would choose to go to a concentration camp!

"'You knew that God was joy,' the angel explained. 'You knew that God was within you. You knew, therefore, that the experience of joy was wholly independent of outer circumstances, whatever these might be. But your soul knew that truth is known not in concepts but in being, and that its knowing was merely theoretical; so it, you, chose to *experience* the truth in the most extreme circumstances which life on Earth could offer.' And so it was. Thus she came to know the truth through her experience; and radiating joy in these horrifying circumstances was able to bring joy into the lives of those around her."

I could see the point he was making and longed to be able to live it.

"The story throws an interesting light on human freedom and imagined 'victimhood'," he suggested. "Yes, we're free, but only relatively so at the conscious level. As the evidence from past-life regressions reveals, it's at the level of soul where we make our key life choices."

After this, my philosopher retired; and we sat back to enjoy the atmosphere of the restaurant. Three fiddlers arrived and played traditional Irish music. Not greatly inspired, we left disappointed.

As we drove towards The Boghill Centre, Roderic's mother's former home and donkey stud, where I was booked to stay, I wondered again what I was doing with someone like him. He was so free and unlimited, not bound by conventions, or the need for security or money. He was totally committed to following his own unique path wherever that might lead him, floating in and out of society at will. One of life's explorers, serious seekers. He'd lived so many lives in so many countries in just one lifetime. Why were we together? Could he be more than just my holiday lover, guide and chauffeur? I had my doubts. While he lived in Ireland, I was deeply rooted in Holland. Above all, though, was the fact he was so much older. As his hand alighted affectionately on my knee, I even questioned whether I wanted any further physical intimacy. But there was something special about his energy that attracted me greatly. And I felt so at home with him.

Boghill was chaotic, but pleasantly so. It was now a music centre, run by a Dutch woman married to an Irishman, Sonja O'Brien, who had just hosted a ten-day workshop for harpsichord players. My healing course cancelled as I was told on arrival, it was an ideal base from which to explore the Burren.

Chapter 5

An Ongoing Workshop

Elly

The Burren was extraordinary, with its unique rock formations and abundance of flora. After an hour or so of driving, Roderic stopped the car suddenly and parked alongside a stone wall.

"There's something really special about the land we're passing immediately on our left," he said. "I don't know what it is, but let's investigate."

With the stone wall blocking our view, it was only partially visible. Getting out, I peered over it. What I saw and felt took my breath away. In the small rocky field midst a scattering of hazels was a dazzlement of flowers of many shapes and colours. The whole area radiated a powerful energy which felt almost too holy to enter. Yet, at the same time, it appeared to beckon. So we climbed over the wall silently in awe.

The very ground at our feet seemed other-dimensional. As elsewhere in the Burren, the rock formations had been carved out by wind and rain, playing the roles of landscape architects, designing the most exquisite sculpted enclosures for flowers which they could imagine. Every inch was so precious we hardly dared put our feet anywhere, only doing so with the utmost care as if treading the most sacred land on earth. It was a feeling we both shared, sensing an almost tangible presence of nature spirits. We had entered, it seemed, a devic realm; and stood there motionless.

After a timeless silence, I felt drawn to a particular plant. Tuning into it, I heard it faintly but surely yelling at me: "Wake up! Break out of your shell! Step into your power! You are a healer. Use us! Communicate with us! We are waiting for you." Tears rolled down my cheeks. I was moved by this recognition of my role as a healer. Although I had been working with kinesiology and flower essences as a physiotherapist, I had always felt that I had to apologise for doing so, since these practices were not recognised by my profession. In fact, I had received a letter from the local head of the Department of Health in Holland informing me that they were forbidden, along with other alternative approaches, despite the most impressive results. In the process, I had not been able to own my role fully, always being on the defensive, even hiding myself. I realized at this moment that I could no longer deny the healer inside me. Nor any longer the invisible realm of nature spirits. Though I had experienced them previously in Holland and Australia, while preparing flower essences, I had never taken them seriously. For the first time, I was convinced I'd be able to communicate and work with them; and made a commitment to do so. I remained enchanted in this sacred space for what seemed like an eternity, expressing my gratitude to Mother Earth.

Returning to the car, we drove off quietly, feeling overwhelmed.

Roderic

Since I had parked dangerously on a narrow lane, which was also a busy tourist route, I had had to return and guide the passing traffic while Elly remained in this devic paradise. Since I had already had many experiences of Nature lifting her veil for glimpses of her mysteries, I'd felt this was primarily an occasion for her.

While waiting, I found a dragonfly on the wall. A transparent blue. I had never seen one with such a colour. Seeing it was dead, I could examine it closely. In *The Language of the Birds*, I reflected on the possible significance of its appearance. I knew that it represented illusions symbolically, though not in the way these are generally understood. It speaks of the facade of outer appearances, which we call 'reality' though it's merely superficial. While we dismiss what's behind Nature's veil as mere dreamtime, in fact it's another dimension, even more real, of Life's wholeness. The dragonfly represents the elemental world of nature spirits and its wisdom. Found upon one's path, it signals their presence. It may also indicate, as Jamie Sams and David Carson suggest in their Native American *Medicine Cards*, that it's time to break down the illusions one holds that restrict one's ideas and actions. This, I realized, was what was happening for Elly; and that my role in the circumstance was to serve the feminine.

Elly

In the afternoon, we walked deeper into the rocky landscape and found a place to rest. There was a formation of rocks laid out flat in an unusual manner. With a central triangular stone and other large ones pointing outwards around it, the arrangement looked like a star. I spread myself out on the biggest one, luxuriating in the sun with eyes closed.

All of a sudden I felt a hand moving across my belly. The sun was warm, the rocks were warm, his hand was warm. Relaxing more, I allowed it to explore. Slowly, as if savouring every moment, he undid my jeans, and his hand slid down further, descending to my most intimate sensual areas. Here his fingers moved gently backwards and forwards. My body writhed, undulating on the rocks, finding its rhythm in harmony with his. I just lay back and let things happen, my quiet murmuring turning into a roar as I groaned my pleasures into the landscape.

It was another landmark experience, not because of the obvious enjoyment, but because I didn't feel I had to respond. I'd always felt under pressure to do so, wondering, "Is *he* being satisfied? Does *he* expect *me* to have an orgasm? Etcetera", all of which meant that I couldn't fully receive. But now I did nothing. I was just in a timeless space receiving, enjoying the waves that flowed rapturously through my body. This was a healing. It was possible because of his attitude – giving, loving and accepting, without expecting anything.

Roderic

Not expecting, yet expectant! – for I too was aroused. While to have made love with her on the sacrificial altar of these rocks, arrayed so uniquely in this strange lunar landscape, would certainly have added another dimension, the moment seemed complete in itself. It was a pleasure to have her laid out before me and dare my interventions; a pleasure to find her so soft and yielding, a feast for the taking; a pleasure to play her erotic keyboard, savouring the notes that responded to my touch, and coax her through the waves and crescendos that brought her to her final ecstasy. Ostensibly the giver, I received much.

55

Elly

In the evening, we went to a pub in Kilfenora where there was a gathering of musicians. The star performer was our hostess, Sonja, playing traditional Irish music on her fiddle. She seemed able to play melody over melody over melody all at the same time, introducing one after the other, almost with the challenge, "I bet you don't think I can bring in one more", and then she did. Her dexterity had us riveted. The pub in its entirety was captivated by her charm, a mixture of genius and angelic presence, childish playfulness and master virtuosity. Even the sullen began clapping and laughing. Others danced on their chairs. I had come to Ireland to hear traditional music, not expecting it to be played by a Dutch lady. Even the Irish acknowledged her gifts and flocked to accompany her.

Back at Boghill, we collapsed into bed, though not yet depleted. Our bodies were drawn together like magnets. It was now my pleasure to give to him. As he laid back in anticipation, I took my fingers on a little dance and followed with my lips. I relished his body, so open, vulnerable, and yet so male. What intrigued me were his tiny buttocks, smaller than my breasts. I enjoyed my oral explorations and his responses, though I was a bit concerned that he was sharing his delights with whoever was in the next-door room, the walls being so thin. Otherwise, I felt completely at ease, surprisingly since I hardly knew him.

Early the next morning, I was wondering whether to return to Cork with him or remain at the centre as intended. It was pouring with rain. I didn't want to be stuck in such weather, surrounded by boggy fields and far from the nearest village. Maybe he is my ticket to sunshine? Yes, it seems. So we headed south.

Knowing my interest in pre-Celtic sites, he suggested we go to Lough Gur. "It's one of the most ancient in Ireland. The landscape records over 5,000 years of history. It has the largest stone circle in the country with over a hundred stones and a lovely atmosphere." As the weather had changed, with blue sky appearing, I agreed enthusiastically.

On arrival, we explored a wood and found a spot on the shore of the lough, where we had a picnic.

56

Hovering around us were blue dragonflies. "Exactly like the one I found yesterday," Roderic exclaimed. "I wonder what they're saying to us."

While discussing this, a man approached, wearing a T-shirt with a dragon on it. "According to legends, dragonflies were once dragons," said Roderic. We both laughed at this coincidence. "They are definitely telling us something," he insisted. "Maybe about illusions."

Were devas an illusion? I wondered – those I believed I'd experienced in the Burren. Was our relationship one? We'd found such a beautiful place and I was so enjoying the moment that I didn't feel like going into depth on the subject. Also, I was particularly enjoying Roderic, feeling soft, sensual and womanly towards him. He was giving *me* back to *me* on all levels. I felt so peaceful in his company. He mirrored my gestures playfully, laughing lovingly even at my crooked teeth: "No, they're not crooked," he assured me. "They're just dancing." Feeling so accepted and loved was a gift. So whether our romance was illusion or not, I didn't want to know.

"The Full Moon is due in a few days. We could do a ritual to celebrate," he suggested.

"Shall we swim naked in the ocean?" I responded.

"*You* may like Arctic waters, but *I* am more at home in tropical lagoons."

"Do you know the Game of Transformation?" he asked as we moved from our bench and spread ourselves out on a carpet of grass. I'd heard of it, but never played it, and looked forward to doing so as I'd been told it was powerful. "It can take two or three days, or more," he said, before launching into a description. "On the surface, it's a board game played with dice, but there's nothing random about it. What it consists of in a nutshell is putting questions to the Universe and receiving insights that lead you to the answers. You can put one on any subject requiring clarification in your life. You could ask, for example: Am I in the right relationship? Should I change my job? What is my life's purpose? How can I increase my financial prosperity? ... and so forth. While playing with a piece which represents your soul, you receive feedback on four levels – the physical, emotional, mental and spiritual."

I was excited by the idea.

"The Game only works," he emphasized, "because you invite into the process your guides, guardian angels and other beings of Light. You recognize their participation while playing, because of the perfection you discover, the spot-on relevance of everything that takes place. Otherwise, the randomness in throwing the dice would be meaningless, even absurd. At the same time, it reveals aspects of your character, fixed patterns, resistances and blockages, often hidden, which may be standing in your way. So, while it's fun, it can also be intense. I've been using it in workshops for the past twenty years with people from all over the world. It was developed at Findhorn in Scotland and has changed many lives – including my own dramatically."

We decided to play on our return to Cork.

Before leaving Lough Gur, I bought a Celtic cross in a thatched cottage-shop – a fertility symbol, I realised later, reading the label. A mile further on, we came to the Grange Circle with its one hundred and thirteen stones. We walked around it clockwise before entering from the east. Happily, we were alone.

"Wouldn't it be lovely to get married here?" As I was thinking this, Roderic said it. Another synchronicity that blew my mind. And also scared me. Was it really meant to happen?

We shared our vision of the celebrations. "A feast with a roasting lamb in the middle, with people singing and dancing all around," I suggested. "Yeah! With flowers in their hair, drums beating, fiddles and accordions playing," Roderic added, gesticulating wildly. "Women's and men's circles and rituals," I imagined, becoming more excited. "The groom riding in on a white horse and bearing the bride away," Roderic fantasized, taking me in his arms and whirling me in a dance.

The wedding took on a dimension of impending reality. Could he, Roderic, really be the one? What will be, will be, I thought, with a sense of inevitability, as if my soul had already decided. But I had to get rid of a lot of resistance, as he didn't fit my image of an ideal husband, whatever that was; and I was concerned with the difference in our ages, not from my own point of view but in terms of what I imagined others would think, my mother, sisters, friends and neighbours – which, of course, was ridiculous.

My hand slipped into his as we walked. I really love this guy, I thought. At the same time, I don't know what the hell I'm doing with him. My mind was buzzing all the way back to Cork and Kristin's.

On our arrival, her first question to me was: "Well? Did you have a romance?"

"Why?" I asked reservedly.

"Because you look so good."

"We explored a little," I replied minimally.

The following day, she flew to the States. Roderic had agreed to look after her house and bouncy dog, Nero, a red setter, in her absence, so we stayed on. I had four days left.

The weather wasn't great, so we started to play the Game of Transformation.

"We each have a piece which represents our soul," said Roderic, while laying out the cards. "First we are born, then we move around the board, gradually up through the four levels from the physical to the spiritual, having various experiences on the way."

We began by formulating our questions, both asking, "What kind of a relationship would I like to manifest?" while I also asked, "What is blocking me from stepping fully into my power?"

We had great fun. I saw Roderic in his element. He was a gifted teacher, highly perceptive, and looked beautiful.

I moved quickly through the physical and emotional levels, encountering no setbacks or blockages, but got stuck on the mental. My biggest fears were stepping out of my security and speaking up my truth in the now moment. The feedback showed that I was constantly looking outside of myself for sources of direction rather than following my own inner knowing. I picked up so many cards relating to birth, purification, break-through, rebirth, transformation and adventure, making me feel there was a major change ahead. On the spiritual level, the Game invited me to consider my wildest dreams in a relationship. What did I want? Lots of love, fun and magic, and support on all levels. "Yes," I jumped up and shouted, stretching out my arms to the sky. "Yes, I am ready." Nero barked his approval.

Roderic had a problem being born in the Game; that is, he had a caesarean operation. Thereafter, his setbacks and challenges were on the physical and emotional levels. Significantly, since he had not been open to an intimate relationship for the past few years, he drew the card: *"Taking high risks in relationships brings equally high rewards."* After processing this, he received the confirmation: *"You have broken through your closed door of isolation."*

Though we played for two days, the Game remained unfinished. "The first time that has ever happened in twenty years," said Roderic. Evidently, we had unfinished business.

Chapter 6

A Celtic Marriage?

Elly

We spent my last day at his cottage. The area was so beautiful and peaceful, I realised again how I longed to live in nature rather than in the city with its noise, dirt and concentration of people. The sun was shining, not a puff of wind, so we walked to the beach. It was empty except for a heron stalking the shallows, gulls on the waves, and cormorants drying their wings on the rocks. The tide was out and we paddled on the water's edge. I was amazed by how many different shapes of seaweed were lying around – tiny leaves, sponges, bubbly fronds, fans of palm, and lengths of cord metres long. "That's sea lettuce ... that's bladderwrack ... that's kelp ... that's *chorda filum* ... that's carrageen moss, very popular in Ireland and used for making jellies and thickening soups," Roderic pointed out, familiar not only with their names but uses.

Roderic

I was not counting cormorants nor so intrigued by seaweeds. Elly was off to Holland in the morning. Was this the end of our relationship? It seemed to me to have only just begun. But, if we were to continue, how? Also, what was it for her? Was it a holiday romance or more? I needed to find out. My mind was buzzing at a fast rate.

Elly

We walked back to the dry sand and lay cosily together. Since I had my period and wasn't feeling so warm, I was wearing one of Roderic's long woollen sweaters. Comforting me, he placed a hand on my belly.

"Wouldn't it be lovely if we had a baby?" he asked suddenly.

It was the way he said it that touched me. I was surprised by the intensity in his proposal: and sensed a longing in his voice. Nobody had ever asked me that question. It was such a poignant moment. In a flash, I saw pictures of a meditation I'd had in France with a lover and child, the fertility cross I'd bought at Lough Gur, and the 'Guardian Angel' of Birth which had appeared as the central theme of my Game, all coming together. I felt the desire not only to step more fully into life but also to bring it forth. Yet I didn't know what to answer. If I said "yes", which I felt like doing, it would change my life dramatically. I'd have to leave my job, home, family and country. Was I prepared for this? It would be wonderful to have a baby and share the beauty of the process. But I didn't say "yes" and didn't say "no". We lay there for a long time.

Roderic

One had to divine Elly's feelings as they were not always put into words. When they surfaced like bubbles from her depths, I grasped them as they appeared and coaxed them into articulation. At a mental level I needed clarity. We could be two boats sailing in an ocean separately or we could guide them to meet. While life is characterized by uncertainties, one can reduce their probability with clear intentions. Either one does nothing with the opportunities that present themselves or one can choose to act decisively. While one can go with the flow, one can also influence its direction. 'Let's just write to each other and see what happens' was not an option I'd go along with. Holiday romances tend to fizzle out after a few hot and whining letters. We both needed clarity, I felt, with an understanding if not agreement on a common aspiration.

Elly

As we lay on the beach, Roderic broke the silence, with yet another astounding idea. "Let's have a Celtic Marriage," he proclaimed.

"A what!?" While a *Celtic* marriage sounded strange enough, the one word 'marriage' gave me more of a shock, the idea of a longterm committment frightening me.

"What *is* a Celtic Marriage?" I asked.

"One in which you make a commitment for a year and a day. It was the practice of some Celtic tribes ..." I was relieved. "At the end of this year and a day, you decide whether or not you want to renew the arrangement. If you do, you can extend it for another year and a day, or change it into something else. Each is free to make the choice."

"No divorce in the middle?" I asked, half joking.

"No. Once the commitment's made, it's honoured for the period."

We discussed the idea and got quite excited. It did seem to have great advantages. I could live with Roderic for a year and a day without having to make a decision binding me for the rest of my life. At the same time, I could experience what it would be like to have a commitment. I had never dared to step into one. At this moment in time, I wasn't open to a lifelong contract and wondered if I ever would be, having a fear of being locked into a situation or trapped in a routine in which the flow of life and my opportunities are restricted. I like to feel free to go wherever I want whenever I want; and have deep and intimate sharings with others, which doesn't mean having sex with them, without the usual feelings of jealousy and ownership. Besides, in all truthfulness, how can you make a promise for a lifetime? My truths are changing and evolving: How can I be sure, let alone promise, that I will feel the same in twenty years' time, or even ten or five? Or even that I will be the same? Or have the same aspirations or goals? So, would I honour a promise once made or my truth as it has become? That would be a real conflict.

But, for a year and a day, I would have a period of security in which I could fully explore and express my truth without fear of losing my lover; and at the end of it, I'd be free to leave the relationship without guilt for not keeping my promise, without the feeling of having let someone down, and, above all, without any sense of failure – because it would be part of the deal in which we had allowed each other freedom of choice.

Roderic

The idea of a Celtic Marriage for a year and a day had come in a flash. I had read of it somewhere, but couldn't remember where, nor any of the details. Later, I found a mention of it in John Matthews' *Elements of the Celtic Tradition*. "Trial marriages of 'a year and a day' could be contracted in May," he wrote, "particularly at

Beltain, a time of major gatherings and fairs, generally held around the first of the month." It was also a time for divorce, when couples could come before a brehon, a public official, and declare their relationship at an end, as ancient Irish law tracts record. It seemed perfect in modern day circumstances, ours at least, with a clear format which could embody whatever intentions and understandings we wished. It would provide a direction, ensure continuity and give us time to reflect on what we really wanted. It was a more realistic and manageable time frame. It also seemed to offer a good balance between freedom and commitment. But I could see that Elly wasn't quite ready. Though she loved the idea, she needed time to digest. At least I had made my intentions clear.

I did not tell her of my request to the Universe for a soul mate and that, in my convictions, she was clearly the answer. It would have put too much pressure on her.

Elly

Late in the evening, seated outside his cottage, I was enjoying my last hour of being in nature, looking up at the stars, breathing in the vastness and silence, when a bat swooped. Others followed. I counted seven. What mysterious little creatures! I wondered what their message was. I went inside and picked a card at random from Roderic's pack of Native American *Medicine Cards*. Out of forty-four furry, feathered, and sea-dwelling creatures, I drew the Bat. I wasn't so surprised anymore by such magical synchronicities. I had enrolled on a course in miracles it seemed.

"If Bat has appeared in your cards today," the commentary advised, "it symbolizes the need for a ritualistic death of some way of life that no longer suits your new growth pattern. This can mean a time of letting go of old habits and of assuming the position in life that prepares you for rebirth, or in some cases initiation." Once again, the same universal feedback: Time to let go of the old and step into the new. Exciting but scary!

What a month I'd had! I was ready to go home. To reflect on all I had experienced before deciding what to do.

Roderic

I was ready to get back to work and finish the final draft of my book, *Father, Son & Mother Earth*.

As I drove her to the bus station in the early hours of the morning, we were not inspired to exchange words. Silent touches expressed what we felt. Not one for long goodbyes, I hugged her briefly and left.

Elly

Far too briefly! I was quite dismayed.

Sitting in the bus to Dublin, I pondered on my two disastrous weeks with Jonathan and two blissful ones with Roderic. "What a cosmic joke," I thought. I'd come to spend time with a beautiful guy, expecting a fun, romantic relationship, being in nature, exploring the countryside, intimately sharing our lives. Instead, there had been no sex, no romance, he was not interested in my inner life, we had rushed from city to city, and, during the only free time we'd had, we'd been trapped in tents by pouring rain with me brooding on my unfulfilled longing for companionship and physical closeness. In a nutshell, a taste of hell! Then I had spent two weeks with Roderic, much older than I, who was joyful, enthusiastic, humourous, wise and loving, and had given me everything I'd ever dreamed of, except that he was not a Greek god with golden curls. I felt ashamed that I couldn't wholly accept him. For the first time in my life, I had met someone with whom I could be fully and truly me at all times on all levels. At the same time, I had felt truly at home with him and found peace.

Two weeks of misery, followed by two weeks of paradise, it was as if the Universe was showing me something: "You thought everything you sought was on the outside! Well, it's not! First and foremost, all that matters is on the inside." The Game, too, had reminded me that beauty was primarily on the spiritual rather than physical level. Yes, but ...!

I also wondered if I would ever see him again. Was he really serious?

Stuck in limiting circumstances, it was time to move beyond them. He had the key, I felt, to open up unexplored areas of my being, as well as to the next steps in the unfolding of my life. There were so many things I could learn from him. There are not many with whom you can discuss nature spirits, angels, past-lives and other aspects of the reality and wholeness of life, and who can speak out of their experiences. I had also encountered a lot of magic and wished to spend more time in his company, learning how to draw it into my life. While being with him was an ongoing workshop, sometimes quite intense, it was challenging, fun, and encouraged my growth. The sensual and erotic side was also better than ever before; and with our knowledge of tantra, though rudimentary, it promised to be more so.

"He is my way out," kept repeating in my head. Was this the promptings of an inner knowing, my soul guiding me? Way back in March, wondering what steps I could take, I had received the words, "Wait until the summer". Well, I had just lived through it intensely. Now, clearly, I had choices before me.

An invitation to spend a year in Ireland? What could I lose? I could leave my job temporarily. I would have to leave my rented house for a year anyway, shortly, while it was being reconstructed. A Celtic Marriage for a year and a day, with a lovely being in a lovely place, seemed like a gift from heaven.

Chapter 7

Love as a Long Conversation

Roderic

When I returned from taking Elly to the station, I found a coloured drawing of an angel on my bed, robed in purple and holding a flower, with these words: *"Thank you, Beloved. I wish you lots of happy hours dancing, singing, and nurturing yourself. It's great to be with you. Elly."*

The question was: Will she or won't she want to continue our relationship? Perhaps, when she gets back to the familiar realities of everyday life, she'll find she's awoken from a dream? Or, feeling so secure and comfortable in her surroundings, she'll ask herself, "Why should I give up all this and plunge into the unknown?" and conclude that it's far too risky, especially with a guy like me – whom she'll rightly see as without roots in any particular society and rather unpredictable. I took Nero for a walk and pondered on the situation.

In terms of my request to the Universe Elly was everything I had put out for. We blended with ease and harmony. She was a delight to be with. I adored her. Grounded as she was in her feelings and body, she would be particularly good for me. Undoubtedly, through her influence, I would become more grounded, particularly in my own sensual and emotional beingness, while growing more fully into my own feminine. I sensed a huge potential in our relationship, love-filled, playful, mutually beneficial and creative.

On the other hand, she had just stepped physically out of my life and that could be the end of it. While I had the certainty in knowing what I thought and felt, there was the uncertainty of not knowing what *her* responses would be, and therefore the next steps. One could easily live in a state of anxiety; but I had been down that road on enough occasions to savour the absurdity of this, a victim's road. One can control one's thoughts and feelings *or* be ruled and even tormented by them. Knowingly or unknowingly one chooses. Intentionally or simply by default one chooses. I chose to be aware of my feelings without being ruled by them. Above all, not to be attached to outcomes. At the same time, with obvious preferences, I made the clear decision to keep all options open, particularly our lines of communication, while taking things simply day by day, however the river of life flowed. I was, of course, open to facilitating that flow and even pushing it a little!

I returned to my writing.

Elly

Surprisingly, arriving home late in the evening, I found a postcard from Roderic already on the floor. The picture was of a dove flying over Ireland with the word 'PEACE' printed on it. Before going to sleep, I drew from my pack of *Angel Cards*. It, too, was 'PEACE'. Yet another synchronicity! Our magical connection was very much alive, undiminished by the seas between us.

I spent the next two days in bed, digesting and processing everything that had happened during the month. It was quite an emotional time. Do I really want to take any of the dramatic steps that seemed so clear in Ireland? I was hovering on the edge of a breakthrough. But, do I dare break out, leave my security and go adventuring, dare to be free, go out into the unknown, to love and be loved? Dare I trust my intuitions rather than the fear-filled reasonings of my mind? My way of living isn't allowing me to explore and express myself according to my deepest desires. It's all about daring. Do I really dare to jump?

A letter arrived from Roderic, which I ripped open impatiently. Headed "A Flash of Inspiration", he suggested coming to Holland the following month. Oops! This *is* becoming serious. If he wants something, he goes for it, I'm beginning to see. Am I ready for this? He also suggested I visit Ireland in October when I had a week's holiday.

His proposals obliged me to become clear. I wrote to him:

It's been hard coming home. The Game of Transformation and you have been stirring me up, bringing unresolved issues to the surface. I had a sort of healing crisis …

You've touched me deeply. I feel the pain of being locked inside of myself and somehow you've given me the key to unlock this. Your loving acceptance has helped me love myself and I'm so thankful for that. It was the first time I'd experienced love, space and freedom. Do you understand what I mean? …

Roderic was not coming from a point of neediness. He seemed so completely happy in himself. While independent, he was fully open to sharing. My decisions and attitudes didn't seem to affect him. Whatever I did or said never made him feel uncomfortable. All this gave me the space and freedom to be, without feeling responsible for his happiness. It's wonderful when someone takes full responsibility for how he or she feels, rather than being dependent and feeling a victim, blaming others or life. This was new for me and helped me stay centred.

Roderic

I enjoyed the space in our togetherness, which allowed us to communicate from our separate positions. I particularly appreciated her openness as she shared her processes. Our love was becoming a long conversation. As she wrote:

Keep writing. It's so much fun coming home after work and finding your letters. I'm feeling better now! My 'wet-suit' has come off. I've changed my concept 'life is hard' into 'life is fun' and hope this will change in all the cells of my body. I have a strong desire to let go and be spontaneous …

This weekend, I'm giving a Reiki 1 Course. I'm looking forward to it, as I love to work with the healing energies and see the miraculous changes they bring, and the excitement of people when they discover that they too can feel the energies flowing through their hands ...

Elly

A letter arrived from Roderic almost every day. If one didn't, I was a bit disappointed. I loved his handwriting, bold, flowing and artistic. Even my neighbour commented as she noted the envelope while standing on my doorstep. This time, he reflected on relationships and gave me wisdom-quotes to think about, ending on the note, "You're a delight and I love you."

Roderic

Clearly, she was also a delight to herself:

> I awoke this morning with the church bells ringing and lay luxuriously in bed knowing it was Sunday. My body felt warm, soft and sensual. It wanted to move. Seeming to have a life of its own, I let it do so. My yoni was moistened and open, longing for you to come inside and move with me in a slow erotic dance ...

I felt like jumping on the next plane. Aside from being provocative, it was clearly an invitation. Sounding the note of a tantric priestess, which I'd strongly suspected she had been in ages past, she continued with an account of her morning ritual:

> I used 'the inner flute' to bring my sexual energy up and through my chakras and felt great. I could have done this for a long time, but when I reach a certain level of intensity I stop. Maybe I'm too scared to lose control.
>
> Do you know 'the inner flute'? It's a breathing technique used by tantric practitioners. You breathe your energy through your sexual organ up to your seventh chakra and down again before letting it out, while moving your pelvis up and down. It's wonderful to share this with someone!

What with flutes, organs, and church bells ringing, this was an unusually musical letter!

Elly

Roderic's response arrived along with a four-page essay on jasmine.

What a deliciously erotic letter! … which sent my cellular, metabolic and bio-vibrational rates shooting up several octaves in a matter of seconds. Thank you for your daring in sharing. What an achievement to be able to have such an experience on your own. It also made me want to be able to de-materialize, travel on a beam of light at the speed of light, and re-materialize beside you. My eagerness to be with you in a slow, warm, moist and sensual dance is overwhelming. However, until then, I am keeping cool. As for "I'm scared to lose control", don't be. We'll crash that barrier, but wait for me!!! …

I was feeling a bit nervous but also excited by his impending arrival into my space and bed.

After dinner, I read his essay. While I had always loved jasmine, drinking teas of its flowers, using its oil in massage and burning incense sticks for its lovely smell, I had never realized how its vibrations affect the subtle energy-centres of the body. I was particularly interested in its enhancement of spiritual awareness in sex, which is the essence of tantra, as well as its stimulating properties.

The following day, a poetic account arrived of his *Spontaneous Chakra Walk Around the Gardens*. I loved the poem, a long one, especially its ending when, coming from the Root, he arrives at the Crown Chakra:

For the crown chakra
   I breathed in the deep colours of the Lavender,
      being the closest to violet.
I didn't eat these either.

But smelled them instead
while imagining a golden light
streaming in from the inner/outer Cosmos
down through all the chakras
into the Earth
and up again.

Then I remembered:
I'm not simply human
but a god awaking.
And I linked across the ocean
with my companion of the soul
and playmate,
A goddess awaking.

Roderic

Nero's barks announced the postman – who, with his special knowing, always placed any letter from Holland on the top of his delivery, handing it to me with his toothless grin. Yes, another from my beloved, this one more serious, about a suspected past-life remembrance in a concentration camp.

This afternoon is sunny. I enjoyed being in the garden, chatting with my neighbour, Agaat. Later, I started reading "Beyond The Ashes". Maybe you know this book? Written by a Jewish Rabbi, Yonassan Gershom, it's about cases of past-life remembrances by those who lived during the Holocaust and are now reincarnated. It's fascinating. Sometimes I have very strong feelings of being a reincarnated Jew. But I don't know for sure. How would one know? When I read that a lot of Jewish women were sexually abused before they died, my body resonated with strong feelings of recognition, even identification. When I write this down I feel very emotional.

Are you able to see former life patterns or sense their energies?

After meeting Elly, I had come to the conclusion that the past-life dimension was certain to come up for her sooner or later, as it had done for others whom I had met, who were committed to their learning, healing and growth. But was this the beginning of a remembrance or merely a sympathetic identification? I wondered. She went on to describe the fears and pains she held, which she felt had no origins in this life. How deep are the roots of the pains we carry! We may look in vain to find their causes in our current lives, the usual approach of psychologists and psychiatrists. Barbara Ann Brennan, acclaimed as one of the world's most gifted healers and teachers, writes in her *Light Emerging*: "According to my observations of the human energy-field during healing sessions, past life traumas always underlie the chronic present-day problems that are difficult to resolve. When traumas from this life are cleared to a certain extent ... the past life trauma that is buried under them arises to the surface to be cleared." If we want to comprehend the human psyche, writes Norman Mailer in his biography of Marilyn Monroe, then "we must question the fundamental notion of psychiatry that we have but one life and one death." "It is time," he suggests, "to look upon human behaviour as possessed of a double root. While the dominant trunk of our actions has to be influenced by the foreground of our one life here and now and living, the other root may be attached to some karmic virtue or debt acquired in lives we have already lived."

My intuition was that what was emerging for Elly was the beginning of a remembrance, which could be explored by going deeply into her feelings. If she wished to do so, perhaps I could support her. I had been working with the raw material of my own remembrances for the past twenty years. With a passionate interest and after extensive studies, I had also been using my knowledge in assisting others. However, I didn't intend carrying on a correspondence on the subject, since, aside from being complex, days if not weeks might be involved in processing. Instead, after a preliminary exchange on the phone, we decided to discuss the subject at our next meeting, which wasn't far off. Meanwhile, I came across a book called *Etty*, the diary of a young Dutch woman, Etty Hillesum, who had also been in a concentration camp. Her diary, a deeply moving account of her thoughts, feelings, philosophical reflections, loves and insights during a three-year period (before she, too, died at Auschwitz) was published in the early 80s and acclaimed throughout Europe. Elly had read it, I discovered; and could have written it herself, for there were many similarities in the psyches of the two. She, Etty, puzzled over many of the same personal issues. In her love life, for instance: Etty's lover, Julius Spier, who was also her teacher, a professional counsellor trained by Carl Gustav Jung, was twenty-eight years older. While she loved him deeply, the difference in their ages disturbed her greatly. Elly's predicament too! *On the one hand*, Etty wrote: "The bond between us has never been as deep and as strong as it is now. With every fresh step the relationship seems to gain in intensity and all that went before seems to pale in comparison, so much more many-sided and colourful and eloquent and inward does our relationship become all the time." *On the other hand*: When the finely cut face of a youth thrust itself between hers and his, she realized to her dismay how old he looked: "I had a kind of snapshot realization then: I would definitely not want to tie my life to his for good. But really such reactions are so mean and unworthy. They all revolve around a convention, about marriage. My life is in any case bound to his for ever, or rather it is united to his. And not only my life, but my soul as well ... It really is mean and petty and unworthy to think whenever you happen to be pleased with his looks, 'Yes, I will marry him and stay with him for ever,' and whenever he looks so old, so age-old, so ancient – and especially when a fresh young face appears beside his, to think, 'No, it's no good.' These attitudes simply must be rooted out. There are so many – how shall I put it? – impediments to truly deep feelings and relationships, relationships that transcend all the bounds of convention and marriage. And the real problem is not even the question of convention and marriage, but the preconceptions one carries about in one's own head." Yet she wrote later: "To put it quite soberly and bluntly, the difference in our ages is too great." Thus she oscillated back and forth, from acceptance to resistance, from loving to denying, never finally

74

resolving the issue – one which Elly, as she realizes, carries within her, to be resolved, for Life has presented her with a more or less identical situation, filling her with a mixture of longings and doubts.

Elly

Doubting is an exhausting mode. My body has its knowing, my soul has its knowing, but my mind is a turbulent sea of conflict. For years I had been dreaming of the perfect husband, lover, which included marriage. My picture was a stereotype promoted by the media of glossy advertisements which Roderic didn't fit. My previous boyfriend had also been much older. Why was I drawing this into my life? Was it to resolve a past-life issue? What really concerned me was what other people thought. Or what I thought they might think! I wanted them to agree with me, to be accepted rather than rejected, therefore please them rather than disappoint. While everything was so perfect in being with him, these fear-based thoughts and my dependency on others bothered me greatly. Actually, it all comes down to the fact that I do not dare to live my own truth. I yearned to be centred in my own convictions. To find strength in this, I enrolled on a series of voice and dance workshops which aimed at connecting people with their uniqueness and giving it expression. In these, I yelled, screamed and roared my truths from deep within my belly, which assisted me in making the fundamental shift from constantly looking to the outside for approval, to honouring who and what I was in essence, what *I* believed and what *I* felt.

One night, I received a picture in a dream: I was driving a car. The problem was that I was in the back, while both my parents were seated in front. I could hardly see where I was going. The message was obvious: I should move fully into the driver's seat, take over the controls, and follow my own path. I am here to honour my own truth, not to live by the directions or expectations of others.

When I was staying with Roderic at Kristin's, there was a book by my bed, *Getting The Love You Want*. I asked him to order me a copy and received his comments by return:

When I asked the Universe how one gets the Love one wants, it replied: "By giving the Love one wants."

It's too flipping clever!! ...

I have just perused Kristin's copy. It looks interesting, but – mon dieu! – it makes relationships look so blooming complicated one might sensibly conclude they are best avoided! ...

I laughed. Yes, sometimes it seems much easier to stay away from them. He continued:

However, to be serious: I am open to a relationship with you in which a primary function and dynamic is mutual loving support in self-healing and growth; in which there is a conscious acceptance and commitment to this; in which each is the lover, healer and teacher of the other – though, ideally, we are also our own lovers, healers and teachers, as the wise say. So, do you accept? Think about it. It's a responsibility.

I love the way he puts things, so clearly and consciously. Yes, I'll think about it. He elaborated in a letter that followed:

Ideally, a relationship evolves into a Spiritual Partnership – which, while based on love, includes clear intentions of mutual support on our individual soul paths of awakening, healing and creative unfoldment – as may be summarised by the words "inner growth". This gives a relationship a meaningful purpose, a clear focus, and a rock foundation. Don't you think?

I was in awe. After all, what is a relationship about? I had been looking for answers for years. You fall in love and then what? Marrying, settling down and living happily ever afterwards, didn't seem to provide a meaningful enough purpose, not even in the context of raising kids. Something essential was missing. Relationship as a Spiritual Partnership? – this was it, one which included soul not as an abstract concept but everyday reality. While I couldn't grasp the totality and consequences of it all, my whole being resonated with the idea, as if I had found a long lost treasure.

I liked the way he had described the Cosmic Inbreath and Outbreath during the summer. I had been thinking about it a lot. And if we are on our way back to Oneness with the Divine, the Source from which we come, we all have to clear and transform our negative thoughts, feelings, belief systems, and energies. What better place to explore, awaken and heal aspects of our innermost self than in the context of a relationship, particularly an intimate one? Instead of blaming and fighting and even killing each other for our shortcomings and imperfections, we could lovingly support each other to heal them. Relationship as a Spiritual Partnership, what a wow! I replied immediately:

Roderic

As she wrote:

A Spiritual Partnership, what a fantastic concept! Everything falls into place at the profoundest levels. Of course a relationship is about the awakening and healing of our souls and the support we can give to each other on our individual journeys. I'm longing for it, but am I ready? Deep down I want to say 'yes', but there are still levels of fear and resistance. I want to be with you next week and be completely open to hear, feel and see my truth in this. Commitment is a big step, don't you think? When I was with you, and also when I read your letters, I have a feeling of coming home. I want to follow this feeling, but I'm scared it will change my life completely, though I have a need and desire for this. Do you understand what I mean? I will and I won't, I do and I don't – this drives me crazy!!!

It might have driven me crazy too, but for the feeling that her soul had already made its decision and that it was only a matter of time before she had dealt with her fears and resistances.

I trusted. That was an interesting word. What was I trusting? Elly? No. Nothing on the outside. I trusted what I felt was an inner dynamic, a moving river drawing us both along our destiny-paths. I trusted that whatever was going on was perfect. I was honouring my process with the Universe, which had begun after my request for the ideal soul mate. Having read the signs, she was clearly it. Even if she didn't want to know it yet!

Elly

When 'going crazy', I go dancing, which helps me connect with my innermost Self and get rid of my doubts, at least momentarily.

I can't believe he's here next week.

Roderic

Aside from the pleasures of re-uniting with Elly, I was looking forward to being in Holland which I hadn't visited for over twenty-five years. I had the most unusual connections with the Dutch, which I had never fathomed. Among them: While I was a guest of their Government, locked up in prison, the Dutch Royal Family was staying in my family's former home in Ireland as guests of the Irish Government, enjoying a three months' holiday by the sea. A strange exchange! I could relate many others. While I had developed a great admiration for the Dutch, I had tasted little beyond fleeting images of the land they inhabited. So, I looked forward to roaming it freely.

Elly

Feeling a bit nervous, I took the train to meet Roderic at the airport.

Sometimes I know in the first moment whether I'm going to say 'yes' or 'no'; and if it's 'no', there's little that can change it. What would happen if I had this feeling when he stepped off the plane? Perhaps my love for him was an illusion? Was the magic only for our time in Ireland? Maybe he was just a friend or my wisdom-teacher? It's so easy to dream when you're writing letters. If I sense a 'no', what will I do or say? Suggest he takes the next flight home? I know from my experience I can be quite horrific.

His plane was late. That didn't help.

Suddenly, there he was.

Chapter 8

Four Walls,
a Floor & a Ceiling

Elly
I could see him through the glass as he waited for his luggage, a tall agile figure, wearing white trousers and a polo neck, with a long brown fur-collared coat and a Mongolian fur-lined hat. He looked special in the midst of all those people, not simply by the way he dressed, but with his radiant air of confidence. After all, he was not as strange as I'd imagined, more sophisticated, in fact quite elegant. It was fun having time to observe and prepare myself.

"Yes," I sensed deep down, "I like him."

Gosh, I thought, he looks so extravagant, a man of the world, used to the best when he's not in the wilds. Will he be bored in my simple place? Maybe we should go to Amsterdam first? As he came through the doors, my whole body felt ready for a passionate welcoming. He was so enthusiastic seeing me. "I'd forgotten how beautiful you are on the outside," he said. "I'd been focusing on the inside." I smiled happily as I sank into his arms, soaking in his smells, which seemed to carry the lifetime of his experiences in many countries.

"Let's sit down and have a coffee before we decide what to do," I suggested. It felt so good to be with him again. He lit me up with his sparkling eyes, flowing spontaneity and joyfulness. As he touched me intimately to my embarrassment and delight, I knew Amsterdam was no longer an option.

Roderic
We arrived in Leiden, a university city of ancient buildings, canals, bicycles, great charm and lively atmosphere.

"What peacefulness!" I remarked as we walked through the courtyard garden to her house, built in 1694, as a plaque on a wall informed me. Inside, white spaces, simple elegance and a sense of sacredness. Flowers everywhere, a red rose on the table, welcoming me, deep purple in her upstairs drawingroom and a vase of sunflowers in the bedroom. We drank wine to celebrate and hardly saw daylight for the next twenty-four hours as we rediscovered and devoured each other in waves of quiet and passionate embracing.

"Let's go to the market," she suggested, late the following morning. I love such places, the pulse of people, colourful and bustling. I was struck by the variety of produce, of fish, cheeses, flowers, herbs, and other bounties of the earth, being sold by Turks, Moroccans, Indonesians and Dutch. After stocking up for the weekend, we wandered along the banks of canals where people sat on terraces drinking beers and coffees. Coming from a world of mountains, bogs and trees, it was like walking onto a film set. Over the centuries, the Dutch had created a rich, beautiful, and well-ordered environment. It felt great moving around it. Also to be in love.

Elly

He kissed me passionately on a crowded street.

"Don't be so shy," he said, as he held my body against his and I glanced around anxiously. "The world loves lovers," he purred into my ears.

Roderic

We slept, ate, made love, talked and talked, occasionally meditated or gave each other Reiki, danced and tranced. Aside from shopping and a bike ride into the countryside, we never left the house, except for Elly who had two days at work. As for roaming freely around Holland, it was back to four walls, a floor and a ceiling, this time voluntarily, deliciously cocooned.

Elly

"Wait for me before you crash any barriers," Roderic had written in one of his letters. I did and we did. It was such a gift that he had mastered the art of semen retention and could enjoy sex without the usual male urge to rush into orgasm. Without this hurried drive, I could relax. Often I had been so frustrated that sex was over even before I had warmed up. Now, we had time to be timeless, to be fully open to each other as love flowed between us. I had desired such a lover and now I had one. All day long, we bathed in the glow.

Roderic

It is not well considered how depleting ejaculation actually is. On each occasion, between two and five million sperm are discharged, with all of the glands, organs and vital energies contributing to this production. Over his lifetime, the average male ejaculates five thousand times, which amounts to roughly four gallons or fifteen litres of a liquid as potent as enriched plutonium! Not only is semen discharged *outwards* but also vital life force. So what, ideally, is one supposed to be doing with it? I knew that the ideal was not simply to retain it but to direct the sexual energy which had been generated *inwards* and *upwards*; and then circulate it around the body. While I had read about this and experimented minimally, I needed practical experiences. In putting out my request to the Universe, I had invoked the assistance of a lover whose knowledge qualified her to be my teacher. I was excited knowing that she was now by my side, evidently, though not yet in her awareness, a once-upon-a-time tantric priestess. We had fun sharing our knowledge and experiences on these subjects, while nibbling snacks, typically Dutch, of smoked eel and salted herrings.

"When I practise the Microcosmic Orbit, as Taoists teach," said Elly, "I circulate my sexual energy by moving it from my genital area up along the spine, into my head, filling it, using my tongue against the roof of my mouth as a switch, and then letting it flow down the front of my body through my throat, heart, solar plexus and belly, back to the genital area, completing the circle."

"Sounds like a contortionists' performance!" I responded playfully. "How do you do that?"

"Well, I have to stimulate myself first," she smiled, "to create the necessary energy."

"That must be fun." I interjected. "And how do you move the energy?"

"By directing it with my awareness, intention and breath. On the in-breath, I draw the energy up my spine; and on the out-breath, I release it down my front. Doing this in a continuous cycle, I not only increase my energy but open the channels through which love can flow more fully and freely. This is especially so when I breathe through blockages and release stored up emotions. Overall it's a wonderful process, which also greatly increases vaginal sensitivity. It's the basis of enlightened sex."

"What about your orgasms?" I asked.

"They have changed dramatically. The practice leads to a full bodied, heightened as well as prolonged orgasm … which is in sharp contrast to the one confined to the genitals … which certainly gives a quicker thrill but lasts only a few seconds. For the male it's the same process. And rather than being depleting it's vitalizing. This is so important. All males should know these basic differences, don't you think?"

"Definitely. They should all be sent to specialized schools where they can learn the essential arts of lovemaking!"

Elly

While I was eager to explore all the dimensions of more enlightened sex together, especially the practice of consciously directing one's sexual energies, this was for later, I felt. Now, while we were still in a basic discovering-each-other phase, I preferred to go more playfully in a spontaneous flow.

Roderic

"Would you like an awakening of the senses?" Elly asked one wet and windy afternoon.

"What's that?" I enquired: "Mine are already on full alert."

"It's a special treat, a feast of touch, tastes, sounds and smells. You lie back and simply receive."

Sounded irresistible! Favoured by the weather, our journeys had become inner.

While I showered, Elly prepared the room, creating, I imagined, a temple space. She came to collect me, tied a blindfold around my eyes and led me in fully naked. The room was warm. She led me to a mattress covered with velvet, on which I layed in silence and darkness.

I became aware of a smell. It was a rose.

I breathed it in deeply. It became the totality of my experience.

I felt a tingling touch on my right foot, which moved with scintillating slowness up the inside of my leg. It was a feather.

Lightly brushing intimate parts it then travelled back along my left leg.

Return to stillness.

Suddenly, tinglings in both feet: Now there were two feathers, gliding upwards in spiralling movements. In wind-rushing flights they swept around my penis, charming it from its slumber like an uncurling snake, before moving onwards.

Return to stillness.

A soft, wet, jelly-like object touched my lips. I couldn't imagine what it was. I explored it with my tongue, mildly sweet, almost odourless, and erotic to touch. She pushed it between my lips. It felt like a giant milk-dripping nipple. Was it a fruit? It was unrecognisable. She moved it rhythmically in and out phallically. I sucked it phallically.

Return to stillness.

There was a noise like the showering of raindrops which came and went in waves of crescendo and subsiding gentleness. A tribal rainmaker? Its cascading sounds washed over me refreshingly.

Another smell invaded my nostrils. Sandalwood? I flashed back through time, embarking, it seemed, on a journey of remembrance. I was in 18th Dynasty Egypt. But another sensation followed, far too quickly, then another, returning me to the present:

To the sound of a Tibetan bowl humming, a warm mouth engulfed a toe.

As smudging smoke of sage pervaded the room, deep over-tone chanting rose from the silence.

One by one, I savoured these delights, which came from the void out of stillness and darkness, and returned to it. Focusing on each as if nothing else existed, awareness and pleasure were greatly heightened.

Indian flutes. A warm liquid poured onto my belly. Hands, with the touch of an angel, spread it gently around my body ...

I felt alive and deeply at peace.

Elly

I love connecting people with their bodies, challenging them to be fully present and alive. They can enjoy the richness of life so much more. The importance of being fully in one's body is greatly underestimated. In our western culture our relationship with it tends to be characterized by disconnectedness and denial. While feelings are separated from thoughts, they are also largely separated from the body. Historically, in our religious traditions, the body became denied with the delusion that this served Spirit. It did the very opposite. One can neither feel whole nor experience oneness when denying the body; whereas, the more it is awakened, the more Life can flow through it and the more Spirit can be experienced. The result of our denial is that most of us are not at all at home in our bodies. While some walk around as if their bodies were simply a mode of transport, others seem to be running around like headless chickens, hardly knowing where they're going or have come from. Disconnectedness is apparent everywhere!

For me the body is a primary reality. As I've come to realize, working with Reiki and kinesiology, it has its own intelligence and knowing. When I listen to it, I learn truths about myself at all levels of my Being. Everything I've ever experienced, every thought and emotion, is stored and reflected in it. Working with children, I have also discovered this to be true. Some can remember feelings and thoughts they had in the womb or during delivery. Listening to my body was the start of my healing journey. It never lies. The challenge is to ask it the right questions. Above all, my body is the temple of my soul and an expression of it, a meeting point of heaven and earth.

Roderic

The next day, I shared with Elly the fact that I had put out a request to the Universe for the ideal soul mate the week before we'd met; and my conviction that she was it.

Elly

I was astounded when I heard this, as I had done exactly the same almost a year earlier, and had completely forgotten. Searching through my old diaries I found my request and showed it to him.

We both laughed looking at the picture I'd drawn of my soul mate to be. I realized how perfectly he fitted my description, down to the smallest details. I only regretted I hadn't been more specific about age!

Is the Universe really so obliging – I in Holland, Roderic in Ireland, both putting out our request and having it fulfilled so precisely? Clearly it is. Having my physical specifications matched – 'tall, agile, with wild jumping hair' – that was the most surprising aspect, convincing me even more that he was the one. Yet, while I could see this, I could hardly believe it. It was like watching myself in a movie, being in it and yet outside of it. The same was so with our proposed Celtic Marriage which felt both real and unreal. I couldn't believe it was me partaking in all of this. Why wasn't I doing what everyone else was doing?

Later, we cycled to my favourite wood a couple of miles outside of Leiden. Here I showed Roderic the tree under which I'd sat when I'd made my request, still astounded how I'd completely forgotten, though the Universe hadn't.

Roderic

We hugged the tree, a giant sequoia, thanking it profusely. There was a wonderful feeling of love and oneness between the three of us.

Elly

"Will the magic I experienced with Roderic in Ireland continue to be a feature of our relationship?" I had wondered before his arrival. Numerous incidents had left me in no doubt. One morning, at the railway station, on my way to work, I passed a flower shop with an abundance of blooms spread out in baskets along the street. One struck me in particular, a pink rose. Normally, these are not displayed singly, since, if someone wants to buy a rose, they choose a red one. I had decided to buy that special pink one on my way home in the evening, but, after a day at work, I had forgotten. I was hungry and dreaming of roast chicken. When I opened the door of my house, I was welcomed by – yes, you may have guessed – a pink rose *and* a chicken! Roderic had bought a whole roasted bird which he'd laid out on a plate on the dining-room table with a single pink rose in a slender glass vase beside it.

This was how it always was, being with him: ongoing inexplicable magic. It made our relationship special and gave me the feeling I was on my right path and the Universe was supporting us. Feedback from others also encouraged me to believe so. "I've never seen you so womanly and radiant with love," both my neighbour and my colleague at work remarked. I was still dependent on comments from the outside! Yet, while everything was saying, "Go for it," I continued to hesitate, my certainties coming and going in waves. Would this ever stop? Why couldn't I simply plunge into our relationship and fully enjoy it?

Chapter 9

Doubts & Despair

Elly

When Roderic left Holland, I was devastated. Only after a week of being unable to write could I share my thoughts and feelings:

Saying goodbye to you at the railway station was also saying goodbye to the magic, the love and joy. All of a sudden I felt left out, not being able to keep in touch with you, myself or the magic.

It took time to find the reasons, and I've found some ...

Deep down I feel love for you, but it's blocked. I have discovered that I have been holding the unconscious thoughts, 'love is not for me' and 'I'm not worthy'. When feeling your love, a very destructive part of me stood up to respond. It wanted to destroy everything beautiful I've experienced with you. It was such a dark and negative energy. Yuk! I let it all come out. I cried, trance-danced, and felt weak as a jelly. But it has given me some space in my heart. A tightness has started to relax. During the night, I felt scared to death by the idea of letting go of old situations, but also felt I would die if I remained in them. I felt trapped ... Letting go of mind-control, honouring what's in my heart, fully trusting my intuition without knowing where this might lead me, is scary. Trusting in the flow and magic of life represents a hundred and eighty degree shift. I need a re-birth! ...

This letter is heavy. I'm heavy! Sorry I'm not as positive as you, at this moment. If you have time to send me some supportive energy, please do.

I got several letters but didn't feel like answering them. He was in such a different mood, enthusiastic, optimistic, making plans, flowing down the river. A note arrived on our proposed Celtic Marriage:

Are you ready for this to take place on 1st May next year, at the time of the Celtic festival of Beltane? I'm going to invite a Celtic expert and 'Master of Ceremonies' to assist in conceiving, creating and organizing the event ...

This was all too quick for me. "Don't push the river," I thought. At the same time: "I want to be ready for this." I replied:

I feel overwhelmed at times, especially when you sent me a copy of 'Our Celtic Marriage' with concrete plans, commitments, etcetera. I'm eager to step into the boat and float, but it brings up deep old fears and pains. I'm still fighting the demons in the cave of my inner world. I'm so scared that I'll be swallowed by you when I open up and give love. Maybe it's the fear of losing control? Or have I had strong negative past-life experiences with marriages? I see pictures of men who were very nice to me before marriage and then afterwards they suppressed me, beat me, and cut me into pieces ...

I hope you can accept that I cannot surrender to you, to love, to life, until I've cleared old stuff. And I will!

"Are you living on another planet?" he asked, jokingly, not having heard from me. He was very understanding:

Happily, love is not measured by letters. Your first arrived on the eighth day of my return. I guessed you were processing. It's great to be so in touch with your feelings and to let them all come up into the Light of consciousness for insights and healing. Really great. Thank you for sharing your feelings.

"Breathe in Joy," the Dolphin says.

He had written on a sheet of light blue paper with waves and a dolphin splashing across it. In a communication that followed, he went more deeply into answering my cries from the darkness:

Beautiful, delicious Elly! ... In relation to your last letter, I awoke this morning with possible insights. I'll begin by quoting your passage: "I'm so scared I'll be swallowed by the other ... I can see pictures of men who suppressed me, beat me, cut me into pieces ..." On the principle that it's <u>we</u> who are the cause of all that happens to us (though we may not appear to be) and that we're not the victims, we know in theory that it's YOU who sets up these situations, so let's consider how you may be doing this.

One way is by sending out conflicting signals to the universe:

Let's consider one of your fantasies – that of being tied up, with arms and legs bound with rope and spread out as if you were on the rack, then raped. Yummy! I'd love to do that for you! And the universe doesn't mind responding to that kind of a signal at all! In fact, it's doing so all the time. But what are this and your other messages saying? Seemingly:

"I want to be overpowered and disempowered."

"I want you to take me, take me, take me, while pretending that I don't."

"In the process, I don't want to give anything."

In this negative passive state of receptivity (which YOU have set up), there is no possibility of an outward flow of love. Which is just how you want it:

"If I was to give anything, I would lose all sense of being overpowered and disempowered. Then it would no longer be a rape, but an exchange, which is what I don't want, for I don't want to give. I want you to take me and go on abusing me.

"Suppress me, beat me, cut me into pieces," is the ultimate in this.

Additional pay-offs in voluntary self-disempowerment and in being such a victim: "No need to take any responsibilities in choosing, loving, giving of myself. I'm so disempowered (tied to a rack) I can't possibly do so."

How wonderful the Universe has been to you: Answering your desires!!! It's been giving reality to your fantasies - enabling you, in various lives, to experience the consequences of your thoughts and attitudes. Consider your possible past-life in a concentration camp, where you were obliged to surrender to sexual abuse. Some would say you were a victim. But it's _you_ who draw such situations into your life, _you_ who create your own futures. You fantasized ultimate self-disempowerment and Life gave you the ultimate experience of it!

How mightily wonderful the Universe is, giving us eternally, unconditionally, ALL we ever ask for! _We_ have the thoughts, feelings and desires, and _It_ gives us the realities.

It responds by virtue of cosmic principles and laws. There is 'Energy follows Thought', 'As Within, so Without', the Law of Cause and Effect, the Law of Attraction, the Law of Resonance, and so forth. But the underlying one is this: The Universe responds to what YOU put out.

Though some of your desires are in the unconscious, you put them there and can get them out. Once you assume the responsibility, you can re-programme yourself.

Have you had enough of all these victim experiences? Do you want to change all this? To choose love? To give out of your freedom, joyfully and unconditionally?

In giving love unconditionally, it's impossible to be overwhelmed and swallowed by another. Have you noticed the Sun being overwhelmed? It shines its glorious light

91

continuously, probably blissfully, without ever asking to receive anything.

Love wants to give. Fear does not.

Love wants to give, for giving is expansive, a gift for the giver as much as the receiver. Fear, which holds back, is contractive.

The more we give, the more we are given to give, is the Cosmic principle.

In any event: Choosing love and going with its flow is MUCH MORE FUN, life-enhancing and life-fulfilling – though it may seem risky.

Love and a Huge Hug

What a letter! My body, my primary truth-detector, came out in goose pimples and a familiar tingling energy moved up and down my spine, confirming its truth. I needed to read it again and again. I made a pot of green tea and retreated upstairs to lie on my bed.

Is it really I who have been responsible for drawing situations into my life? For creating them even? Have I really been disempowering myself? I needed time to get the full picture.

I remembered an event of a few years earlier, when I was preparing for my initiation as a Reiki Master: For a week, I'd been imagining a big fire into which I'd thrown various possessions belonging to my past. Shortly afterwards, while at work, I was called by a neighbour urging me to come home fast as my house was in flames. The upstairs room in which I'd stored all the things I'd wanted to get rid of was almost entirely destroyed, while all that mattered to me was left untouched. That was magical. "Are my thoughts so powerful?" I remembered asking myself at the time. "Did I create the fire?" I had suspected this only, not daring to conclude that I had actually done so. "Thought creates," Roderic had told me. In so many words, he was doing so again.

"I want to stop being a victim and reclaim my power, taking responsibility as the creator of my life," I declared. "I've had enough of being 'the poor little me'." While I'd been realizing the need for this over the years, I now felt ready to make the shift.

While an insight may come with a flash, however, integration takes time and involves inner work. I needed to review my life and its patterns in the light of my new understandings. I gave myself Reiki and felt the energy flowing through my hands, nurturing my body, mind and spirit. "All is well. I am with you," Great Spirit seemed to whisper.

I felt deep gratitude towards Roderic for having taken me seriously and given me so much clarity on these life issues. He was not playing to my 'poor little me' image but helping me see myself from my own soul's perspective, holding up a mirror while tapping me gently on the head. I'd been scared he wouldn't accept my processes or that he'd reject me because of my heaviness, he being so joyful.

While in Holland, he'd left me the manuscript of a book he'd just finished, *A Million Dollars or The Godhead*, yet to be published. I realized that he'd also had his period of doubts, struggles and dark night of the soul; that his wisdom had come from his lived experiences. Travelling the path of the Fool, he had become the Wise Man. While I wasn't 'in love' with him in a wow-wow tear-my-heart-apart sense, I felt a deep love connection. Being with him was so rich and refreshing. I had to stop dreaming about the idealized man based on superficial stereotypes and fantasies and step into the reality of love and live it. Being with him was also a great opportunity in which I could resolve my fears and resistances. Finally, I was convinced that our Celtic Marriage for a year and a day was perfect for me, keeping things open while giving me the support and security I needed as I stepped from one way of being into another. If I didn't jump in this time, I'd never be able to experience the fullness love offers. Deep down I knew he was the right man. "He'll come with the wind," a psychic had told me in Australia, "and with him you'll find Love, Truth and Compassion." This was Roderic. For the first time, I felt sure. I missed him and let him know.

Within a month of his leaving Holland, we re-met in Ireland at Kristin's house.

Chapter 10

Becoming a Creator

Elly

We walked along the cliffs with Nero through harvested fields of barley, breathing in crisp fresh air. As we paused for a hug, Nero took off on the trail of a rabbit.

"You yell," said Roderic after his efforts had failed to recall him. "You've just done a voice workshop!" So I yelled wildly, more for my pleasure than to summon the wayward, for I was clearly too late, as he'd vanished over the horizon.

"Look!" exclaimed Roderic, his attention diverted. "Fat hen!"

I turned around but saw no bird anywhere, neither fat nor skinny. "What are you talking about?" I asked. He bent down to pick small green leaves. "Fat Hen is one of the most delicious plants to eat. We'll collect some for lunch." We boiled it lightly and fried it in butter. It really was delicious, succulent with a tang. "A gift of nature," he said: "It has more iron and protein than spinach and more vitamin B1 and calcium than cabbage" – the nutritional value of wild foods being one of his favourite studies.

After lunch, we sat in the conservatory with tomato plants and a young mimosa. "What are we going to do together?" he asked, leaning towards me, sniffing my white musk and nibbling my earlobe. "What are your dreams? ... apart from being licked from head to toe at least four times a day!"

On the eve of a major decision to give up everything and move to Ireland, the question was certainly relevant. What *would* I do all day long?"

"So, what *are* your personal dreams?" he asked again. "One needs to be clear about these – don't you think? – or, as often happens in a relationship, the dreams of one become submerged by those of the other. Ideally, they should harmonize and be mutually supportive."

"I agree. I've seen this happen often."

The sea sparkled. Autumn sunlight blazed through the glass. It was certainly a day for coming to clarity.

"We create our own realities," he reminded me, "whether we're aware of this or not."

"Tell me again."

"We create by every thought and feeling we send out into life."

"Do you really think we are so powerful?"

"Far more than we imagine. Thoughts are powerful. Thoughts plus feelings are even more so. They create literally. Our realities of today are our thoughts, feelings and desires of yesterday. One way they create is via the universal, Cosmic Laws of Attraction. We set up magnetic fields that draw people, things and circumstances to us; or us to them."

"You mean I'm a sort of magnet?"

"Precisely. Powerfully so. Deliciously so," he chuckled.

Nero was licking my leg. "See!" he exclaimed. "Even he can't resist you! We've been creating our selves and realities for lifetimes, mostly unconsciously. Now, waking up to what we've been doing, and how, we can create consciously. Isn't that exciting, incredibly exciting?" His enthusiasms were always delightfully boyish.

"Yes, it is," I agreed and smiled, encouraging him to proceed.

"But we must know the laws and principles involved. The 'Rules of the Game', I call them, for that's what life is." He looked at me, wondering if I was yet convinced, and continued: "To see life as a game, to see the fun behind the seriousness, to be its conscious player rather than an unwitting pawn or victim, imagine how wonderful that would be, how liberating."

Yes, I would love that, but I wasn't quite there yet. Stepping into the role of a creator was new to me. Clearly it involved major shifts.

"Everything is possible," he declared, as if the world was his oyster, "but first one must be clear about what one wants. What *are* your dreams?" he persisted.

My mind was still locked in limited concepts. Thoughts of money and the possible lack of it had been blocking my imagination. I had many fears and resistances. All of them had been preventing me from daring to dream of whatever I might want to be or do.

"Your dreams, the ones I'm referring to are those of your heart," he sounded the words sonorously, "its yearnings, the primary impulses of your essence, the unique potentialities of your soul, seeking their manifestation and expression." He paused to let this sink in – his gentle, smiling, knowing eyes fixed upon me. "Without honouring the dreams of your heart," he warned, "you'll never have the feeling you're on your right path, nor any deep sense of fulfilment. Knowing and honouring your dreams is your primary responsibility. Daring to go for them, that's the challenge."

It was a moving speech – 'moving' for it urged me to empower myself, not so much by its words as by the charge of his energy. He was shaking me, trying to awaken me, obliging me to become clear about my deepest desires, my innermost truths, and bring them to the surface.

"You're right," I agreed, "I've never allowed myself."

This wasn't wholly true. I'd honoured my dream by making the commitment to become a Reiki Master, when I had to find ten thousand dollars which I didn't have, believing, trusting and knowing that it would come – as it did.

"It's not always easy," he acknowledged. "First, we have our minds to deal with, which usually have a thousand reasons why something is not possible, why one's dreams are unrealizable or we have no right to follow them. Sometimes these make perfect sense, perhaps even most of the time. At least, they appear to. But, if one accepts them, they can keep one in limitation for the rest of one's life; and the mind will tell one how clever one has been, how splendid one is – though, in accepting its limitations, one's heart and soul have been denied – one's whole Being betrayed in fact, for the role of the mind is to serve them, heart and soul."

I could feel the truth in this.

"The limitations?" he questioned. "Most of them never existed. Only in the mind that gave them a reality! But: "Argue for your limitations and they're yours," as Richard Bach said in *Jonathan Livingstone Seagull*. Or was it *Illusions*? That's exactly how it is."

"What if you don't have any money?" I asked. "Isn't that a true limitation?"

"Only if you say so."

"That doesn't seem real."

"Only because you say so!" he repeated and laughed, amused by my perplexity.

"Come on! Be serious!" I requested. "Without any money you're completely stuck," I insisted, even though I'd experienced that this wasn't always so.

"That's what I thought, once upon a time," he confessed. "It's what the logic of the mind tells one with its limited awareness, perspectives and knowledge. From its point of view it's unarguably right, though in my actual experience it seldom is. I've been stuck without money many times before finally discovering the principles involved. Absence of money was never the problem. *I* was. If you like, I can share my experiences."

Luxuriating in the conservatory, bathed in sun while protected from a biting wind, I listened with absorption.

"When I was twenty," he began, "I'd been stuck for two years in an accountant's office as an apprentice, supported by my father for I wasn't getting paid, doing something I hated. It was my parents' wish and sensible from their point of view as it promised a career with excellent prospects, virtually guaranteeing me security and success. Yet none of this interested me. It was their dream, not mine. But what could I do? Having no money of my own, I felt completely trapped. But was I in fact? No one was holding a gun to my head. So why didn't I quit?"

He paused before answering, as he rolled a cigarette. "Because I was afraid," he resumed. "Fear ruled supreme. I feared to face the inevitable consequences, a state of destitution and the family dramas. I feared to let go of the security in which I lived and step out naked and alone into a world that terrified me. I was a bundle of fears with close to zero confidence … But, one day, I'd had enough. Not living my truth, not following what was in my heart, my dreams and aspirations, denying my own Being, I discovered that I was dying a little each day. Happily, finally, I plucked up enough courage, walked out of the office and never returned, to everyone's dismay. In worldly terms, a thoroughly foolish act – which resulted, of course, in instant chaos: I had no capital, no savings, my father cut me off, I couldn't pay my rent, I'd nowhere to live, with no more than five pounds in my pocket, and was soon wondering where the next meal was coming from. Now, what was I to do?"

At this critical point, he went to the toilet, leaving me in suspense.

While Nero battled with a bumblebee against a windowpane, I had time to ponder. What a decision to let go of everything, simply in order to be true to oneself! Yes, I wondered, what next?

"First, I had to ask myself the question: Who/What am I?" he resumed on his return. "A poet? Yes, by aspiration. A philosopher? Yes, a passionate truth-seeker. Hardly good livelihood material! Besides this, I had one other passion: Art. Hardly more worldly; but at least I had a dream, though in my circumstances it was thoroughly unrealistic: To open an art gallery ... 'That is absurd!' my mind said immediately: 'You know no artists, no critics, no dealers, nor even collectors. And, above all, you have no money. Not only is it absurd, but completely impossible!' But that's what I decided. And that's when I first experienced magic."

"Tell me all about it." I was really excited.

"Three weeks later, having obtained premises and decorated them, I opened a gallery in the very heart of fashionable London. I had been offered a place, a large basement, rent-free initially, which I converted." He recounted in detail. "The moment one sets one's heart on something and commits oneself to it, the Universe supports one, I discovered: All kinds of things happen, which would never otherwise have done, with assistance arriving unexpectedly on one's doorstep. That is how it was. A few months later, I was travelling around Europe, organising exhibitions, visiting artists, museums and galleries, attending international gatherings, buying and selling paintings. Not the impossible, as the mind tends to tell one, but great success in a very short time."

"I've read something similar in Paulo Coelho's *Alchemist*," I commented. "If you really, really want something, the whole Universe conspires with you to achieve it."

"Exactly. But you must have the courage and trust to go for it, despite whatever obstacles."

As ever, one story followed another. Needing to be convinced, I had no wish to interrupt.

"When I had the idea of setting up an international gold smuggling organisation operating between Europe and the Far East, I knew nothing of the business and was once again destitute in London. Literally. Here again, my mind could have said, 'This is impossible'. In any event, I decided to proceed, and six months later I was fully operational with offices in London, Brussels, Geneva and Hong Kong. By this time, I had trained my mind, which had given up arguing that things were impossible."

"But some things must be," I insisted.

"Of course. But not always what our limited minds tell us."

"What *is* the primary limitation?"

"Our belief systems. We need to look at our beliefs about money in particular and how we relate to it. 'Money first and all else follows' is what our ignorance, fears and conditionings tell us, which implies in so many words that money is our God, the primary power and source of what we need. Being the Christians we are, or claim to be, we'd never agree that that is what we believe, but that is what we're demonstrating every day by our thoughts and actions without having understood one of the primary teachings, 'Seek ye first the Kingdom of God and all else will be given unto you.'"

"Yes, but what does that actually mean?"

"Little if one doesn't understand that God, his Kingdom, and the source of all we seek, are within us."

"How does that help?"

"Let me say it in modernday words, those of Deepak Chopra, I think: "In aligning with our innermost Selves, we align with the power that manifests everything in the Universe.""

Deep down I sensed the truth in all of this. But it would take some time to become fully convinced in all the cells of my body. It was in total contrast to the ways of my culture. I would need my own experiences before I could fully trust this new approach.

After a lengthy discussion, we paused for cheese and a glass of Dubonnet.

"In worldly terms, it comes down to this," he announced suddenly, eyes alight and smiling: "Daring to be foolish! Foolish in the wisest possible way!" he added and laughed. "You must go beyond the reasonings of your worldly mind – which, says the worldly mind, is foolish! You must let go of your fearful attachments to security – which, says the worldly mind, is ludicrous! You may even have to say goodbye on occasions to your worldly 'common sense' – which, your worldly mind will tell you, is pure insanity! Instead, you must honour the impulses of your heart, your intuitions and deepest inner knowings, though these in their wisdom may defy all reason. For this you must go within and listen. This will bring you to another level. Another level of the One Game of Life!"

He was seriously foolish, that's what I liked about him.

"Let's get back to you and *your* dreams," he suggested: "If you leave aside all the limitations, whatever you perceive them to be, all obstacles and attachments, all concerns about where the money is going to come from, all the reasonings of your mind which tell you this or that is not possible, and listen only to your heart and soul ... what do these tell you when you put the question, 'What are my dreams?'"

I really didn't know.

"Allow them to be ridiculous," he encouraged, "even impossible, if they want to be, neither limiting nor judging them. Then, when you're clear about them, we can explore together what *our* dreams may be, what *we* want to create."

After this torrent of stories and insights, once again I needed time to reflect. Maybe months! The main point for me at this moment was the realization that I, we, could create what we wanted, that we had the freedom to do so, and also the power. My first step was in owning and coming more fully into the energy of this. We'd have time then, I hoped, to come to clarity.

After a brief tour of West Cork and Kerry, during which we revisted the Round House and my lover tree, I returned to Holland.

Roderic

What did *I* want to create? Little on the outside right now. With books to complete, my energies were focused on writing. What *we* would choose to create would emerge out of our being together, I felt. The first step was Elly's move to Ireland, which was certain to be alchemically intense.

One area in which I hadn't stepped into my role as a creator as fully as I was able was in the creation of myself – "the highest creation for man," the Taoist master Mantak Chia calls it, "creating oneself consciously." Somehow, my primary responsibility, working on myself, was the one to which I managed to give the least attention, lulling in a kind of existential laziness. Elly, I had observed, was far more seriously committed and centred. Though I had a quote from Ramtha pinned to my bedroom door as a reminder – *"My life became fulfilled when I took hold of all my understanding and focused it on myself"* – most mornings, I simply walked past it!

Chapter 11

Lovers, Teachers, Healers

Roderic

*Nero is curled up on the floor
and it's pissing with rain ...*

We were back to love as a long conversation, a thousand miles of land and sea marking our separation.

Elly

One of the discussions we had was on the seemingly opposing demands of individuality and oneness in the context of a relationship, on which Roderic wrote:

Ideally, neither should diminish nor detract from the other. And neither is to be sacrificed. Rather, they're for mutual support and enrichment. But how?

While we'll be separate individuals living together, we'll also be living 'as one' – not in the sense of being joined at the hip but in belonging to a larger whole. But how does one do that without restrictions on individuality? If a relationship is to work, individuality should become more empowered, more extended, more enhanced. That's the challenge.

Feeling the oneness, making decisions and acting from it, how does this feel for you when you've been living on your own for so long, with you alone as the centre of reference?

Roderic

Her response, written over days:

How do I deal with the relationship between 'individual identity' and 'oneness'? I still have a fear of losing my identity if I step into 'oneness'. I'm still suspicious, still not trusting 100% that the other will support me. I have to gain confidence in the fact that I'll be enriched by the relationship and that it is not only asking <u>from</u> me; that it is supporting instead of exhausting me.

Love and dependency have always been connected in my experience with relationships becoming locked up in negative, manipulative or limiting patterns. Dependencies developed and freedom was lost. Can it be otherwise? Love and freedom, with support for my true Self, on an equal basis, is new for me. I long to feel the oneness <u>and</u> my individuality at the same time.

Acting from a consciousness of oneness, I think I know what that means – being aware of the need of the other as if it were my own and being responsive to it. Yes, that'll be challenging. With you, it's easier to keep in touch with my essence as you're always reminding me to do so – with your continual questioning 'What do <u>you</u> want?'!

This weekend, I felt moved – yes again into tears – when I thought of you and how loved I feel. Maybe I wrote this before, but, layers of protection have come off, and I now feel on a deeper level what it means to be loved for who I really am.

Roderic

On my second visit to Holland, there was less inseparable togetherness, with each of us being more active in doing our own thing. While Elly, with quite a full programme, was giving Reiki workshops and attending her physiotherapy practice, I was writing. We had a vivid illustration of the fact that when each honours their own truth life works out perfectly for both. For example: One morning during a weekend, as I was working downstairs, she was upstairs, lying in bed, possibly lazing, possibly reading, possibly expecting me to arrive with a cup of tea. Already engaged for over an hour, I was in the middle of a flow. Suddenly, I stopped, and pondered. "Can I really continue what I'm doing and ignore her? Maybe I'm being selfish?"

The first thought which came to mind was the principle, 'honour your truth', which is generally though not always synonymous with following one's flow, in this case one of inspiration. Such principles are not absolutes and can easily result in a lack of consideration. The second thought that came was that it isn't appropriate for the happiness of one to be dependent upon the presence, actions or decisions of another, something we had often discussed. Neither of us wished such a dependency, which inevitably violates or impinges on the other's freedom. On the other hand, it isn't appropriate to exclude the other and their needs from one's awareness. So, do I continue or not? I decided to do so.

At the same time, though I didn't know it, Elly was thinking to herself: "I hope Roderic's not waiting for me downstairs and isn't angry that I'm ignoring him, not serving him breakfast or coffee, as I want to finish what I'm reading." Though she had planned to read only one chapter, she was now half way through the third. That was her flow. "At the same time," she told me later, "I was reasoning with myself that if you needed me, you would come up. Maybe you were busy and didn't want to be disturbed." These were *her* respectful considerations.

The outcome was that when I had finished my flow, closed down my computer and was on my way upstairs to connect with her, Elly was already on her way down, having just finished her third chapter. What precision of timing! It confirmed that we were both in harmony with 'the flow'; and that, while functioning as individuals, we were attuned to the underlying oneness.

If she had acted otherwise: Elly, out of an inappropriate concern for me would have stopped her reading and come downstairs, busying herself with breakfast while invading my space, in which case neither of us would have been happy and might have become irritated. Or, similarly, if I'd gone upstairs, we would have been out of tune with each other and our selves, going along with a situation that suited neither of us – *each believing we were pleasing the other*! Ridiculously.

This seemingly minor event was, we understood, of major significance. It was a resolution of the paradox, following our individual paths while living our oneness.

Elly

It was so much fun discovering and exploring together how cosmic principles and spiritual truths touch every little detail of our lives and relationships.

Roderic

An important discovery during this trip was that we could live so harmoniously in such a small space. Further, that I could follow the flow of my writing and she could accept my occasional unsocial rhythms. Hers, more sociable, included Reiki meetings with students at her home. During one of these, which I attended, we gave each other treatments. I enjoyed seeing her at work and observing the gentle loving way in which she practised this healing art. Highly sensitive, she was aware of the presence and condition of the subtlest energies throughout the body, and shared her insights. A healer-priestess in her element, she was particularly gifted in inspiring as well as empowering others.

As I had lapsed in my own practice ten years earlier, she gave me a refresher course, reminding me of the symbols and hand positions. She also encouraged me to treat myself: "Reiki is a great way of loving and nourishing yourself and becoming more aware of the flow of energy throughout your body, which is what you want. It's such a pity, when you have these tools, not to be using them," she added tenderly one evening while stroking her fingers through my hair.

I could see that I needed her support in grounding my own healing abilities. I had been told that I had x-ray powers in my hands which could have dramatic effects. I had experienced this once in a spontaneous healing. To develop this ability, I needed the kind of support I received from Elly. Frequently, I was far too much in my head instead of heart and body.

"Awareness of the flow of subtle energies is also vital for the most ecstatic sex," Elly reminded me, while snuggling up. I had really begun to appreciate the truth of this, not simply as a concept but energetically.

Elly

After Roderic's return to Ireland, his input into my healing and learning process continued by letter. I had been extremely angry with my boss and shared this with him. "What do you think?" I asked, expecting a reply of sympathy and support, I being the victim, after all! Instead, not unusually, he pointed out that far from being the victim, *I* was the cause. It was in *me*, he insisted, and *I* had to look at it. I had a huge resistance to this, fully convinced that *I* was right and it was my boss who needed to change. "No," he insisted, the cause was in *me* and *I* had to look at it. As he explained:

First there is the person who is angry. Then there is the person who appears to be the cause of this anger. This seems straightforward. One causes the anger by his behaviour and the other, the so-called victim, experiences reactions. The victim says to the former: "You've made me angry; I'm becoming ill with the anger you're causing; You are to blame."

First point: You don't have to live in automatic reaction mode (that of the 'helpless victim') when someone pushes one of your buttons and you respond in a predictable way. Whatever the other does, you don't have to be angry. You have many options: You can laugh, understand where he's coming from and be compassionate, and so forth. The truth is: You can choose how you want to react. This is the 'creator mode'. This means claiming full responsibility for how you want to experience life. While life is always as it is, how you experience it is how you choose. Such is your freedom. On the other hand, so long as you're carrying anger in your system, ever ready to be triggered, you're not free. So it's not a question of denying what's within. It is _your_ anger, remember. Not his. However, my main point is this:

In the context of any relationship, each individual must claim 100 percent responsibility for causing/creating whatever goes on in that relationship, particularly in a close or intimate one. Must? Because that's how it is. The real question is not "Why is _he_ doing this to me?" as if _he_ has a problem; for, even if he has, that's wholly irrelevant. He is simply acting out _your_ psychic drama. He's in your life (with his problem) because you've drawn him into it for this purpose: to trigger _your_ problem and bring it to the surface, so you can see it and (if you choose) own it as _your_ problem and heal it.

The moment you've healed it in you, he doesn't need to be there any more. Either he'll be withdrawn from your life or he'll cease behaving the way he does. You know you're healed the moment he ceases to be able to push your buttons. He can try as hard as he likes, but you'll simply smile – not in any superior way but with understanding and gratitude – for, with his behaviour, he's giving you a gift. Meanwhile, you can beam golden light at him!

"No," I still resisted. "He's my boss. He's the one who's got to beam at me!"

Later, helping me to understand my anger, Roderic took me through a step-by-step process, inviting me to write down all the reasons, large or small, why I was so angry with him. So I did, and made a list, numbering them up to 20:

1) I'm angry with my boss because he…
2) I'm angry with my boss because he …
3) I'm angry with my boss … and so forth …
          … and sent it back to Roderic.

Responding, he wrote:

Step two, as you know, is leaving out the other person 100 percent. It is not what <u>he</u> is doing that is important, but how <u>you</u> are reacting to what he is doing. Your reactions tell you more about you than him. He may simply be reflecting aspects of you back to you. – aspects you deny as being part of you, or don't want to see because they are buried in your subconscious... Therefore one thing you can usefully do is sit in front of a mirror and speak out your list, <u>addressing it to yourself</u>.

This was eye-opening, also embarrassing. Clearly the problem *was* me! I was projecting unresolved authority issues with my father onto my boss and also aspects of my self I didn't like, my shadow side. Later, I reflected on my inner dramas: How important it is to know what emotional baggage we are carrying; and to deal with it so we're not dumping it on our partners or otherwise polluting the environment. I could so easily be doing this with Roderic.

Roderic

This dumping of unhealed aspects of past relationships onto current ones may be occurring in ninety-nine cases out of a hundred. It made me wonder about me and my mother!

Elly

By Christmas, we'd have known each other four and a half months. Preparing for the occasion, he presented me with a proposal:

Hi! Ho!!

Don't let's buy each other Christmas presents this year. Rather than buying and exchanging objects, let's share gifts of our Selves. Suggestion: We could each write six 'gifts' on a card that we would like to offer the other person; put each card in an envelope (beautifully wrapped and/or specially created); and give it to the other, who could then call upon the gift whenever he or she felt like receiving it. Such as: "It's my great pleasure to offer you a Reiki treatment for an hour."

ALSO: In addition to the above, we each have another six cards, on which we write down six gifts we'd like to receive from the other. Like: "I'd like to be tied to a rack and licked from top to toe for an hour."

This can be fun as well as call forth creativity. Many possibilities. In a playful way, we can explore our gifts to each other as lovers, teachers, healers. Do you agree?

Roderic

The ritualised gifting of objects on specified occasions is not one of my pleasures. Rather than feeling obliged by expectations, I prefer to be moved by inspiration and spontaneity. I was delighted with her response:

Great! I've lots of ideas already, popping up like mushrooms. The only thing I don't agree with is the number 6. Why not 7? – as in 7 days, 7 chakras, 7 colours of the rainbow and 7 steps to heaven? So, I'd like to give and receive 7 presents. Maybe I can finally experience your healing hands? I have sore bones and you've never healed them!!!

I added up the presents to be exchanged: Seven to give and receive for each of us, totalling twenty-eight. Since the enjoyment of each could last an hour, would there be any time left for eating and sleeping?

Elly

We celebrated the season at Roderic's seaside cottage, our Love Bubble, as we called it. Instead of cutting down a tree, we created our own ritual totem with driftwood, shells and seaweeds from the beach.

The highlight of the week was indeed exchanging our gifts, which we laid out on the floor between us. Roderic's to me were in seven envelopes, hand decorated, each with an image and words on its cover. One, a priestess rising from a lake with a glistening sword in her hand, bore the words 'TRUTH', 'CLARITY' and 'PURPOSE'. Inside was the gift: *"I offer you 1 to 3 days of processing, gentle and relaxed, in clarifying your Higher Aims & Purposes and Your Next Steps in Life."* Lovely, though he'd been doing this ever since we'd met! Another, sunflowers blooming by a wood, was headed 'NATURE', with the gift: *"A Simple Introduction to the Tibetan Secrets of Youth & Vitality."* I was curious. Given his age and vitality, they must have been working for him. A third, with the image of a lotus, headed 'PEACE', 'JOY', 'BEAUTY' and 'SENSUALITY', offered me: *"One Sensuous, Scintillating, Loving, Massage."* Wonderful to feel his hands over my body! ... The last, stuck with a red-and-blue airmail envelope with stamps from New Zealand portraying our magical Dragonfly, marked with the words 'ADVENTURE', 'PLAY' and 'MAGIC', was addressed to both of us, and offered: *"A Honeymoon in New Zealand."* My body leapt.

Roderic

What delighted me about Elly's gifts was the originality and beauty of her presentations. "I'm not creative," she'd once insisted. "One of the most absurdly self-limiting concepts I've ever heard," I'd responded. "We are all aspects of the Divine, the very nature of which is creativity. So you in essence are boundless creativity. You just have to give yourself permission to express yourself without preconditions, restrictions or judgements." So I was impressed. She had accepted the challenge, using her imagination to the maximum, and spent hours in the design and making, employing a wide range of images and materials, *collages* and *assemblages*, wrapping each as a precious gem. The first package contained an exotic red-feathery snippet from a cabaret artist's wardrobe on a white card with gold stars and a red shoe, offering me *"A Strip-Tease Dance in a Seductive Setting."* That should shake the berries off the hollies!

The second contained an invitation to a voice workshop. "You have such a special voice," she enthused, as I read it, "mellow, deep and dark. I want to hear it come out fully in its richness, to hear you roaring like a cat on heat. Uncontrollably!"

"Born in the year of the Earth Tiger, I should be quite good at that," I replied.

110

"May be it will reveal an aspect of your Being you haven't yet discovered," she suggested.

Another gift promised *"A Way to Heaven"*. The card, with a hand-drawn flute looking like a phallus pointing skywards, surrounded by golden stars, was my ticket to a fifty minute workshop entitled *"The Inner Flute"*, a Tantric breathing technique for raising energy to one's higher centres, otherwise known as *"The Way to God through Sex"*.

"Which reminds me," I replied, taking her hand and drawing her towards me. "I have one more special gift."

"What's that?"

"A demonstration of the art of Tongue Kung Fu."

"Sounds terrific."

I had been preparing for this. The tongue, as we know – moist, warm, remarkably flexible, soft yet possessing a file-like roughness – has wonderful powers of sensual stimulation. The Taoist master, Mantak Chia, calls it "the first strategic tool in lovemaking," which can by itself "wage brilliant love campaigns" when we learn to use it properly. Less known, it is also a means of directing one's life force, *chi*, into one's lover prior to intercourse. In this it can be like a magic wand, sprinkling bliss wherever it touches.

Naturally, wishing to be able to gift my lover the greatest of pleasures, I had prepared myself by undertaking a specialised training, which consisted of three basic exercises, each of which, Serpent Tongue, Hook Tongue and Slap Tongue, as they are called, are conducted with an orange suspended with a string at mouth level. In the first, one focuses on a thrusting in and out movement, making one's tongue firm and sharp-pointed and lashing out at the orange in the manner of a viper. In the second, one focuses on up and down movements, while extending the tongue as far as possible, trying to hook the orange as one licks up its side. And in the third, one focuses on sideways movements, forcibly slapping the orange with the tongue. These develop its strength, flexibility and nimbleness.

But an orange is an orange! Now, with my beloved, I could explore the possibilities from toes to ears and nipples to vagina, sprinkling bliss while tasting honey! My great ambition was to so excite her that she'd scream her delights to the gods in the heavens.

This would cause her to release what the Taoists call her "elixir of moon", a female equivalent of male ejaculation, believed to contain a super powerful elixir of *yin* essence. It was a quest which could take several months, so I had read, being no easy accomplishment.

Chapter 12

Time to Say Goodbye

Elly

Back home, I felt as if a veil had been removed from my eyes, enabling me to see more clearly. I felt deep gratitude towards Roderic for giving me so much loving acceptance despite my doubts and resistances, even rejections; and showing so much patience. I felt blessed. I was more than ready to leave behind all this and jump into the new. The time had come for decisiveness and action. Clear in theory, but challenging in practice. It took me a week before I could utter the fateful words to my boss, "I am leaving." It was a significant step and test of my commitment. Happily he proved to be understanding and supportive. I was greatly relieved. It was as if I'd stepped out of a harness, though I had three months' notice to honour yet.

My biggest fear was that having given up everything, Roderic would change his mind, or we'd split up even before we'd started, and I'd have to find my way myself. But deep down I felt I had to do this anyway. The professional limits imposed upon me were no longer acceptable. I needed space and freedom. I was ready for new ways of being and working, new ways of relating to the Earth and Cosmos, and particularly to my own Self – my higher or innermost self or soul. Indeed, I was ready for a whole new orientation and lifestyle.

Strangely, one of the most challenging parts of letting go was giving up my membership of the local tennis club, which represented the cutting of my roots, social and cultural, through which I was implanted in my home base. But one thing I knew for sure: Before the new could come in, the old had to go, or the magic would not happen. In my relationship with Roderic, it was always happening:

One crisp and sunny morning I went for a bike ride to one of my favourite lakes. To my surprise, on turning a corner, I came face to beak with a huge stork. Over the years that I had been cycling around I had never seen this magnificent bird, which I'd thought was extinct in the region. Arriving at the lake, ten minutes later, three swans flew low over my head with a mighty whacking of wings. Several birds crossed my path that day, most unusually. What's up? I wondered. Were they telling me something?

When I arrived home, I couldn't believe what awaited me, a card from Roderic on which he had written "Follow the Birds!" without any explanation. I had to call him. He giggled knowingly, as if he was part of a mischievous conspiracy.

"What did you mean by 'Follow the birds'?" I asked.

"Watch how they appear in your life," he replied, "crossing your path. They'll give you signs, guidance, which you can learn to read."

"How?"

"Observe, listen, tune in, and ask. But, first and foremost, be aware, so you can see the patterns. Until you do, how can you read them?"

Reflecting on this synchronicity, it seemed to me that the Universe was confirming once again that I was on my right path, with magic part of my new world opening up.

I experimented 'asking the Universe'. Firstly in simple ways. "I want Roderic to call me this morning," I requested and imagined him doing so. I had no idea he was travelling at the time, driving from the west coast of Ireland over the mountains to Cork in the south. If I had known, I would have realized that there was almost no chance of him responding as he had no mobile phone. However, he called within thirty minutes: "Why do you want me to call you?" he asked, letting me know that he had picked up my signal. I was astonished.

"To see if I could make you call me via the Universe," I replied. "Otherwise," I added jokingly, "I have nothing to say."

"Well, now you know what a power you have over me!" he laughed. "Yours to command, mine to obey! I received your message as a clear strong impulse."

He made me happy with his joyful voice.

Roderic

Whenever I heard hers, I wanted to jump on the next plane.

Elly

Late February, Roderic arrived in Holland for his last visit before I joined him. I delighted in his hugs, his playful and romantic nature. He presented me with a family ring with my favourite gems, turquoise set in gold with a crystal, which symbolized our commitment. We had a great evening at the theatre and fabulous lovemaking. Later, I told my friend, Joyce: "Finally, I'm through with all my doubts. I'm now ready to go to Ireland. I love him."

Thereafterwards a downward spiral:

My beloved mother rang. I had been seriously affected by her fear-based questions and her reasonings that made perfect sense: "How will you live? What will you do in Ireland all day long when Roderic is writing? What will you do to make money for your old age?" and so forth. In other words: "You can't live your dream. It's impractical, impossible, and stupid even to think about it. Life is full of danger and uncertainties. Material security counts for everything." So: "Stay where you are, here in Holland. Don't take risks ..." Now, she was singing the same tunes all over again.

The whole situation was a set-up by the Universe, to test me on my new resolutions, commitment and clarities, I was convinced. But I wasn't great in responding. I was thrown back into doubts again. One day I had none, the next they were flooding the floor!

I wanted to resolve them once and for all and needed some time on my own. So, while Roderic was exploring the bookstores of Leiden, I lay in my bath and reflected. Was I really doing the right thing? I thought of the chat I'd had with a senior member of our church while ice-skating in town a short time earlier. I had shared that I was going to Ireland to live with my partner. I had always seen him as a liberal thinker but his response surprised me: "How unlucky you are," he said. "Why don't you find a young man in your own area?"

If I listened to all these voices I would never go to Ireland; and maybe I would stay in the same job and the same house for the rest of my life, unhappy and unfulfilled, fulfilling only the expectations of others rather than honouring my own head and heart.

At the same time, applying the principle of 'as within so without', I had to accept the possibility that the doubts and fears expressed by my mother and the church member were reflections of my own. When I stopped doubting, others would stop projecting onto me, or their projections would simply bounce off. So, how to stop doubting?

I added hot water to the bath and chewed some licorice.

Every relationship has its challenges, I realized, whether its age differences, racial, religious, social or financial status. Maybe they are there to prompt one to look deeper into particular issues. I was challenged to see and accept that age is relative; that while the body ages, the soul is timeless. The innermost essence of Roderic shone through his sparkling eyes which were full of life, enthusiasm, playfulness, wisdom and love. I was being invited to let go of my limited perceptions and love unconditionally. When I do, it is so, so liberating. The age issue had brought up so many aspects to look at and heal within myself that the challenge had actually been a gift. One of the underlying reasons for my doubting that Roderic could be my soul mate was my misconception about soul mates. I had imagined that there would be love at first sight, no doubts, complete surrender, total admiration, no issues to work through, and so forth; but I can see now that a soul mate, as one's spiritual partner, is *the* person to press your buttons and bring to the fore all your unresolved, unhealed pains and patterns; and that is great! Seeing things positively, I realized how lucky I was to have a soul mate whose impact was so constructive and supportive. Roderic was obliging me to let go of the job I didn't like any more and create the life I really longed for, which, though it felt scary, also felt great, even though I didn't have a clue what I'd be doing and where the money would be coming from. I didn't have to give up everything I loved, as my victim mode was suggesting; I was simply releasing the parts of my life that were no longer supporting my growth and well-being. My family and friends would still be there. My home was not attached to my house. Besides, I wanted to be able to feel at home wherever I was. And what a blessing it was to be able to live in Nature so close to the sea. My heart started to sing. A shift was taking place within me from a feeling of victimhood into one of gratitude.

I stepped out of the bath, put on some nice clean clothes, played Bach's *Matthew's Passion* loud, and started cleaning my living spaces.

"You look radiant," Roderic remarked on his return.

"Yes, I'm in love!" I responded, giving him a big hug.

We decided to go to a movie, *You Got Mail* with Meg Ryan and Tom Hanks, which brought home to me the fact that I was living in two realities: an outer one in quest of romantic love, living my life with job, theatres, parties and family; and an inner one of higher self, auras, past lives, and intense personal processing, with Roderic being very much a part of this. As if intentionally to emphasize the difference, he commented comically before the movie started: "I wonder how many people here know that they're sitting on their root chakras?"

I laughed. Looking around, I saw a hall full of teenage girls, all dolled up, their eyes glowing with desires and expectations, seemingly eager to meet the man of their dreams. Looking through their eyes at Roderic, it seemed unbelievable that he could be my lover. Yet, from the soul's perspective, that of my own inner knowing, our relationship was perfect, as I now realized. I relaxed and enjoyed the movie, warmly holding the hand of my beloved.

Afterwards, we went to a pub decorated in classical Greek style and run by Indonesians. I felt radiant with love and laughter and could have danced on the tables. But we had to leave it shortly as it was closing. We walked back through the town, enjoying the architecture along the canals. At home we danced to Bob Marley; then Sade's *This Is No Ordinary Love*. Having dissolved my doubts completely the flow of energy between us became incredible. We were enfolded in a bubble of Love and Light. Merged in a blissful oneness, it didn't matter whether we cuddled, made love, or just layed beside each other.

Roderic

After days of this soothing elevating glow, I left for Schiphol Airport.

Elly

Soon, the following popped through my letterbox:

Hi, Beloved!

It's great being back at my seaside cottage. So cosy, with a lovely energy. It's going to be a bit small for two, but we'll manage. It's a beginning, a small seed. We'll nourish it with loving attention; then have a big tree. I've already begun re-organising to create spaces for your arrival ... All very domestic!

I'm writing this on the dining table. I wish you were here lying on it. Then I could make love with you. Wow! My warrior spear is hard with the thought. I'll have to cool down before continuing! ...

He was gearing me for my new life:

No vehicle at the moment. It's the first time I've been here without one. Interesting. Four miles walk to post this letter ...

And no more bought coffee. Here you'll have to dig up your own dandelion roots!

No car, no telephone, an hour away from the nearest village? Here I am in Holland, a sophisticated civilization with a rich social and cultural life and all facilities available within walking distance, and I am about to let it all go – job, house, family, friends, and financial security – to live with my lover in a tiny cottage with no outside world other than nature. Am I really prepared for this? Yes, I concluded: I am more than ready for a break and a life without pressures ... for freedom, stillness, open spaces, and Earth-relatedness ... above all for a life and a relationship that honours the essence of who I really am ... a spiritual being! Ireland, here I come.

"I see flames above your head, yearning for adventure," said my friend Sophie while reading my aura in the candle-lit corner of a restaurant in Haarlem. "It looks as if you've reached a point on which you've been working for many lives. You are going to fulfil your soul's destiny."

This was one of the first of my goodbye encounters. I felt it important to take time for these, for, having completed one phase of life and about to embark on another, it was a significant moment of passage, one I didn't want to pass without honouring. Besides farewells in restaurants, homes, pubs and sauna, I wanted a ritual to celebrate the transition. Rituals are essential in life. They can be healing, fun and transformational, and we don't have enough of them. While we have let go of old ones which no longer serve us, we haven't created new ones that meet our needs today. Above all, I wanted to create a time and space for sharing and celebration, in which I could express my love and gratitude and feel supported in my next step.

So I invited ten of my best women friends to join me in a one-day event in a sacred space in a sacred circle; and asked each to bring three things, a crystal or other favourite object to put in the middle of it, a dish of food to share, and a gift in the form of a poem, song, dance, drawing, hug or whatever inspired them.

We met at ten in the morning, beautiful women, all on their own spiritual paths. We sat in a circle on velvet cushions and began by introducing ourselves, each lighting a candle as we took turns explaining why we'd come.

"I experience spirituality in a different way from you, but I too love rituals," said Inge, "that's why I'm here."

"I've done a lot of things in my life without marking or celebrating them," said Joyce, "and realize how important it is to take time for special events like this."

"It's a milestone in your life and a party I want to celebrate with you," said Marion in her cheerful manner.

My sister Hilda cried, realizing she'd miss me terribly.

Maria too was moved to tears, while declaring she'd nothing to say. "But I want to feel how moved I am." So she sobbed while we waited silently.

After all had spoken, we held hands, as a unifying energy of Light and Love flowed through and around us. I was touched by the openness and surrender of my friends. And honoured that they'd come.

We split up into groups of three and gave each other a four-handed massage with natural oils and flower essences. It was a great pleasure seeing those I loved giving each other so much attention. As four hands moved tenderly around the front of my body, I could have yelled with delight, but remained silent, smiling, not wishing to disturb the others.

It took a few minutes to transform our parlour into a space for feasting. After savouring the dishes each had prepared, we returned to our circle.

"I want to hold and rock you with all your friends," said Maria, looking at me in her special endearing way. They stood in two lines, holding hands with the woman opposite. Invited to lie in the cradle they'd created, they swung me back and forth as a mother rocks her baby, giving me a great feeling of intimacy and connectedness, of being nurtured and loved unconditionally. Afterwards we sat in silence, moved by what we had experienced.

One after another each handed me a gift, something she'd created or of symbolic significance. After each presentation we hugged, feeling the warmth and softness of our bodies. Agaat had made a beautiful jewel box decorated with a dragonfly and containing spiral snails, knowing how I loved spirals. "Yes, how she does!" echoed my sister, who seized the moment to give a wise and humourous talk on 'Elly and Spirals'. Marion read her favourite poem and handed me a turquoise, the gemstone of travel: "Both my boyfriend and I have blessed it, holding it in our hands for a while, to wish you luck on your journey." Wil, whom I'd known since I was ten, spoke about power, reminding me that I'd once written to her questioning the value of our friendship and suggesting it was over; and telling me what a shocking but powerfully healing effect my honesty had had on her. We hugged intensely, happy we'd continued. "Yes," agreed Ingrid, "and what's so nice about Elly is that she's vulnerable and powerful at the same time." Joyce brought many gifts, including a tiny bottle of whiskey "as old as our friendship". Plus, she jumped around taking everyone's photograph, her special talent. Diana had waited to be the last, hoping she'd know what to say by then. She did. "I have been so impressed by this gathering of women," she said. "In my experience, they're always competing. Here we share, nourish and support each other, and it's mighty." As Agaat noted with a Dutch saying, *Delen is helen*, 'Sharing is healing'. All agreed that I was taking the right step. It was wonderful to be so enthusiastically supported. They'd all known about my doubts. Overwhelmed by their attentions and support, I said very little; but I had written each a short note on a beautiful card expressing what I wanted to say, presenting it at the end of the day along with a packet of my favourite incense, Nitiraj Original, an ancient blend of natural oils, resins, gums, aromatic herbs and spices.

Chapter 13

Sacred Promises

Elly

I had made the most consequential decision of my life and the moment had come when it would be irreversible, at least for a year and a day, as Roderic had arrived in Leiden to collect me.

My house was stacked with boxes almost ready to be despatched, to Ireland, to be put into storage, or thrown or given away. What a wonderfully liberating process it was, releasing what was no longer necessary.

My thoughts were jumping from one world to another, looking backwards to what my life had been and forwards to what it might become.

"What a plunge you're taking," Roderic noted sympathetically. "And what a lot of work for a year and a day," he teased. "You must be really sure what you're doing!"

Yes, I was. It seemed a life time ago that he put his shocking proposal to me, "Let's have a Celtic Marriage," on the beach in Ireland.

"Isn't it interesting how two freedom-loving beings like us can decide to make any kind of a commitment?" He laughed at the irony.

Can freedom and commitment ever be compatible? – we'd wondered.

Roderic

We were making a commitment for a year and a day because we were not happy with the idea of a commitment for life. Nor were we happy with an open-ended relationship without any commitment. So we had an in-between alternative which allowed us a perfect balance, we hoped ... which would enable us to practice the rare mystical art of living with paradox! ... for, from a reasoning perspective, how can you have both?

But, how, as a Christian living in a predominantly Christian society, can one even speak of alternatives? The Christian concept of marriage, deemed so sacred – divinely ordained, so it is claimed – is invested with such a charge of 'truth' and 'holiness', and so deeply ingrained in collective consciousness, and so supported by the laws and customs of the land, who dares to suggest that it can be appropriately replaced by anything else?

Elly

In some way I still felt the Church had its eyes on me, even though I left it more than ten years ago! Even though my particular Church was a liberal one, two thousand years of its doctrines were still imprinted on my mind to some extent, if not also my nerves, cells and bones. I was left wondering what these all had to do with God's love. In fact, what the Church did in the name of 'Love' and 'Truth' made me sad, angry, and sometimes outraged. For example, its historical dictate has been, "Believe in what *we* proclaim as *the* Truth or you will be put to death." I had read that they'd put several million people to death in the Middle Ages, mostly women, for their herbal knowledge and Earth-based spirituality, their so-called paganism; and thirty to forty million just in South America. All in the name of a God of Love!

Only recently I'd realized how I had been conditioned into accepting false beliefs and equations such as "What the Church says equals 'the Word of God'" and therefore "What it says equals the 'Truth'". How far from being so! Occasionally I had broken out in sweats of fear in case I'd be punished for no longer being a member of it or subscribing to its beliefs which, of course, was ridiculous. So I was still in the process of freeing myself.

I was happy when *Conversations With God* by Neale Donald Walsch fell into my lap, as 'God' comes across as a much more compassionate, flexible, humorous and freedom-loving Being; and so strongly supportive of individuals seeking to live their own truths rather than following the dictates of institutions which, as 'God' says, are man-made and based on fear. Above all, He insists on our freedom, reminding us that that's what we truly are: "Eternal, unlimited and free."

Happily, Roderic too insisted on my freedom. While binding me in a commitment!

Roderic

We were both familiar with these *Conversations* and often read passages to each other. Whether they were really with God or simply imaginary dialogues was beside the point. They rang true and were deliciously explosive!

As truth-loving beings we were concerned with the sacred; or, rather, with the question: What *is* sacred?

What about marriage specifically? Is it or is it not God-ordained? Or is it merely a human convention? Didn't we, as Walsch suggests, simply make up the fiction that it is what God prefers? Yes, apparently: According to 'God', "I don't prefer anything of the sort, but I notice that *you* do!"

Elly

This had come as quite a shock to me.

Roderic

But why do *we* prefer marriage, while 'God', seemingly, does not? Because, says 'God', marriage is the only way we have been able to figure out how to bring foreverness into our experience of love. Historically it has been the primary means whereby a female can guarantee her support and survival and the male can guarantee the constant availability of sex. Pretty basic! Thus, a social convention was created, a bargain was struck between the sexes, and a contract made; and since both parties needed to enforce it, it was said to be a sacred pact with God, who would punish those who broke it. Later, when we found that that didn't work, we created man-made laws to enforce it. Walsch, too, had been shocked: "I always thought that marriage was the ultimate announcement of love," he declared. "As *you* have constructed it, it is the ultimate announcement of fear," 'God' replied, whereas "true love is always free and cannot be bound by pledges or conventions."

We agreed whole-heartedly.

So what about sacred promises?

"The fact is that your marriage vows, as you presently construct them, have you making a very un-Godly statement, says 'God'. "It is the height of irony that you feel this is the holiest of holy promises, for it is a promise that God would never make."

"Remember this," He says: "There is only one sacred promise and that is to tell and live your truth. All other promises are forfeitures of freedom, and that can never be sacred. For freedom is Who You Are. If you forfeit your freedom, you forfeit your Self. And that is not a sacrament; that is a blasphemy."

Elly

This is so, so true! What a revelation! And liberation! Thank you 'God'. Thank you Walsch.

While I had ceased believing that a Church ceremony makes a marriage sacred, I still felt the need for some replacement. Something must make it sacred! What does, is not because of any ritual or pledge, but the way you think, feel and act in every moment of being together. It is *I* who am creating the sacredness, I realized, doing so over and over again, revering it in all aspects of life. It *is* in the honouring of truth, yes – but *my* truth, the truth of Spirit as *I* experience it, not in any outer forms. And that is sacred, honouring one's God-given freedom to be able to do just that! I knew I could do it with Roderic. In fact, he flares forth when I don't speak or live my truth.

Roderic

We'd also read Gary Zukav. "All the vows that a human being can take cannot prevent the spiritual path from exploding through and breaking those vows if the spirit must move on," he writes in *The Seat of the Soul*. What happens, for instance, when individuals, locked in a bond by their so-called 'sacred promise', begin to feel drawn along different paths, whether worldly or spiritual? People awake at different times and grow at different rates. While one may be leaping and bounding in a process of accelerated transformation, another may be stuck in a standstill mode, resistant to all change. What does one do then? Does one honour a promise one has made in the past or one's truth in the present as it has become? Is one's truth to be dishonoured and one's freedom forfeited? Either would be a betrayal. Ultimately, Spirit will not be bound.

It is also a fact that endeavouring to secure the love of another exclusively and in perpetuity by means of a so-called 'sacred promise', aside from being unnatural, tends to have a negative effect. The moment the promise is felt as an obligation, you are likely to start feeling trapped by it and resent it. But when you know you remain free to choose, to renew your commitment or not, you'll no longer have the feeling of being trapped. So, better to feel free to choose it over and over! In that light we saw our Celtic Marriage.

Elly

In spite of the fact that I had dreamed of the perfect marriage, I had never wanted nor would I have dared promise a life-long commitment to anyone. The problem with this is that it neither guarantees the love you seek, nor the security; nor does it permit change; and the only certainty in life is change, whether on the inside or outside, or whether you like it or not! As Shakti Gawain writes in *Living in the Light*, "Real commitment makes no guarantees about a relationship's form; it allows for the fact that form is constantly changing and that we can trust that process."

If people stay together because they really want to share deeply and honestly with each other, and there is true intimacy and growth, a life-long commitment is more likely to emerge as a natural development; and that is beautiful. But if people stop being honest in sharing their deepest truths and needs and simply stay together for security, physical or emotional, there may not be much left that is real in their relationship. You may end up, as Gawain puts it, with "an empty shell, a nice commitment but no real people in it."

Roderic

What an ideal relationship is all about energetically is an openness and flow at the very deepest levels between two beings in the vibrant love-bliss state of a oneness which extends, enhances and empowers, rather than limits and suppresses their individualities.

Elly

My main responsibility in a relationship now is not to give away my freedom anymore, or my power, as I have been doing in previous ones. That is paramount. In my view, the biggest threat to freedom in a relationship is emotional dependency, when the happiness of one is dependent upon the presence, actions or attitudes of the other. What attracted me about Roderic was that he was not dependent on me, rather wholly independent. Sometimes I questioned whether he was too much so. I didn't want to be dependent either. Contributing to my sense of freedom was the feeling I could express myself fully, honestly and openly on all levels, especially on the spiritual, without being judged or ridiculed as I had been in the past. I realized that freedom is only found when both individuals take full responsibility for every aspect of their lives, including their happiness, healing, fulfilment and growth. With our relationship evolving into a Spiritual Partnership in which all this was recognized and honoured, losing my power seemed no longer a possibility. I was excited. I had been longing for this. It was new for me. I was now living it.

Roderic

As the wisdom-teacher Eva Pierrakos expresses it in her *Pathwork of Self-Transformation*: "The perfectly mature and spiritually valid relationship must always be deeply concerned with personal growth. When it is, it is built on rock, not sand; while, the moment it is experienced as irrelevant to growth, it falters."

Gary Zukav also writes on the subject: "Spiritual partners bond with an understanding that they are together because it is appropriate for their souls to grow together." As for how long: "They recognise that their growth may take them to the end of their days in this incarnation and beyond, or it may take them to six months. They cannot say they will be together forever. The duration of their partnership is determined by how long it is appropriate for their evolution to be together." In other words, you stay together only so long as you grow together. That's how we saw it, though we'd decided to make a commitment for 'a year and a day' – but *renewable,* as my beloved keeps reminding me!

127

Elly

It was time to celebrate. While we had been talking about a big celebration, I hadn't felt ready for this, neither before nor in the midst of moving house and country.

Roderic

It was Beltain, the Celtic fertility festival. It was the day too when Taliesin, the great Celtic bard, was reborn, manifesting mysteriously in a leather bag at Gwyddno's weir. It was a Full Moon day and the beginning of the Wesak festival, commemorating the birth and life of the Buddha. It was the Dutch Queen's Birthday, a national holiday, with many festivities, streets and terraces thronged with people, with music playing and children selling toys in market stalls along the canals. Altogether a joyful and auspicious occasion!

A bright sunny day, we hired a boat and toured the city.

Later, tiring of crowds, we retreated to the Hortus Botanicus where we sat under a plane tree.

There are trees for dreamers, trees for healers, and those under which one may seek enlightenment. It was under a plane tree that the great god Zeus seduced the lovely nymph Europa, the tree that shaded them being uniquely rewarded, never losing its leaves thereafter. In myth, human consciousness and culture, each species has its colourful history. But all love lovers. And I love Elly.

Elly

"Don't we need a little ritual to mark the beginning of our Celtic Marriage?" I proposed.

"Absolutely," Roderic agreed.

"Close your eyes," he requested some moments later.

I sensed him walking off somewhere, though the soft grass betrayed no steps.

"You may open them," he said, returning in what seemed less than a minute. "We will mark this sacred occasion wordlessly with a long kiss under a cascade of flowers and let the trees and swans be our witnesses … but not before you promise me to live and speak your truth at all times."

"I do. Whole … heartedly … I … do!"

"What about you?" I asked. "Do *you* promise to live and speak your truth at all times."

"I dooooo … ooooo!"

With that, he drew me to him with one hand, while dipping into a pocket with the other, pulling out a fistful of pink and red petals which he flung into the air above our heads.

Such a romantic!

Roderic

We were now married – bound, that is, for a year and a day.

Elly

After saying goodbye to my house, now empty, I walked through the garden and out of the gate for the last time, after twelve years. Agaat, my friend and neighbour, took photographs and wished us well with a warm hug. After much of the previous days in tears, as friends came to say farewell, I now felt at peace and ready for our journey.

We took the Eurostar express train via the Channel Tunnel to London where Roderic had a meeting with a film producer who had offered to purchase the rights of his book, *How to Rob Banks Without Violence*. I was happy we were not flying, wanting a slower transition from one world to another.

"I'm carrying you off to a far away island," said Roderic in jocular vein as the train pulled out of Leiden station. "Abducting you, like Zeus with Europa, to her delight!"

"Wonderful," I sighed.

As we headed towards the Belgian border, leaving familiar countryside behind, fragments of thoughts, people and talks, flashed through my mind – including my precious ninety-seven-year-old grandmother who had come all the way from Friesland to meet Roderic. Saying goodbye to her, I'd had a strong feeling I would never see her again. I rested my head on Roderic's shoulder, so relieved I'd made my decision. It felt so right. We were on our way and there was no way back. Drifting into doziness, I reflected. This was the first time I'd ever committed myself in a relationship. If Roderic had asked me for a life-long commitment, I wouldn't be sitting beside him now. On the other hand, if he hadn't asked me for some form of a commitment, I wouldn't be sitting here either. It is nice to have a clear time frame. I have the security of knowing that we'll be together for the next twelve months, enjoying each other's company, sharing each other's love, knowledge and wisdom. We are both more likely to treat the relationship with the maximum of respect knowing it will be coming up for possible renewal.

Though I had just begun a Celtic Marriage and was off to a supposedly Celtic country, I knew little of the Celts; but I had bought books on the Druids and sure liked this custom.

"They were a freedom-loving race," said Roderic as our train rushed on, "who clearly understood that every human being is intrinsically free. That's what I like about them."

That's what I liked about him too.

"Their cultures honored the dignity and freedom of women and their equality amongst men in all aspects of life, particularly when it came to marriage and divorce, unlike in Roman and Christian societies where the inferiority of women was taught by religion or enforced and perpetuated by customs and laws, as it still is in many places ..."

"That, I find so incredible," I interrupted with disgust, "that any religion should preach that women are inferior in the eyes of God."

"For the Celts marriage was a purely social and contractual arrangement, not at all religious," Roderic flowed on. "It took many forms: monogamy, polygamy, polyandry and concubinage."

"Yes?" I was surprised how many there could be.

"But in whatever form it took, the rights of both parties, of both men and women, were protected by laws. In any dissolution, separation or divorce, they were treated as equals. A marriage for a year and a day, which was real but could also be a trial event, was one of their most brilliant innovations."

Knowing I was keen to know more about their customs, he'd lent me his copy of *Women of the Celts*. What surprised me in the little I'd read was learning that both parties in a marriage were sexually free. A couple never swore exclusiveness to each other. They had their own understanding of fidelity: You promised to be faithful in the fulfilment of a common achievement, like the up-bringing and education of children and in maintaining material stability; but promised personal liberty on levels that didn't affect the continuity of the marriage, the primary function of which was procreation. Such honouring of freedom was possible because there was no religion telling them what was 'right' or 'wrong'."

I wondered how it worked out in practice. "What do you think?" I asked Roderic, as I handed him a chunk of baguette loaded with camembert, lettuce, tomatoes, anchovies and olives.

"It's whatever you both decide. As long as you don't impose your choices, there are no rights or wrongs. All is permissible by mutual consent."

"But what do you *feel* about it?" I persisted.

"At this moment, I have no desire for anyone but you, O Delicious One!" he declared nobly, nudging his cheek alongside mine, and licking my ear.

"No, seriously," I insisted.

"One cannot know what the future might present, who might walk into one's life and cause a galactic explosion; but, as I see it, the principle is this: With whomever one is, one shares openly and honestly about what one feels. One can then deal with whatever presents itself in the moment."

In London we saw *Shakespeare in Love*, which made Roderic shed a tear! A deal with the film producer was agreed. Maybe we'd fly to Hong Kong one day and watch it being made. After a two-day walking tour of the city, we took another train west towards the Irish Sea.

Chapter 14

Our Love Bubble

Elly

"I can't believe it! I'm actually here," were my first words on arriving at the cottage. I stretched after our long journey, breathed in the fresh ocean air and entered.

The space inside was rich and welcoming. Taking my hand, he led me to the bedroom. "Now yours," he said. He'd made a great effort to ensure I'd feel at home, creating a space for me by vacating his room, the largest, and moving into his much smaller office, where there was a bunk-bed stacked with books and files. We had decided to sleep separately – my preference, his insistence.

Roderic

No matter how much in love one is, it's vital that each has a space which is a hundred percent theirs. One may hardly ever use it, but that's not the point. Neither is locked into a situation. Having one's own space, one can come and go from it at will, meeting the other out of one's freedom. Sometimes one feels like being alone in one's own energy-field. I do when engaged in any inner work, reflecting or processing. With one's own space, one can find the right balance between aloneness and togetherness. It was also nice meeting in the mornings, a fresh encounter.

Elly

The view from my room was idyllic. I could lie back in the large double bed with its pile of soft cushions and look out the window at the cows and a big bull grazing. When I opened it I could hear the waves pounding. All was beautiful. I was in the right place; and really on my own now, away from friends and family.

On our first Sunday, we had a big clean out, which helped me feel at home. A few spider webs had to go. I enjoyed sucking them into the vacuum cleaner. I painted the kitchen from blue to white, which let in more light.

"Yes," said Roderic. "More light! Goethe's last words."

While I painted, he organised the shelves, particularly his books on healing and diet. Not the usual cookbooks, I noted. He had beautifully illustrated works on preparing wild foods, others on raw foods, juices, nutritional herbology and "perhaps the profoundest work on food and nourishment ever written," he suggested, handing me a copy of *Spiritual Nutrition & The Rainbow Diet* by Gabriel Cousens. We both enjoyed food and wanted to eat the purest, not fanatically but at least as a basic, allowing for the occasional exception.

As we worked, Enya, Sinead O'Connor and Peter Gabriel played in the background. "If we only had croissants," he sighed, "I'd put on our disc of French Café Music."

After living on my own, I enjoyed creating a space together, a haven of beauty, love and light. As we cleaned, we gave love to every little detail, bath, sink, taps, mirrors, windows, fireplace, cooker and fridge. We weren't simply cleaning but building up an energy-field. We thanked the Universe and asked to be blessed with harmony, peace and joy. Roderic invited the angels to join us and make their presence felt. Surprisingly, I became aware of Beings of Light all around me, which I had never experienced before. I felt flooded with love and overwhelmed with gratitude.

Roderic

Gratitude, for me, was an ongoing lesson. I had adopted it as one of my themes for the year. Elly, in her constant expression of it, was my greatest teacher. We decided to express our gratitude aloud daily. There was so much to be thankful for, like pure drinking water straight from a well, unpolluted air sweeping across the ocean, a beach on our doorstep, loving neighbours, birds, trees, wild flowers and peacefulness. We also expressed our appreciation for each other's undertaking of chores: "Thank you for taking out the rubbish, sweetheart," or "for hanging up the washing." The more the gratitude, the richer life became, or, to be more precise, the more richly we experienced it.

Elly

Life is much slower here and I'm still too rushy. When I'm doing the dishes, it's quickly and efficiently as if I've a train to catch, without really enjoying the experience.

"Before enlightenment, washing up! After enlightenment, washing up!" Roderic joked. "Besides, if you don't enjoy what you're doing, don't do it, or find a way of doing it joyfully," he suggested lovingly. "One of life's ongoing challenges, wouldn't you say? We are the creators of our own reality, remember, at least of how we experience it: So let's choose joy."

With such perspectives, I couldn't stop washing dishes!

For the first time in my life, I had no programme, no commitments, nor outside pressures. Yet I wanted to do everything at once, be in nature, sleep, read, chat, clean the house, meditate – *and* do nothing. I seem to switch from one extreme to another: While doing nothing, being passive and receptive, suddenly I feel I have to do something. So I speed up and become almost aggressive, swinging from an extreme of feminine mode to a masculine one, with almost no inbetween. I am not centred in myself, carrying stillness or grace in action.

I still hear voices echoing from back home, "What are you going to be doing all day?" Now I'm here, I'm still wondering! I have no idea what I'll be doing tomorrow or next week? It's a bit scary having nothing planned. While I enjoy doing nothing, I judge myself and feel guilty, coming up with old thought-patterns like, "It's Saturday night and we must do something special." I need to slow down and move into greater depths of stillness.

"The more you go into it," Roderic encouraged me, "the more you'll discover emptiness as fullness, pregnant with life, peaceful and blissful."

Roderic

For Elly, this was challenging. The transcontinental cyclist, conqueror of the Rockies, terror of the Alps, with her capacity for sustaining long bursts of energy, found it difficult to be still.

Elly

Every morning on waking, I read *Ramtha*. Powerful stuff. Strangely, I could see the vibration coming from the book as Roderic handed it to me.

"It's about joy and its realization," he said, "about finding, honouring and daring to follow your own unique path; about self-empowerment and creating your own reality." That's what I was here for, opening to a new approach to life.

"Ramtha is a great teacher," he continued, "an incarnation of Ram, a mighty warrior who lived forty thousand years ago, one of the founding fathers of the Aryan race. The book is a channelling of his wisdoms. "What you are looking for is not on the outside," he reminds you frequently. "Seek and find the God Within; then all things become possible."" I was inspired, if not set on fire, by the intensity of love, compassion and power with which it was written.

Each morning, as I read in bed, Roderic arrived with a hot drink of lemon, honey and ginger. I felt like a queen. On every level, I was being nourished and supported. Our neighbours were all so friendly, bringing us fruit and vegetables from their gardens. Every Thursday, our landlady, Mrs Violet Howe, who lived in the large house on the hill, drove us into the picturesque harbour town of Kinsale to do our shopping. A pint in the pub, The Mad Monk, a stroll along the quay, a browse in the bookshop, boutiques and craft shops, afternoon tea in Café Palermo, with the occasional magical encounter, this was our weekly contact with the world.

Roderic

For the moment, it was all we needed.

Elly

I was ready for an evening in bed with music, candlelight and cuddles, making love. I had read a comical little book on male and female orgasms and was in the mood. But Roderic wasn't.

We discovered we had different rhythms. While I like sex in the evenings, he doesn't. "Don't count on me after nine o'clock," he said. "When I hit the pillow I go to sleep."

I also like sex when I wake up in the morning, when my body is warm, cosy, and longing to be touched. "Please don't disturb me before eight," he said, "because I'm either meditating or writing."

"And not before you've had a shower," he added with a smile. He likes fresh bodies. Otherwise he loves me unconditionally!

When, I wondered, were we ever going to be making love?

Roderic

We never ceased doing so.

Elly

Yes, we were in a flow of hugging, kissing and playful affection throughout the day. But I was counting! I was locked into the idea that if you've just started a relationship, you should be making love almost every day or at least twice a week, especially on Saturday nights and/or Sunday mornings. So, why wasn't this happening? As we didn't sleep together, was it ever going to be possible to enjoy sex when *I* wished to do so? Does *he* set the timetable? Something needs to change. Why can't *he* reprogramme himself?

Roderic

Planned or routine sex turns me off. It's Saturday in two days' time and at ten o'clock in the evening we'll be having sex! No, not me! Not when it becomes an obligation. When an expectation is set up, it puts a demand on one, which deprives one of freedom. Further, if ever this expectation or demand is not met, woe unto the offender! Me! There's massive disappointment. Worse, worse and worse: Feelings of guilt, failure and rejection. All in the name of 'love'! I couldn't give a fuck about Saturday nights! I like spontaneity, with two people coming together moved to do so out of their freedoms.

Elly

Yes, I had expectations and various fixed ideas to go with them; but it seemed he also had something to look at. Definitely, being so defensive!

Roderic

While, on the one hand, I was as open to sex as Elly, feeling little diminution of this primary drive since teenage years, on the other I was easily switched off; firstly, being highly sensitive about my freedom, perhaps too much so, and therefore of its protection: Thus, the moment an event is set up and I am expected to be, to feel or to perform in a certain way, whether it's Christmas, birthdays or Saturday nights, my instinct is to withdraw, closing up before what I sense as a demand. Further: I have a hidden fear, I suspect, of being trapped and devoured by a needy, excessive or possessive love, or anything faintly resembling this.

Additionally, I don't view it as a healthy situation when the happiness of one is dependent upon having his or her needs met by another. While I can give freely, and another may do the same, neither have the right to demand when to receive; nor to move into a mode of disappointment, frustration or joylessness, if and when their demand is not met. We have to have a clear understanding about this. I am not here to fulfil Elly's needs, as she is not here to fulfil mine. We may choose to be aware of them and respond out of our love *because it is our pleasure*; but let *how* and *when* we respond never be other than out of our freedom.

Elly

I agreed with what he was saying. Nevertheless, I was convinced that he was over-reacting. Basically all I'd wanted was to feel that I was wanted and desired, as, in that period particularly with its many transitions, I was feeling vulnerable. When I listened to myself I knew I was in complete harmony with the way we were relating, both sexually and otherwise; but again my mind was in the way, giving me all kinds of reasons why we ought to be making love more often, and on my terms – namely, between sheets and between the hours of nine in the evening and nine in the morning. Also, I was still more concerned about what other people would think if they knew, rather than living my own truth. To be honest, I knew I was playing a game and that my sexual desires were not as I'd pretended.

I had also been angry: Why should he set the conditions and timetables? So I had rebelled, wanting to make Roderic feel bad and generally give him a hard time.

More and more I realized how much anger I was carrying towards men and the whole male approach to life through Church and other institutions, mental, authoritarian and imposing, with no space given to feminine aspects. Later, I read in a book by Ron Smothermon that a woman is often meanest to the man she loves most. Having been treated as a second-class citizen for so long, she has so much anger to express, buried so deep she doesn't always know it. "She'll express it by complaining, by withholding affection and sex, by making you wrong in front of your friends, damaging your ego, etcetera." The healing, he suggests, is in not blaming her but in letting her know that you know where it comes from and that she's entitled to be mean. When he's got the message and she's received his understanding and sympathy, she can let go of her manipulations.

Roderic

And don't we know all about those?!

Of course the female complaint is but one side of the coin. Before the patriarchy dominated human culture, there was the matriarchy. It, too, had its dark side of imbalances and excesses, including ruthless and barbaric exploitations of the male, which he still holds in his cellular memory as deep-rooted fears. So, to protect himself, he has resolved: Never is life to be dominated by women again. For my part, I make sure of that!

The next step, of course, is the balancing of the two principles, male and female, within each individual, man and woman, and in all aspects of life.

Elly

So, how did we resolve all our silly patterns?

Roderic

Firstly, by noticing them!

Elly

Secondly, by admitting what we were doing.

Roderic

Thirdly, by exploring the underlying causes and motives ...

Elly

.... which requires a great deal of honesty, openness, vulnerability and trust.

Roderic

But the more we dared speak our truths and welcomed those of the other lovingly, unconditionally and without judgement, the more doors opened through which love could flow and do so more freely.

Elly

The question, "What am I going to do all day?" was soon answered.

"Let's write a book on our Celtic Marriage," Roderic suggested.

I gulped. Writing letters and keeping a diary was one thing, but a book!? While I aspired to speak my truth, revealing it to the public was another matter. "You mean including all my doubts and our sex life?" I questioned, dismayed.

"The raw truth and nothing but," he replied predictably. "It would be a great opportunity to explore various aspects of relationship more consciously, particularly 'relationship as a Spiritual Partnership'. Then we can share our experiences with others. The world is waiting for an alternative to the currently limited concept of marriage which clearly isn't working anymore for many. We need new models, new perspectives, new foundations and, particularly, examples from lived experiences."

"Yes," I thought, "and it would be fun working together." I wanted a sabbatical from healing anyway.

I didn't have a clue what I was letting myself in for, how much work and discipline was required. And was I creative enough? The question still bothered me. "Of course you are," Roderic insisted, and gave me another chat on the subject, reminding me of the God Within, "whose very essence *is* unlimited creativity and it's waiting for *you* to draw it out."

139

We consulted the Universe. I picked a *Medicine Card*. Rather, it jumped out of the pack as I was shuffling. It was the Spider. "Create, create, create," she said. What could be clearer? "Okay," I agreed. "Let's go for it."

We had a wonderful evening with lots of laughter, whiskey, Pringles, and lovemaking. Not focused on having an orgasm, we simply enjoyed each moment as it came, beginning by sensually oiling each other. He was beautiful in the light of a candle. His body still has a childish openness and receptivity. When he touched me intimately, I felt like roaring, and did. Coming from a town-house in Holland, with the thinnest walls separating neighbours, it was great to allow sounds to come up from deep within and let them out uncontrolled.

We ate a peach afterwards and cuddled into sleep.

When I woke up, he wasn't there any more. He had gone to his room at two-thirty. "I didn't have enough air," he said.

Roderic

So wonderful to have the freedom to be able to come and go happily, without guilt, accusations, and 'poor little me' trips!

Elly

We are living an intense life in our Love Bubble, not going anywhere, simply being together. Living with Roderic keeps one busy, with almost every little chat touching the essence of life. It's been quite an adventure, writing the first chapter of our book. It was scary in the beginning, with Roderic sitting behind his computer opposite me with a look on his face saying, "Okay, now tell me," as if I were the source of all inspiration and progress hung on my every word. But after all the struggles, blocks and hiccups, I felt great having finished the first few pages.

Roderic

Churchill compared writing a book to wrestling with a tiger. Attempting to do so with another was like wrestling with a family of them!

Elly

I find my relationship with Roderic really different from others. He looks at almost everything from the soul's perspective; and is more or less beyond ego reaction. While I am still trying to change him in certain areas, he gives loving acceptance of me as I am, totally and completely. First I couldn't believe it and was suspicious. Later, I discovered he was always like this. It made me feel I could open to love more and more, and really be me. I was coming home to myself. Also, his constant humour, joy and playfulness were a delight to live with, supporting me in letting go of rigid patterns and in daring to open up to life however it wished to flow through me, particularly in being the light and silly me rather than the heavy and serious one.

The tough side was that he didn't let me get away with anything. My occasional irritations and projections came hurtling back as things which I had to look at and heal within myself. It was the beginning of the end of my habitual state of victimhood. Instead, I had to take full responsibility at all times as *the* primary cause of all I was experiencing. Sometimes, I wanted to run away from all this conscious behaviour. It seemed so much easier staying in victimhood with the luxury of blaming circumstances and others.

What surprised me after living for ten years alone, enjoying my independence and freedom, was that I was so hooked on being with him, almost every second of the day. Even when I went for a swim on the beach I felt drawn back into his presence, to be with him, talk with him, and be together in our Love Bubble. So I would rush back.

Having my own space during the night was a necessity. If we'd had to sleep in the same bed every night, I'd have felt trapped. With my own place, I felt free and could withdraw at any time. It provided a balance of independence and togetherness, of sacred individuality in a bubble of oneness.

Roderic

Some people think that their relationship would be over if they moved into separate rooms; and that there would be far less sex or almost none at all. Actually, the contrary is likely to be the case. When two people are apart there is magnetic attraction. When they are together all of the time, the charge dissipates, the magnetic attraction diminishes, no matter how much the two love each other. To increase the charge, there needs to be periods of separation, so that when they come together again it's with a mighty bang!

Elly

Ideally, every couple should have three rooms: One each, which is sacred and secret; and one in-between with a king-size four-poster bed with silk and satin duvets!

Chapter 15

Theme Weeks
For Soul Mates

Roderic

Focused on writing, I was often too much in my head and felt the need to be more in my body. Reflecting on this, I realized there were also other aspects of life to which I was not giving enough attention. Nor was it simply a question of me meeting my needs, but of giving sufficient time and energy to Elly's. One of the reasons she'd come to Ireland was to learn about communicating and working with nature spirits and angels, and we had hardly done more than talk about this. I had an idea. Each week we could choose a subject and focus our attention on it. We could have *Theme Weeks*. We could have one week focused on the body, for example, which we'd call *Body Week*; and another on angels which we'd call *Angel Week*; then maybe an *Awareness Week*; and so forth.

In committing ourselves to a Spiritual Partnership we had agreed to support each other on our individual paths of healing, growing and awakening, so *Theme Weeks* could help us engage in this more seriously. I suggested the idea to Elly, presenting her with a list of possible themes under the heading *Theme Weeks for Soul Mates*.

"Great idea! But what do you mean by *Slave Week*?" she asked bemused.

"For three days, I'm your slave. You're to treat me as one. I'm at your beck and call to fulfil your every wish, dream or desire, to the best of my abilities. You ring a bell or raise a finger and I'm here to do your bidding – instantly, adoringly, efficiently – your perfect slave!"

"Oooh! I look forward to that," she replied with delight.

"Of course you'll be careful not to abuse your power or over indulge in being a bossy boots," I pointed out, "as *your* three days of queenly omnipotence will be followed by *my* three of kingly equivalent."

Thus, *Theme Weeks for Soul Mates* would also give us the opportunity of exploring games often played out unconsciously in relationships, thus freeing ourselves from their disruptive dynamics, while having a great deal of fun.

Elly

Yes, I was excited. This could be a great way of opening up to each other, of becoming more intimate and vulnerable, while challenging me to be more light-hearted and creative. I loved Roderic's ideas, his fertile mind constantly inventing new ways of being and doing things.

"Let's do it," I approved.

Roderic

We began with a *Body Awareness Week,* starting the day with a bath together, with sesame and lavender oil.

"Sesame oil is food for your skin," Elly smiled and rubbed it all over me, making me smell like a tahini sandwich.

"Do you love your body enough?" she'd asked, meaning it was quite clear I didn't. "Do you ever look in the mirror? Wouldn't it be a good idea to stand in front of one every now and then and say, "What a wild and wonderful creature I see in front of me?" and give your body more loving attention?"

"Maybe," I conceded.

"Look how fantastic it has been, serving you for years, never giving you any trouble. It's your mobile home. You've travelled the world with it. Doesn't it deserve the very best in caring and nurturing?"

"Definitely."

We found a body-loving ritual in Shakti Gawain's *Living In The Light,* which consisted of standing naked in front of a mirror and sending positive thoughts to every part of the body, whether one liked it or not, looking for the beauty, thanking it, and generally giving it loving acceptance. Thus we went from head to toe. "Your body has been criticised, judged and rejected by you for years," says Gawain. "It responds quickly to love and energy."

144

Elly

So we told our bodies, "You're wonderful, incredible! You're beautiful! You're awesome! We love you."

I could see it was much more natural for me to do this than Roderic, who had never done such a thing in his life. While he knew it was a good idea, it was challenging for him to get fully into the feeling of it.

We visualized our bodies as we wanted them to be, healthy, graceful, vital and powerful; and energised them by dancing to Gabrielle Roth's *Endless Wave*. In this, she guided us with her sensual voice in a moving meditation around all our body parts, while taking us through her five basic rhythms of Flowing, Staccato, Chaos, Lyrical and Stillness.

While she invited us to move beyond self-consciousness into our wild free spirit, the smallness of our cottage put a limit on our abandonment.

Roderic

We tried to maintain a high degree of body-awareness throughout the week in whatever we were doing. Being fully present, alive and vibrant at all times is challenging, though it takes little more than an act of mindfulness. We practised Buddhist disciplines for this while walking along country lanes. We breathed consciously, directing *prana* or life-force to specific areas, breathing in sunlight, power, joy and other qualities; gave each other massages and Reiki; and did colour and chakra-breathing exercises. We drank water consciously after infusing it with sunlight for twenty-four hours and charging it with positive thoughts before swallowing, water being a conductor of the subtlest energies. Altogether we had a concentrated week, with a balance of seriousness and fun, aware of the fact that in most of these practices we were simply on page one.

Elly

It seemed quite natural to extend our *Body Awareness Week* into a *Sex Week*, which I proposed to Roderic.

"What a fantastic idea!" he replied with his usual wild enthusiasm. "Maybe it is time for a renewed focus on the subject. What do you have in mind?"

I was thinking of various Tantric and Taoist practices such as the Inner Flute, Microcosmic Orbit, PC Pumps and breathing techniques.

Maybe we should call it a *Spiritual Sex Week,*" I suggested.

"What *is* spiritual sex?" we wondered once again, really wanting to get to the core of this question.

"Is it holding a bible in your hand while you thrust your penis into your lover?" Roderic pondered frivolously. "Or is it spreading her out on an altar, offering one's deed to 'the One Above'?" he added with a chuckle. "Or is it something only sanctified by marriage? Or a monk seducing a nun?"

I laughed.

"What do *you* think?" he asked, sitting beside me as I lay in bed.

"Spiritual sex is bringing in the dimension of soul, one's innermost essence. It's about experiencing the oneness of your two souls in a physical union," I replied seriously.

"And how does that happen?"

"By shifting from a focus on the purely physical to an awareness of your own and the other's subtle energy-field. The more you connect with your own innermost essence, the more you are able to connect with someone else's. You can't feel oneness with another if you don't feel oneness within your own being, can you?"

"Not me!" he exclaimed. "Never!!"

"What we tend to do is reach out to the other as if he or she can supply us with what we seek, while what we seek comes from connectedness with our own innermost self."

"You're a real master," he smiled.

"Therefore, from the Tantric point of view," I resumed, "all meditations and exercises are focused on increasing our awareness, bringing us fully into the present, while connecting us with our innermost essence of love, joy and ecstacy, which we can then share as we circulate our energies into a blissful oneness."

Roderic

While I appreciated Elly's focus on the spiritual and shared her beliefs and aspirations, it would never be at the price of renouncing my delight in sex purely and simply as a medium of playfulness, which I believe is a fundamental aspect of Divine Intention.

Later that evening, lying in bed, I decided to consult the Highest Authority on the subject. Rather than directly, I took the lazy approach, turning to Walsch's *Conversations with God*:

"Play with sex," says 'God'. "Play with it! It's just about the most fun you can have with your body … Sex is joy … Sex is sacred too, yes. But joy and sacredness do mix (they are, in fact, the same thing), and many of you think they are not. Play, play, play with sex – and with all of life!"

That's what I believe.

At the same time, I aspire to remember that from the highest perspective "I" am God playing in "My" Creation; and that nothing in Reality is separate, neither inner from outer, nor higher from lower. While sex is a union with my earthly beloved – sensual, loving, playful and ecstatic – it is also a communion with the One Living Presence.

Elly

"Good morning," said Roderic, peering around the door with a smile on his face. "My penis has been on the alert for the past two hours. Full alert! It has come for its morning education! What's the programme?"

Letting his flowery orange sarong slip from his waist, he slid in between the sheets beside me.

Roderic

Suddenly I lost all interest in programmes!

Elly

During my tantric training I had done a number of exercises to increase the awareness of the energy flow within one's body and also one's partner's. One of them was called 'Hugging'. While it's a great way of attuning to each other's bodies, feelings, and subtle energies, it is also a wonderful prelude to more intimate sex. So I invited Roderic to explore this.

"Why? We've been hugging all day?" he replied.

"Not in the way I'm going to show you."

Roderic

We're going to stand naked and hug for ten minutes, motionless," she said, "just observing, just being aware."

"And what's that going to do for us?" I asked.

"Wait and see."

After bathing together, she led me into the living room. "It's warm and cosy here."

This would have to be good to sustain my attention. I was doubtful it would be. While it's wonderful holding one's beloved in one's arms, playing statues, frozen in a pose, wasn't appealing.

But I was greatly surprised. The mounting sensuality as cheek touched cheek, shoulder touched shoulder, chest touched breasts, bellies touched bellies, inner thighs touched inner thighs, not to mention other parts, as various impulses pulsed through them, was absolutely scintillating. Though we stood motionless, nothing was static, as our awareness moved fluidly in a roving delight from area to area. "What a wow!" I exclaimed, as we relinquished our hold.

Elly

We extended this exercise into an oiling, one of our favourite activities.

"What would you like and where?" I asked him.

"Well, if I'm to be your perfumed garden, sandalwood on my brow for a mystic dimension, ylang ylang around my sacral area, rose around my chest and heart, and jasmin elsewhere. How about that?"

Roderic

As she smoothed oil around my most intimate parts, I asked her to linger a while, and used the occasion for Testicle Breathing, a Taoist practice for increasing potency, which I had learned from my occasional bedside reading of Mantak Chia's *Cultivating Male Sexual Energy*.

Elly chose orange, sandalwood and patchouli, which I applied as she directed.

"Okay, that was just a start," she declared. "I'm going to dowse you in grapeseed oil."

"Our best salad oil?!" I queried. "Well, at least it's edible and lickable!"

She put on a CD of slow beating drums. Taking it in turns to dowse each other, we smoothed it around with erotic touch. As my hands slid around her hips and buttocks, she glided into a rhythmic dance, inviting me to do the same. We weaved our bodies around each other, and against each other, snakelike in twists and spirals. As I lay down on the towels she'd prepared, she resumed her slithering dance upon me ...

Elly
I revelled in this event with a childish pleasure.

Roderic
In modern parlance, it was a Peak Oil experience!

Elly
Everyday during our *Spiritual Sex Week* we explored something different, sometimes together, sometimes on our own. While Roderic practised Testicle Breathing, I engaged in similar disciplines, Ovarian Breathing and Vaginal Weightlifting. I wanted to develop my "love muscles". In theory, the building up of these gives a greater ability to squeeze your lover's penis while making love, adding greatly to his pleasure while heightening your own through increased sensitivity and orgasmic intensity. Strength of muscles in this area is also vital in other exercises such as the Inner Flute, designed to raise energy to higher centres. Contracting and expanding these muscles thirty times a day for six weeks is recommended for a real improvement, according to Margo Anand in her *Art of Sexual Ecstasy*. While I had been practising on and off, I had never sustained this. Now, in our *Spiritual Sex Week*, I was inspired again and determined to become a master of this part of my body.

Roderic

"Are you ready to practise the Microcosmic Orbit together?" Elly asked me one evening.

"Okay," I agreed. Todate, we had been practising on our own.

While she arranged and lit the candles and incense, I laid rugs and cushions on the floor. In the sacred arts of sex, such as the Tantric and Taoist, there's an emphasis on the importance of an inspiring space. But while the aesthetic, sensual and mental are one thing and indeed quite essential, far more important is the feeling aspect. So we caressed and cuddled, kindling the flames of a golden glow.

"Okay," she said softly. "Are you ready?"

I was.

"We'll start by moving energies consciously around our bodies and coordinate this with our breathing. Conscious breathing in unison adds a whole new dimension."

"Perhaps we should do this separately to begin with," she suggested.

"Too clinical," I countered.

"Be patient," she insisted. "First we must know what we're doing, then practise a little, after which we can relax into the rhythms with the love and feeling aspect.

I listened as she outlined the next steps.

"The intention is that we breathe our energies into each other's bodies and souls. While I breathe my female essence into you, you inhale it, drawing it in through your penis and up to the crown of your head. Then, on your outbreath, you release your male essence into me through your penis into my vagina, which I will draw up to my head, absorbing it before breathing out again."

"How do I do that?"

"You simply 'think' the energy in, up and out, as you breathe. No great effort. It's as simple as that.

"Of course we have to create some sexual energy first," she added, "or there isn't anything to be raised up."

"Well, I'm happy you've said that," I assured her, "for if there isn't anything to be raised up, I might not be able to participate!"

"For the woman," she began: "She breathes slowly and deeply through her nostrils, when she feels the expansion and heat of the

150

man's penis inside her. She then contracts her vagina and surrounding area – perineum, buttocks and anus – 'thinking' her partner's hot nourishing male energy into her clitoris and G-spot, past the perineum, into the coccyx and up the spinal column.

"When it reaches the head, she holds her breath and contraction for as long as possible, as she keeps drawing up the energy. Then she exhales, as he exhales. As he exhales bestowing his energy, she exhales bestowing hers, releasing all tension. She 'thinks' the energy down the front of her body until it reaches her pelvic region in a wave, and gently releases it to her partner through her G-spot and clitoris. That's her cycle. His, except for the most obvious details, is the same.

"There's a crucial point in all of this," she added: "We're not simply circulating energies but lovingly offering the essence of our beings – nurturing, vitalising, balancing and even healing each other. Theoretically, the more we practise these exchanges, the more explosive and blissful they become."

I loved experiencing Elly as the teacher – one so skilled, adorable and luscious!

We lay down again to begin the practise. After lingering a while as our fires smouldered, I entered a cavern of liquid silk. Yielding as it received my hot pulsing member, it closed upon it firmly in a locking grip. We were ready for our breathing on the first thrust.

Elly

But the moment we started we were totally confused about who was breathing when – in or out, up or down, along the back or along the front. So, while we were all hotted up, I giggled and he flopped.

After agreeing again on how we'd coordinate our rhythms, we tried again. Now our energies became so focused, weaving and mingling, we arrived at such an intense feeling of unity, as the borders between us became vaguer and vaguer and we melted blissfully into each other. I had never experienced anything like it.

Roderic

It was as if, in our breathing together, we had switched from diesel to rocket fuel and gone into orbit.

Theme Weeks for Soul Mates is powerful medicine!

Chapter 16

Encounters in Nature

Elly

Few delights were as great as going out into Nature. Every sortie was a discovery. Each day we picked something different for eating or making drinks. There were hawthorn leaves, blossoms and, later in the year, berries:

"A tea of these makes an excellent tonic for the heart," said Roderic. "In fact, in orthodox medicine, an extract from the hawthorn is used in treating its ailments."

I found it incredible that leaves, blossoms or berries could heal diseases. While I could accept the idea in principle, I found it hard to imagine while holding them in my hands that they could be so powerful. "Sometimes dangerously so," said Roderic. "You need to know what you're picking. A few years ago, a local couple ended up in hospital after eating the petals of a crocus. One lost a kidney. But don't worry," he assured me as I looked at him astonished, "This is one area in which I don't take risks."

As each month passed there was a fresh range of Nature's gifts to be harvested. Horsetail was one of Roderic's favourites. We hung lengths of it in bunches around the kitchen. "It is one of the oldest plants on the planet, descended from a tree which thrived in the swamps over a hundred million years ago. With the highest concentration of silica in any plant, it's good for the bones, which is why it is known as the skeleton builder."

One of my favourite teas to pick was camomile, which seemed to grow mostly in fields with young bulls. So sometimes while wading through quagmires of dung to pluck their sunny heads and feathery stems, we found ourselves having to make a speedy exit. I was surprised at how they thrived in such an environment. Picking camomile in dung made me feel really close to Mother Earth.

Collecting flowers for salads – blazing yellow gorse, orange and crimson nasturtiums, deep blue borage, along with an assortment of leaves such as dandelion, plantain and navelwort – was also new for me. We had soups of sorrel, nettle, wild mushrooms and seaweeds; collected carrigeen moss in rock-pools for thickening soups and making jellies; and, in a nearby estuary, discovered fields of marsh samphire, a kind of sea asparagus, which made a juicy vegetable. One of our most exciting finds was a giant puffball larger than a football, which we sliced into cutlets, and invented a dish which we called a Puffburger, consisting of an egg, tomato and fresh basil between two fried circular chunks. It was fun and delicious.

The more we picked flowers, fruits and herbs for our nourishment, the more I realized that Nature is not simply a place, a physical environment, but that each tiny part has a life-force energy running through it, shaping and sustaining it with a unique pattern, character and power; while able to provide us with everything we need. I was beginning to have a tangible sense of Mother Earth as the womb of all life, to sense her pulse as a living being, and her varying vibrations. I felt profound gratitude for the fact that I had been able finally to uproot myself from the city with its bombarding noise pollution into the peace of the countryside. I had not realized how disconnected I had become from Nature. In the city I was contracted, to protect myself from its invasiveness. In Nature, welcomed by its beauty and depth of silence, I expanded.

I longed to be able to communicate with animals, birds, plants and trees; and wished to honour the commitment I had made in the Burren, the previous year, both to open up to Nature and work with her more consciously.

"Cultivating awareness is what it's all about," Roderic kept reminding me. This was still my challenge. When I first came to Ireland and was meandering along country lanes, with a Universe of life around me, I would find myself locked in thought, my eyes fixed to the ground in front of me, unaware of anything. He used to act this out, mimicking me comically, stooping forward, his head almost at knee level, staring down and scrutinizing the tarmac in front of his feet while moving forward at a fast pace, commenting, "Isn't Nature wonderful?" and laughing. With such vivid demonstrations I came to see that the more I was absorbed in thought the less I was aware of anything around me.

"You need to empty your mind not only to become fully aware of so-called *ordinary* reality, but even more so of subtler vibrations of invisible realms. To become aware of nature spirits, you must tune your level of vibration to theirs. You cannot do that when the mind is buzzing. So first it must become still."

Yes, but while I had spent a lot of time stilling it in Nature, sitting on rocks watching and listening to waves, standing in the woods by a murmuring stream, silently observing the swooping of bats in their evening flights, and generally in meditation, I didn't seem to be any closer to seeing or meeting them.

"Just waiting for them isn't enough," said Roderic. "Do you really ask? You can sit in front of a door forever, but if you don't knock, it may never be opened. Respecting your freedom, they wait for you to ask; otherwise they'd be imposing, which isn't permitted."

So, the next day, I asked, and declared myself open.

Committing myself to opening up to Nature, to reaching out and receiving from her, I had dreamed of meeting beautiful fairies, elves, angels and other beings of Light. But, no such delight. I was in for a shock. The first and immediate response of Nature was a big rat, clawing feverishly on the kitchen window, desperately trying to climb the glass and enter through an open vent.

"Yuk!"

"Well, you asked for Nature," said Roderic, amused. "Here she is!"

I was really frightened and tried to chase the rat away; but she didn't want to go. I ran to the front door to close it. I had a phobia of rats and was in a panic. I had the fixed idea, which I'd got from a movie, that they can jump up to your throat and kill you.

"Isn't Nature wonderful?" said Roderic mockingly.

I was so disappointed. "Let's go for a walk," I suggested. "I want to get rid of the fear in my body."

On our way, we met a hare, which came hopping slowly along the lane towards us, stopping about a metre in front of me. It was the size of a small kangaroo. It sat there a moment staring at me with cool deliberation as if to ensure I was fully aware of it. Then it ran off into a field.

Back home I consulted our *Medicine Cards*, but could find no hare, only its cousin the rabbit, which represents fear. So, seemingly, in *The Language of the Birds*, the hare was telling me to look at my fear. So I did, I really did, until it made me feel sick in the stomach. Reflecting on this, I realized that I was locked into many fearful thoughts about Nature: It is hostile, even dangerous, and it might attack me; it's full of bacteria and viruses that can make me ill; it can even kill me. The rat represented all of these fears: They were dirty, sneaky, carried lethal diseases and were generally obnoxious.

"Fear closes all doors, as you know," said Roderic, who was following my process, refusing to participate except as an observer.

"Yes, but how can I change it?"

"There's only one way: Into love."

I understood the theory, but my fears were deeply rooted, even chronic. As far as the rat was concerned, they were triggered by the tiniest of sounds in the house or a whisper of wind on a blade of grass. "Was that the rat?" I would ask anxiously. In spite of the summer heat and our love of fresh air, I closed every door and window to make sure she couldn't get in. Every time I stepped into the garden, she appeared. I didn't dare wear my summer sandals. Even on the hottest day, I put on my Wellington boots.

"Are you expecting a storm?" asked Roderic, ever amused.

I even skipped my Full Moon walk to the beach in case the rat was lurking in the undergrowth. And the strange thing was that while Roderic was working in the garden she was never there, while she always arrived whenever I appeared, leaping out onto the pathway or scurrying through our patch of nettles or African daisies. One day, he did actually see her, as she popped into view where he was working:

"Aren't you scared?" I asked.

"No. I'm doing my thing and she's doing hers."

I had to deal with this situation as she was spoiling my pleasure living in this beautiful place. I considered my options, which seemed to be either to put down rat poison or move to another place.

"You can keep on moving house as much as you like," said Roderic. "For one thing, there are rats all over Ireland, all over the countryside, even in the mountains, even in the cities. Indeed, there's an estimated fifteen to twenty of them for every member of the human population. The main point is that *you* have invoked this situation."

"How?"

"You wanted to open up to Nature spirits and asked them to present themselves. Nature, of course, has its dark side, but you weren't prepared for this, and you're holding a lot of fear. Fear, as you know, attracts. This rat, evidently sent to *you* personally, is obliging you to look at this fear and deal with it. You can hardly open up to Nature in its wholeness as long as you're holding onto it. You can go anywhere you like and you are going to be *re-presented* with the same 'problem' – though, let's use the word 'challenge'. That's why *I* never meet the rat, because she is *your* challenge. And it isn't going to help the situation by me solving it. I can make suggestions, but it's for you to choose, act, and take responsibility. If I was to deal with it, my beloved, you would be deprived of the learning experience."

"So what do you think about putting down rat poison?" I asked.

"You've been put into a situation which is certain to demonstrate to you what your relationship with Nature actually is."

"It's separate and fear-based," I suggested.

"Precisely. Which is the very opposite of the oneness you seek!"

For years I had been teaching people in my courses that Reiki was another word for life-force energy and that every living being, tree, flower, animal and human, was animated by it as an expression of the one life. Now, being face-to-face with a rat, it was a different story!

"When you see yourself as separate," said Roderic, "you tend to see as hostile that from which you have become separated. Then you want to destroy it. You call it an enemy or pest and invent a pesticide or poison. It seems very practical and the only choice you've got. But it isn't."

"What other choice is there?"

"Cooperation."

"With a rat?!"

"Yes. Talk with her on behalf of all rats. Come to an understanding. Make a deal."

"What do you mean? Just tell her to go away?"

"No. There is no *telling*. There has to be mutual respect, an exchange. There is *asking* her; but, before that, there is recognizing that she has needs too. Even before that, I would say that the relationship between you needs improving – not only personally, but between the rat as a member of her species and you as a member of yours, the human race."

"You want me to invite her in for tea?"

"Not exactly; but you can hardly expect cooperation while you remain in a hostile mode. As we've said, it's all about changing fear into love. First, after so much hatred directed towards rats, you have an opportunity to apologise on behalf of the human race, to ask for forgiveness, and also to thank this species as one of the world's most accomplished scavengers and clean-up operators for its great contributions to the wholeness of life. At the same time, it's about you seeing and acknowledging the rat as an expression of the Divine. Yes, the rat, even the rat."

"Come on!" I replied, in disbelief, though more by way of stubborn resistance.

"Well. If you talk about the oneness of life and Nature, the rat cannot be excluded. As long as you remain in the fear mode, she remains an enemy. And that's not what you want, is it?"

"No."

"So you can start a new way of relating, based on friendship and cooperation, or at least mutual respect and understanding."

"You honestly believe that rats will actually cooperate?"

"Absolutely. I know from my experiences. You're not expected to have a cuddly relationship with them. You must be true to your feelings. You don't have to have rats running around the place. Quite the opposite. This is about mutual respect, which includes respect for each other's spaces. So you say to this one: "Look, I wish you the very best, a life of abundance, and I'm wholly open to living in harmony with you, BUT: You in your space and me in mine. Only then can we have a good relationship." It's the same with humans. Each needs their own space and to respect that of others."

"Let's be practical," I said, eager to deal with the immediate situation.

"Okay. I'll give you an example."

"After a long chat with a family of mice that had been decimating my strawberry bed," he told me, "I proposed a solution, which, in short, was this: "You leave my bed alone and I'll plant an additional quarter of a bed next to it, exclusively for you. You don't touch mine and I won't touch yours, except to keep it weeded. One year later, I was able to judge the results. All of the strawberries in my bed were left entirely untouched, while piles of decimated unripe fruit littered theirs. What they thought they were doing with them, I never found out. They all rotted."

"As I said," he concluded, "despite the seeming craziness, talking with the mice turned out to be a thoroughly practical approach and solution, much more wholesome, playful in fact, than the usual hostilities, pesticides and slaughter. Of course you can pooh-pooh the idea, but first you must try it."

I wondered what *I* could do with the rat. I didn't believe I could do anything. My fear was too strong and I lacked conviction. But I'd got the message.

"I'll come over and put down some poison," said Dennis, our neighbour and caretaker of the estate on which we lived. I didn't feel able to say, "No, don't worry, no need to do anything, I'll have a little chat with her. That'll do the trick." So I let him come. He put down two pipes half a metre long with blue powder in them, one beneath the kitchen window and one near my bedroom.

He returned the following morning. "They didn't eat much," he noted. "It'll take a few days."

"Oh, my God," I thought: "Does he mean there's more than one?"

Poisoning really seemed the only option. I was too scared. But I felt worse and worse about this, especially when I saw the rat with its pup, which made her seem more human.

On the second day, the baby rat died. I found it lying on its back outside the front gate. The evening before, when I was about to fall asleep, I had felt the Rat Deva entering my room. While it wasn't visible, I could sense its presence, a large energy-field hovering above me. I was so scared I hid under my bedclothes until it had gone. From underneath my duvet, I thanked it for giving me a lesson about fear, but wasn't ready for any further communication.

The day the rat died, she peered up at me as I was looking through the kitchen window. I could see she was in pain, drugged with poison, and flies all around her. Pitying her, I sent her Reiki to ease her suffering. As I did so, she looked at me again and came crawling towards me. I stopped giving her Reiki, afraid I was bringing her back to life! A few hours later, when I saw her on the other side of our cottage, lying on her back close to where her baby had died, another ridiculous fear arose: Maybe, before she died, she'd told all the other rats in the neighbourhood that I was a serial killer and they would all come and get me!

I had a basic fear of life, evidently, seeing it as hostile rather than supportive, which was blocking me in opening to its love and beauty.

After the rat, a wren came, appearing in exactly the same spot. I had never seen such a tiny bird and watched it through the kitchen window. Later, it left its calling card on our doorstep, a tiny feather.

Some days afterwards, while reading in the living room, I heard the penetratingly demanding sound of a bird at the front door, which was open. I looked up and saw the wren coming in. It hopped into my bedroom, came out, and hovered in the hall, gazing at me. "There you are. Tweet, tweet!" it seemed to say. What touched me was that this little bird had risked its life to visit me. There was so much love coming through it from the Universe.

Seeing life as hostile, I had always felt I had to fight to survive. It seemed the wren had come to tell me I was valued by the Universe, that I was heard and seen and worthy of its love. It was telling me to trust. Tears of gratitude and joy flowed down my cheeks.

Next, I turned to plants and trees. Less risky, I thought.

"A tree can tell you anything you want to know," said Roderic, "but don't take my word for it. There is no substitute for being with trees, attuning to them and opening up your own lines of communication. They are living energy-fields with their own intelligence. That is a fact."

Looking at them, I realized they were not trying to be anything other than what they were. "I am what I am" is what they were saying, which gave me permission to be uniquely what I am.

Roderic gave me an article on how to work with the healing energy of trees by the Taoist masters, Mantak and Maneewan Chia. "They're the most spiritually advanced plants on earth," they believe. "Subtle energy is their natural language. As your understanding of this grows, you can begin to develop a relationship with them. While they can help you open your energy channels and cultivate calm, presence and vitality, you can reciprocate by helping them with their blockages and devitalised areas. It's a mutually beneficial relationship that needs cultivation."

Casting its shadow over our cottage was a large sycamore. Here beneath it, armed with a set of instructions, we opened ourselves to the flow of its energies. Absorbing these, we circulated them through our crown and root chakras as well as the roots, trunk and crown of the tree. Following a nine-step programme, we called our practice *Tai Tree*. Our experiences were complementary: While I felt the flow circulating from the top down, Roderic felt it from the ground up. A difference in yin-yang polarities, we concluded. Sometimes, when I embraced the tree and connected to its roots, I found myself shaking as if I were holding a pneumatic drill, which totally convinced me there was an exchange of energies. It was a significant experience opening me up to another level of awareness in the presence of Nature. Happily it was followed by many others. Whever I tune into flowers, I experience an overwhelming feeling of love and oneness.

I was also drawn to the sea and its creatures:

One day, while seated on the rocks, a school of dolphins passed by. I was bewitched by their strength, speed and elegance, as they moved through the waves. Though they were gone in a flash, they reappeared over the next four days, playing around at the edge of the bay. I had been asking to see one ever since arriving at our cottage, but had had to wait. I had spent hours, weeks, even months, just sitting at the seashore, but it was only after I had made a commitment, going down there daily to meditate and tune in to them, that they finally showed up. This, for me, was another example of how the magic starts happening once you have a clear intention and make a commitment. It is the same in love relationships, I realized. Without a commitment, little can happen.

Nature, my schoolroom!

Chapter 17

Healing with a Past Life Dimension

Roderic

It was winter, wild in the countryside, with wind howling, rain pelting, and bitterly cold; but cosy and warm inside, with a fire crackling. Not weather for venturing outdoors, but perfect for inner journeys. We were about to make a discovery, a key in understanding of mysteries of our Selves.

One day, I discovered a lump on one of my breasts. Slightly alarmed, I went to consult a local doctor, who confirmed that it was indeed a lump. "You'd better have it checked at a hospital to find out whether it's malignant or not," he advised. So I went to one in Cork, to its department for breast cancer. "It doesn't appear to be malignant," said the specialist, "but you should have it removed by surgery."

While I had a great respect for the medical profession, I had huge reservations on its approaches to healing. It appears to work primarily with two options, either to cut away a disturbed area, which might sometimes be necessary, or stuff its patients with drugs, often with dangerous side effects. It doesn't seem to spend much time addressing the causes. One doctor actually told me that he didn't have any time at all for this. I am convinced that when you cut out or treat an ill part of the body without looking into the causes at different, often at non-physical levels, the symptom will reappear sooner or later, maybe in another place or form.

So I wasn't prepared to accept the word of these experts. I was determined to find the causes myself, so they could be dealt with. Therefore I declined an operation. Better than any doctor, I had my own resident holistic health practitioner:

"Why don't you use your skills as a kinesiologist and ask my body for information directly?" I suggested to Elly. Bodies know:

They have their own intelligence. We, or any doctor, however skilled, can sometimes only guess what a body lacks or what the cause of a condition is. And if there is a deficiency in a rare trace element, for example, extensive and costly tests may be necessary to ascertain this by orthodox means, whereas, simply by asking the body, one can find the answer in a few minutes – provided one puts the right questions!

How is this possible? By a method of extreme simplicity! While professionally known as kinesiology, it is more commonly known as muscle-testing. While putting a question to the body, for example, you exert a light pressure on a muscle, such as on an outstreched arm, and observe its resisting or yielding response, which will signify either a "yes" or a "no". The response is instant. Either it will remain outstretched or it will collapse. One of the first things that can be established by this method is whether the cause of a condition is primarily on the physical, emotional, mental or spiritual level, which is of extreme importance. Without this information you can spend a fortune and a lifetime seeking the cause on the wrong level, while uselessly, wastefully and even dangerously applying 'remedies' on the wrong level. Strangely, while kinesiology was and continues to be developed by doctors, there are not many of them who are familiar with it. While I had attended a couple of introductory workshops on the subject, Elly had been using it in her practice as a physiotherapist for many years.

Elly

"Hold an arm out in front of you," I requested in a clinical mode, ready for our session.

"First things first!" Roderic replied smiling, drawing me reluctantly into an embrace. "All good things begin with a hug! We may be engaged in a healing process but the underlying reality is that we are sharing love and having fun." I agreed. About to become far too serious, I yielded happily.

"We also begin by welcoming our angels and other beings of Light and inviting their assistance," he suggested. Of course! It was a challenge remembering this. We took it in turns reminding each other.

"Think of something joyful," I began when we were ready, his arm extended. I needed to establish that his body's response system was in order, so it could give me clear positive and negative feedback. Normally, when presented with a positive, its bioelectrical system holds firm, enabling the muscles to maintain their strength under pressure. On the other hand, when presented with a negative, the same system responds by short-circuiting, and the arm collapses – the muscles, having lost their strength, being unable to maintain their position under pressure.

"Something joyful? How about you?" he replied playfully, "you lying on the floor, naked, with raspberries and cream on your belly!"

When I put a light downward pressure on his arm, it resisted strongly, a positive response that signified "yes". "You should do it some time," I suggested. "Now think of something which would cause you stress."

"Mr Bean being run over by his mini!"

When I put the same light pressure on his arm, it wavered, resisting partially. "Obviously, this wouldn't cause *you* enough stress."

"Sorry, Mr Bean!"

"Try again."

"How about someone getting to the raspberries and cream before I did?"

"Do try to be serious," I pleaded, wondering whether the session was going to work.

"Okay," he agreed. "I'll think about something really scary."

When I put the same light pressure on his arm, it collapsed immediately, a clear negative response indicating a "no".

Having confirmed his bioelectric system was in order, giving clear signals, and that he was now in earnest, I asked his body for basic information under the following headings, to find out in which was the priority for healing the lump: *Structure*, relating to the purely physical, including any blockages in the immune system. *Chemical*, relating to allergies, levels of toxicity, or mineral or vitamin deficiencies. *Emotional*, relating to traumas or negative feelings or thought-patterns stored in the body. *Electromagnetic*, relating to the functioning of the chakras and the flow of energies through the meridians.

His body informed me that the primary cause of the disturbance was chemical; and I was able to trace this to a specific supplement that he'd been taking. He stopped doing so immediately. Having pinpointed the cause and taken the obviously appropriate action, the lump disappeared naturally in three weeks, never to return. Thus, an operation, great cost and much unnecessary trauma were avoided!

Roderic

It was around this time that I decided to give up smoking.

I had a sneaking suspicion there was a karmic dimension to this, that the habit was connected to a situation in a previous life, possibly in the sixteenth century, in Elizabethan times, certain memories of which I had been able to access quite vividly. But, if there was such a connection, could it be established simply by testing the responses of muscles? The idea that one could ask one's body for information on events of over four hundred years ago seemed extraordinary. Yet, why not? "There are more things in heaven and earth than were ever dreamed of in your philosophy," as Hamlet said to Horatio.

I already knew from personal experiences that the body carries past-life memories at a cellular level; so, on reflection, it seemed more than possible. I was excited by the thought of being able to access such information, on the spot, in a question-and-answer session.

"You can ask your body anything you like," Elly had said.

"Have you ever used kinesiology to explore past lives?" I asked.

"No. I wasn't taught this. Nor would I have dared to do so as a physiotherapist, as it would have been considered too far out."

"A pity," I replied. "Doctors, therapists, the whole medical profession, need an education in metaphysics. They are far too limited in their approaches to healing."

"Yes! That would certainly revolutionize the system. It would also make communications with doctors easier and more wholesome. One could talk about consciousness and the soul withour fear of ridicule."

"Have you ever heard of kinesiology being used to explore past lives?" I asked.

"No."

"So, let's do it. We might be the first."

"I've never understood," she declared, "how it's possible for the body to hold past-life memories when it's not the body which reincarnates but the soul or higher self."

"Because," I suggested, "the body is not simply bones, flesh and blood, but an energy-field, a multi-dimensional energy-field, existing and vibrating at different levels of frequency. The physical is merely the visible dense aspect, a materialization at the bottom end of the frequency scale of what is largely invisible, while the soul is an energy-field penetrating all levels. Its memories, which it carries through Time, impress themselves on the physical body. Some people even have physical scars from a previous life at birth."

"Incredible when you really think about it," Elly enthused.

A few weeks later, I read a passage in Jane Roberts' book, *Seth Speaks*, affirming this: "The body does not only carry memory biologically of its own past condition in this life; but indelibly with it, even physically, are the memories of the other bodies that the personality has formed in previous incarnations." This also seems to be supported by the evidences of well-documented researches in the United States and Canada, using techniques of past-life regression.

Elly

It was encouraging to know that this was happening. It's so much more real to look at the whole person, including his or her past lives, which have such an impact on the present one, than focusing exclusively on the physical ailments of hearts or livers, which may be expressions of imbalances on deeper levels. Again, it's taking the soul, and multidimensionality of our beingness, into consideration as part of our wholeness.

Roderic

It was time to put our beliefs to the test; so we continued putting questions to my body, having established, first of all, that there was indeed a past-life dimension to my smoking.

But, before proceeding further, I wanted to be sure of the accuracy of the answers. We needed a method of questioning which would exclude any possibility either of Elly or my body being influenced by what I at the level of conscious mind already knew or suspected. Fortunately, while I remembered some details of my Elizabethan life, I had never shared them with her; nor had I ever mentioned that I'd had a life at that time. I wrote down a number of questions, both relevant and irrelevant, suggesting that she put these silently to my body in whatever order she liked, so that I couldn't hear, and my mind would have no way of influencing the response. "You may also add questions of your own," I suggested. "Then I'll really have no idea what you're asking."

In response to her first question, my arm collapsed immediately.

"What did you ask?" I enquired afterwards. "Whether you were a woman! Your body had no doubt about that," she chuckled.

The key questions and responses were as follows:

"Is your habit of smoking connected with your immediate past life in England?" No. "With your nineteenth century life in Austria?" No. "With your fifteenth century life in France?" No. "With your sixteenth century life in Elizabethan times?" Yes.

This confirmed my suspicion.

Elly

I was excited playing detectives, though I knew nothing of Elizabethan times.

Roderic

I had another question for her to put: "Is your habit of smoking today linked with your use of tobacco during those times?" No.

This surprised me greatly. It also validated the muscle-testing process, since my conscious mind, suspecting a link, had anticipated a "yes". My body's responses had clearly contradicted my thoughts on the subject. But I was puzzled. What could the nature of the link be? Needing a clue, I addressed my higher self and awaited a response.

It was a good time to pause. We had prawns to grill, wine to chill, and Manchester United was playing Real Madrid.

An answer came the following day, quite unexpectedly:

After working under pressure unnecessarily, I felt exhausted and lay on my bed, listening to the wind howling. Elly gave me a Reiki, followed by a massage, during which she sensed a huge difference between the energies in my left and right legs, those in my left being far weaker. "It feels relatively lifeless, as if you're not fully in it." It was then I remembered that I had been partially paralysed down my left side towards the end of my Elizabethan life, before being executed.

I was intrigued by this connection between my two lives.

"The left side of the body is linked with receptivity and the feminine," Elly reminded me. Both of these, evidently, were yet ongoing issues for me, as I had thought I had dealt with them sufficiently, having been working on them for years; but my body was indicating otherwise. "Do you also realize," said Elly, "that your habit of smoking results in a major dulling of your receptivity? Maybe a part of you has concluded unconsciously that it's safer to perpetuate that state?

Early that morning, I had turned a few pages of Barbara Marciniak's *Earth*, channelings from Pleiadians, and was struck by the following statement: "Whatever issues you have not dealt with and peacefully cleared in your personal history will form chaos in your body," they warn, emphasizing the importance of this during the current period of the Earth's evolution when energies of higher frequency are pouring into the planet: "As the energy increases, blocks in your physical, mental, emotional, and spiritual bodies are magnified ... A tremendous and radical change is taking place within your physical body, and we cannot emphasize this enough ... So, to avoid burnout, *listen* to what's inside you."

It was time for me to stop and do just that, to switch off from any activity on the outside for a few days and go inwards, deeper into what had already been presented, and exploring whatever else might come up. If I didn't do so voluntarily I might be obliged to do so.

Seeking additional feedback, I picked a *Medicine Card*, suspecting it would either be the Frog, signalling my need for purification linked with smoking, or the Bear, confirming I needed to go into hibernation. It was the latter, reversed. "Become like the

Bear and enter the safety of the womb-cave," it advised. "Attune to the energies of the Eternal Mother."

Yet I prevaricated.

Another event signalled synchronistically: The supply of electricity for the area got cut off. I was no longer able to work on my computer.

I love this kind of magic and ever marvel at the way the Universe works. When it gets little or no response to its promptings, it tends to become increasingly forceful – first the little tap, then mightier, ever more dramatically, whacking you on the head or otherwise bringing you to a halt.

Sometimes, before taking the appropriate action, I need to hear the message three times! Out of curiosity, seeking further confirmation, I picked an *Angel Card*. On it was a picture of an angel on a motorbike halted at red lights. It was marked 'OBEDIENCE'. What could have been clearer? I resisted no more.

So I curled up in bed, bear-like, burying myself in the darkness of a womb-cave of duvets, and began reflecting. I invited to the surface whatever needed to be looked at and resolved, examining in detail various patterns in my lives, current and previous. Involving events and relationships over centuries, this was intense. Elly, supportively by my side for much of the time, gave me drops of Angelsword, one of her Australian Bush Flower Essences, to facilitate receiving clear information from my higher self, including the most distant memories. I went ever more deeply into my Elizabethan life, its themes and events buzzing in my head. Why a weakness on my left side in two lives? I wondered. What resistances, blockages, unresolved issues, if any, did I still carry in relation to receiving and the feminine?

Elly

It was wonderful to witness his process, which he shared with me in detail. Step by step a picture began emerging.

Roderic

In Elizabethan times, my relationship with the feminine had been represented by the Queen, who had showered me with gifts and favours. Thus I had become powerful and wealthy. The down side

170

was that whenever I fell out of favour, I had the carpet pulled from under my feet, becoming thoroughly disempowered – eventually, in physical terms, paralysed. Her love had been conditional. But this former life could not be considered in isolation.The pattern continued. The same themes and issues ran like threads throughout other lives up to the present. In my current one, I had repeated centuries-old patterns quite dramatically. Receiving was dangerous, I had concluded; so, defensively, while generous in giving, I had switched off on receiving, unconsciously, on the feminine receptive side. Power, fame and fortune, these too were dangerous: they promoted the envy and treachery of others which had resulted in my downfall and ultimate demise, costing me my life on more than one occasion. I had to root out these patterns and associated fears and remove them from my system one at a time. Even in this life, I had been showered with gifts by a queenly figure, over a million dollars worth, seemingly unconditionally, re-enacting my Elizabethan drama; and, once again, I had had the carpet pulled devastatingly from under my feet.

Applying the principles with which I was familiar, it was obvious I must have been doing this to others at some time. "As you do unto others, it will be done unto you," as Jesus warned, though he (or his commentators) had failed to qualify with the crucial addendum *"in this life or the next"*, without which his words make no sense whatsoever. Thus one learns, through the experiencing, either in this or subsequent lives, what it feels like to be on the receiving end of one's own actions. Hopefully then – after a few howls of "this is utterly insufferable behaviour!" – one wakes up, recognizing that the causes lie within one's own being, and resolves to heal the pattern. If the past isn't fully understood and the wisdom extracted, it will repeat itself in one form or another, again and again. Manipulating others as if they were pawns on a board? After long and deep reflections, buried in my cave of duvets, I realized the extent to which *I* had been doing just that. But I had thought that I'd already cleared this pattern. Perhaps not fully enough! Or perhaps I had let go of it but not replaced it with a clear, positive and intelligent alternative.

Elly

While it seemed that Roderic had cleared many of his patterns on a mental level and was indeed into a new approach, there were still fears locked in the energy-field of his body, which meant that he was blocked in his ability to receive. I had discovered this a year earlier, the first time I gave him Reiki, in his Round House, when the energy flowing through my hands had simply bounced off him.

There was another occasion when I'd vividly experienced his rejection of the feminine. It was while playing the Game of Transformation with my friend Joyce from Amsterdam, a counsellor and hypnotherapist. While trying to connect him with his feelings, the pains and fears he was still carrying in his body, which we could clearly see and which the Game was showing, we had to put up with his impenetrable defensiveness and clever reasoning for which we were no match. It would take a hammer to crack open his nut, we'd concluded. He had given us such a hard time that we'd begun doubting our abilities. At one point, I'd screamed out my rage and frustrations, smashing a pillow on a chair. "I've come to an end," I thought, "and can go no further." I'd even felt like flying back to Amsterdam.

My great delight now was the feeling that he was ready, open, willing, and quite vulnerable. Through Kinesiology I could communicate with his body directly and he could not deny my intuition. There was no escape anymore! Nothing worse than having one's intuitive feelings ignored or rejected! We had found an approach that worked for both. So I was excited that he was now exploring his feelings of rejection of the feminine and healing them. It had all started with his desire to stop smoking, which had eventually led us to the underlying causes.

Roderic

It's strange to think one can reject both love and healing, but apparently so. I came into this world rejecting my mother, who in turn rejected me – at least, as I experienced it – passing me into the care of nurses and nannies before leaving the family household. This dual pattern, *my* rejection of the feminine and *its* rejection of me, had a long history.

Elly

"Tell me about it," I requested, arriving beside him with camomile tea and honey waffles, wondering how it might affect his life now and me as his partner.

"I can trace my relationships with the feminine back about four thousand years," he began in a matter-of-fact way, "but the rejection pattern has only existed, as far as I know, for the past five hundred."

I was no longer amazed by such statements. Having known him for over a year, I had come to believe and also feel that everything is possible, that life is unlimited and so are we, much more than we think.

After relating his past-life patterns in relation to the feminine in considerable detail spanning centuries, he ended with their most recent and increasingly more extreme expressions:

"In my previous life in the first part of the twentieth century, my denial of the feminine became total. Not simply women were excluded, but everything representing the feminine in principles or qualities. I lived a harsh life in the desert, adventuring as usual, before retiring into a tormented though creative isolation. I came into my current life to address these imbalances," he said.

I felt blessed that we had the time, tools and freedom to spend on our healing, As we lay cosily in bed, I could see the rain sweeping horizontally across the valley and invited him to continue.

"First, as my soul had decided, I had to re-experience these and other situations; then choose again, hopefully more wisely. So, at different stages of my current life, I have found myself involved in various past-life re-enactments, similar in terms of circumstances, psychological ingredients and human characters, thereby obliged to re-confront all of the same unresolved issues. For example, I re-played the Habsburg drama, also in Austria, also with a young Baroness, with more or less all of the same ingredients, excepting my title and the historical costumes; and with no loss of life happily, but I ended up in prison."

Though I knew that fact could be more improbable than fiction and didn't doubt him for a second, I still felt some resistance to accepting this reality, the utter strangeness of it. You can read about

173

past lives as an abstract concept, but that they can have such an impact on the realities of everyday life is quite astonishing. Hearing stories of actual experiences from the mouth of your lover who is lying beside you is riveting.

Roderic
It is wonderful to be able to share such profound and intimate details, and explore them with such fruitful outcome, in a safe and supportive environment with a kindred spirit and loving partner.

Elly
I was still wondering if Roderic had fully resolved his problems with the feminine and if there was any connection with *our* relationship.

"The feminine I'm referring to doesn't have much to do with women," he replied. "Not primarily. They feature as actors in what are essentially inner dramas. What I mean by the feminine and masculine are *yin* and *yang* principles, aspects of one's psyche, imbalances in which tend to cause havoc. Therefore they require understanding. As you know, the masculine principle is represented by left-brain activities and intellect, and the feminine by right-brain, feelings and intuition. Both need to be functioning in harmony or they malfunction. The masculine principle seeks to impress itself on life by imposing, which tends to prove disastrous as we've seen historically. Basically it works from the top down, starting with ideas, concepts, belief-systems. It is more concerned with the grand scheme of things, the overview, the universal, its primary connectedness being with the abstract." Even though I was familiar with this, he gave examples, his clarity refreshing my knowledge on the subject. "The feminine principle, being receptive, allows things to unfold" he continued. "There's great wisdom and power in this, generally unappreciated by the masculine. Basically it works from the ground up, organically, like nature, with a small seed that it nurtures. It is more concerned with the particular and personal, its primary connectedness being with the Earth. The feminine approach is not to be underestimated. Its seeds too can grow into billion-dollar enterprises. It's taken me a long time to appreciate the fundamental differences in the two, and longer still to change my way of being and operating, which has resulted in many a 180 degrees shift."

I ushered him on.

"My path of exploring the feminine, of rediscovering and integrating it, led me into giving up my worldly projects, leaving cities and returning to the Earth, opening up to Nature, feeling into her and so forth, picking up a spade, digging the soil for months on end, sowing seeds and nurturing them, creating and cultivating gardens."

"So, how do I as your female partner now feature in your life?" I asked, still wondering about his past-life relations with women, whether as mothers or lovers.

"As long as I live with the male and female aspects of my wholeness reasonably well-balanced, in loving and harmonious relationship within my self, my outer relationships will reflect this," he replied. "Thus, I've drawn you into my life, beloved!"

More than symbolically he drew me into his arms.

"I, as one aspiring whole being, am now able to relate to the female, *you*, as another aspiring whole being, I hope," he added, releasing me from his embrace. "The dependencies, projections, neediness and traumas, have gone. What remains are the joys of being together, being mutually supportive, mutually respecting the freedom of the other, while growing, exploring, sharing, creating, and generally having fun together."

We snuggled up warmly.

"There's yet another aspect," he declared, pulling himself up from beneath the sheets. "What *is* man's yearning for the feminine? What *is* our yearning for the opposite sex? It goes way beyond instinctive urges and has nothing to do with horizontal relationships."

I, too, emerged from the cosy darkness. "*Horizontal* relationships?" I murmured. "What do you mean? We've been horizontal for about three days!"

"That it has nothing to do with relationships on the outside, is what I mean. The primary yearning, built into our psyches, is union with the Divine, with our own souls. On our evolutionary path, as cosmic beings waking to who and what we truly are, it's for the return to Oneness. From the male perspective, in Jungian terms, it's with the feminine *anima*. When we, as males, project this outwards onto a woman, we're in trouble, ever looking for the ultimate and our completeness in the other; and ever failing, for it's not where they are found."

"And so?" I asked.

"To keep relationships healthy, we must remember that the primary relationship is a *vertical* one – that is, within our own Beings, with our own souls or higher selves. Again, it's putting first things first. Becoming whole and complete within our selves is also the primary task. The outer comes as a reflection of the inner; in any event, as a function of it."

"You mean that all our relationships are a mirror of the one we have with our Selves?"

"Largely, yes; and it gives one such a feeling of freedom, and of being in control of one's life, knowing that all begins on the inside and that when you want to change anything, or something in a relationship, this is where you do it: On the inside."

"Gosh!" I exclaimed. "What a difference that would make in all our relationships if this principle were understood and applied."

"It's more than a principle," he added. "*As Within, So Without* is one of the basic Laws of Life."

Roderic

During three days and nights of hibernation, with many an interlude of sharing and cuddling, I had brought enough issues to the surface, with their roots in many lives, to keep me processing for weeks. All had begun with Elly's massaging and the question-and-answer sessions with my body, marvellously intelligent being that it is. Marvellously intelligent being that she is!

Elly

It was a moving process getting the clarity on deep-rooted causes of fears and anxieties going so far back in time. For me, there was no denying the reality anymore: We are all on a journey through many lives. I felt humbled by the vastness of our unfathomed natures carrying so much mystery; but also inspired by the fact that it's accessible when we allow ourselves to be open and ask the right questions. It's time to take account of these past-life dimensions in our healing approaches.

Chapter 18

Going with the Flow?

Roderic

Celandine, primroses and violets were appearing in the hedgerows, along with early flowerings of wild garlic. Blossoms were bursting on the blackthorn, pussydown on willows, and the buds of chestnuts were swelling. The hills around us were ablaze with gorse. Daffodils, narcissi, primulas and anemones had begun bringing colour back to gardens. Birds, chirruping, fluttered hither and thither, busily collecting twigs for their nests.

Our cottage, though modernized, was an ancient dwelling with thick stonewalls and small trellis windows. On a bright sunny day, it was dark as a cave. Cosy, warm and womb-like, it was ideal for hibernation in winter, a time for inner work and creativity; but with spring stirring, then emerging, I became increasingly restless. Our afternoon walks were not enough. My body longed for a fuller emergence into the expansiveness and vibrations of Nature. Above all, it felt the absence of light. If I really listened and responded to its impulses, I'd be outdoors all day, finding some activity to keep me there; but I was held back by a fear that if I didn't keep a tight rein on myself, focused on our writing, which meant staying indoors, our book might never be finished.

Sometimes it takes an outer circumstance to wake one up, jolt one out of a rut, which is what happened. One day, our computer packed up, and having spent most of an afternoon trying to remedy the defect, I gave up. Providence at work, we sensed. But what was it telling us?

"To stop everything and have a break," said Elly with a tinge of excitement. Perhaps, but the computer still needed fixing; and the only person I knew who could do so on the spot was a friend, Mike Tanner, who lived a couple of hours away in Bantry.

"Let's visit him," Elly suggested. "We can rent a car and find a nice place to stay overnight. Maybe tour the Beara Peninsula and visit the Buddhist Centre?"

"We could go for a week," I proposed, carrying her suggestion further. "It can be one of our *Theme Weeks.*"

"A *Recovery Week*?" she joked.

"No idea," I replied. "Maybe the theme will suggest itself as we go along? How about *Going with the Flow*?"

"Great!" she replied.

"But whose flow? Yours or mine?" I joked.

At the same time, I was also serious, for the two flows might well be different or even in conflict. In fact, 'going with the flow' may not simply be a holiday issue but a lifelong one and a key one for couples. How is it to be achieved *jointly* without the disempowerment of one while yielding to the preferences of the other?

Elly

"Let's go to the Aran Islands!" I proposed. I had always wanted to visit them. It was one of the few areas in Ireland where Gaelic was still spoken and I wanted to connect with traditional Irish culture. I had seen images of women in black shawls seated at the doors of thatched cottages knitting sweaters, waiting for the return of their fishermen husbands, staggering home under baskets laden with the day's catch. It sounded fascinating.

Roderic

Ah! Already a plan! Going with the flow, yet having a plan! Can the two be compatible? To be free to respond to the magic of the moment, I wasn't in favour of having any plan at all, though just one seemed okay. We both wanted to meet Father Dara Molloy, a rebel Catholic priest who lived on one of the islands, Inis Mor, the largest, where he'd founded *An Charraig*, 'A Spiritual Centre in the Celtic Tradition'. We had seen him on television two days earlier in a documentary, *The Celtic and Christian*, conducting a marriage ceremony in a field beside a ruin. I had also come across him through his quarterly journal, a subtly subversive publication, *Aisling*, and noted that he offered his services conducting Celtic

179

Rituals, including weddings. Perhaps he'd conduct a ceremony for us? We wanted an officiator with whom we could work in creating something original.

Elly

We both knew we wanted to renew our agreement. After nine months of living together, our love had deepened, we had built a solid foundation, and there was more to explore, enjoy and create. The possibilities of growth seemed endless. Besides, our book wasn't finished! We'd have an official celebration with family and friends.

I was intrigued by Dara's open approach and wanted to attend his Sunday morning 'Celtic Eucharist' to get a sense of his personality. So, having fixed our computer in Bantry, the trigger for our journey, we headed northwest.

Roderic

It was Friday. To be in time for Dara's Sunday Morning Service on the island, we'd have to catch the ferry the previous evening, which meant driving directly to the harbour area with little flow possible.

We had planned on crossing the River Shannon. There was also a ferry there, leaving every sixty minutes. Rather than hurrying, we decided to relax, and caught one with seconds to spare. As I switched off our engine, the deck-gates closed noisily behind us. "What perfect timing!" I exclaimed, not realizing how significant this precision would turn out to be.

Elly

It was a delight to drive along the coast of Clare again. Although there were no flowers, the Burren was still spectacular. While rocks can be really rocky – that is, harsh in their rockiness – those of the Burren are soft, almost silklike, vibrating richness. We stopped for tea in the fishermen's village of Kinvara, weaved our way through the suburbs of Galway City, and arrived at the docks of Rossaveel just as the last ferry to Inis Mor was pulling away from the quay.

Roderic

We had missed it by seconds! After five hours of casual driving from the River Shannon, we could have missed it by twenty, ten or even five minutes; but no, we'd missed it by seconds. Again, precision-timing! Two such events on the same day, one after the other? This was quite explicit. "There are no meaningless coincidences," I declared to Elly. "I feel sure there's a message in these two situations, something fundamental we have to grasp."

Over the past few months, we had had several experiences connected with time and timing, so the two events were not without a context. Time is a framework set up by the Universe for learning experiences, as we had discovered: It had been teaching us about patience, trust, when to act, when to be still, when to go forth, when to withdraw, when to plan, when not to do so, and so on. One can either be its slave or its master. Locked into time-schedules we are deprived of freedom; and our openness to the flow of life, with its many possibilities, is greatly diminished. Frequently, by setting up programmes with deadlines, I, no other, make myself its slave, creating pressures that don't otherwise exist, sometimes from a lack of trusting, sometimes from the left-brain's illusionary habit of believing that it is in control or can be. Thus do I struggle to push the river! Vainly, for it flows as it will!

These split-second timings had put me on notice. Since we'd set the theme of going with the flow, I felt sure we were about to be challenged on more time-related issues during this journey.

But how were the two events actually connected? I puzzled as we lay in bed in a nearby inn, while Elly, clearly bored by my obsession, drifted off to sleep.

On neither occasion had we been concerned with schedules, though we had been aware of them. So it wasn't due to the success or failure of any conscious efforts that we had arrived at a particular place at a particular time. It seemed to me on reflection and to my amazement that catching one ferry by a few seconds and missing the other by the same margin had been consequences of our *intentions*. While we had had a clear intention to catch the first, we had had none to catch the second, feeling that it would be better to spend the night on the mainland so we could arrive fresh in the morning. Our awareness had registered our intentions and the results on the outside were a function of these, so it seemed.

Elly

A rough ride of forty minutes across high-rolling seas took many passengers through varying shades of green. Sea, wind, waves, the rawness and power of the elements, I loved it.

Expecting peacefulness, our first impressions of the tiny capital, Kilronan, where we landed, were of bustle and aggression as bus-tour operators competed for our custom. "The city bank," said our driver, pointing to a small bungalow as he drove up hill on the way to Dara's house. "It's open one day a week. That's if the helicopter comes with the money. The island is nine miles long and two miles wide, with a population of nine hundred people, twelve hundred bicycles, and three thousand miles of stone walls made out of necessity … otherwise, in this land of rocks there'd be no fields." It had the tiniest I'd ever seen.

As we stepped off the bus, a tractor appeared, driven by the priest himself. "Make yourselves at home," he said, pointing over a hill. "I have an appointment with the Minister for the Environment who's flown in from Dublin, so I'll join you in a couple of hours."

His centre was small, with dormitory accommodation for ten, and three volunteers in residence. The cottage where he lived with his wife, Tess, and three small children, was a few metres away. So lovely to see a priest with a wife and children. It seems much more natural and wholesome than the celibacy prescribed by the Roman Church.

"Help yourself to food," said Stephanie and James, pointing to the cupboards. "We're going for a walk to harvest for dinner."

"What are you looking for?" Roderic asked enthusiastically.

"Wild leeks, garlic, mussels and limpets."

"Limpets, what are they?" I asked Roderic when they'd gone.

"A cone-shaped shell-fish which clings to the rocks and is as tough to chew as a piece of leather. You'll need the jaws of a dinosaur!"

Roderic

"I've left the Church but *not* the priesthood," Dara emphasized on his return.

"What do you mean?" I asked.

"Well, mostly it's the other way around. Priests leave the priesthood but not the Church," he clarified with a twinkle.

No longer believing in institutionalised religion, he wanted to bring spirituality back into everyday life, one that connected Spirit and Earth, the local environment, its people and their life-styles, seeing sacredness in everything, celebrating and living practically with a sense of it.

"Returning to the roots of one's own culture," was among his key phrases. "We mustn't forget the old ways of cultivating. Once, there was nothing here but rock." He told us how the soil on the islands had been built up over centuries, its fertility maintained with sand and seaweed brought up from the seashore annually. "We have to get back to living wisely, simply and wholesomely on the Earth; above all, sustainably." I liked his messages, which he demonstrated practically in everyday living.

Elly

I didn't take part in their discussions, feeling uninspired and losing interest. While Dara had taken courageous steps, he seemed to have 'Church' still imprinted all over him. But had this to do with him or me? He didn't have the kind of power I'd expected, magical, mystical and charismatic. Maybe it was a woman I was seeking? Besides, I was beginning to wonder if I was really ready to organise a big wedding celebration, the kind we'd imagined. It didn't seem part of the flow of the moment. So I didn't feel inspired to enquire about Celtic rituals and ceremonies.

"Let's go to the village," Roderic suggested, as we left Dara to sniff out the island.

It wasn't where I wanted to go, but I didn't say anything, hoping we'd find a path along the way for a scenic walk.

This is where my problems resurfaced, as I slid back into an old pattern. If *I* wasn't clear what *I* wanted to do, I followed someone else, disempowering myself in the process; and, later, resenting doing so. But I couldn't make up my mind. Did I want to rent a bicycle? Roderic didn't and it was pretty windy. Did I want to go on a bus-tour just to get a quick overview of the island? Dara was offering guided tours: Perhaps that would be more interesting? Were we going to be here two days or five? Should I or we just wander around the coast?

"Would you like a lift to the ruined stone fort of *Dun Aonghus*?" a tour-guide asked, stopping his vehicle at the edge of the village.

"Dinner will be at six-thirty," Stephanie had said, so we had about three hours.

"*You* decide," said Roderic emphatically, which put me on the spot.

Roderic

I had no intention of imposing my flow on Elly; nor any wish for her to follow mine graciously, denying what she felt. Rather, I wanted her to communicate her feelings clearly; then, after sharing our desires, intuitions or preferences, we could decide which to follow. That seemed the most intelligent, balanced, harmonized approach.

Elly

My usual way of ensuring harmony with my male or even female companion was to ask him/her what he/she wanted and align myself with that, sometimes happily, sometimes disastrously. Usually disastrously! – for after a while I no longer knew what *I* really wanted, which made me angry and frustrated, negative conditions I turned on myself. Generally, in my relationship with Roderic, as on this occasion, I was challenged to connect with what *I* wanted, and speak it out.

"*Dun* what? What and where is that?" I stuttered. I didn't want to say "yes", nor say "no". I wasn't centred, felt switched off, and wasn't in any kind of a flow; on top of which, I felt rushed. "Okay," I said, with despairing resignation: "Let's go."

Roderic

Elly's lack of clarity and indecision challenged my patience, since she was neither in my flow nor her own.

Elly

I couldn't believe how quickly I'd fallen back into the old pattern of not speaking my truth and switching off completely. Part of my problem was that I'd come to the Aran Islands with fixed ideas, high expectations, and had been disappointed so far by both the island and the spiritual centre, feeling neither to be as sacred as I had expected. I was still hoping to go somewhere where I could find 'It' – whatever 'It' was.

Roderic

Clearly 'It' was not found at Aonghus' Fort, summer residence of the Celtic god of love. In a nutshell, the afternoon was a disaster.

Elly

The evening more so! When I'm not centered I become an observer and usually a heartless, judgemental one. Everything irritated me, especially Roderic, who came across as the all-knowing teacher, serious and arrogant, not as the mystic fool and poet that he is, with humour and playfulness. I felt like shooting him. Why did he need to impress people? I'm so bored with mental chatter.

Roderic

Thus speaks the imbalanced female, into her feelings while denying the mental!

Elly

… whereas the imbalanced male goes over the top in his bla-bla-bla and is wholly disconnected from *his* feelings!

Luckily we slept in separate dormitories.

Am I with the right guy? I wondered. While I appreciate his knowledge and wisdom, I can't stand his all-knowing tone. If he acted like that with my family and friends, I'd feel embarrassed. Why can't he communicate in a relaxed and witty way? Is this his method of keeping his distance and avoiding intimacy? … Why do I always want to change people? Why couldn't I accept him lovingly as he is? He too could judge me for withdrawing from conversation, for not bringing any colour to the exchanges, for having been so dull and boring. I turned, churned, and puzzled all night.

Roderic

I slept like a log.

Elly

The next morning, Sunday, to which I'd been looking forward, I was still brooding and went for a walk, keeping my distance from Roderic. The stone walls made me feel even more angry, trapping energy into tiny boxed compartments, blocking my space. I felt like throwing the stones back into the fields, all three thousand miles of them!

Still in a state of mental and emotional chaos, though tactfully restrained, I joined the small informal procession of seven adults and the three small children of Dara and Tess as they descended by narrow path steeply towards the sea for a celebration of 'Celtic Mass'. As we arrived at the ruined chapel of *Teampall Chiarain*, built by St Ciarin, it was cold and windy with threatening rain. We assembled on the leeward side, where we each picked a stone and placed it on the wet grass before sitting on it.

Roderic

Mass in Nature! I remembered the words of George Russell, one of Ireland's greatest writers, a poet, visionary and reformer: "I think of the earth as the floor of a cathedral where altar and Presence are everywhere."

We were surprised that there was only one visitor, expecting far more support for Dara's initiative, his note being Celtic Spirituality, and the Aran Islands being outposts of the Celts. But these Gaels were still under the yoke of Rome, bound by habit to their local congregations.

From his article on 'Spirituality and Sustainability' in *Aisling*, we had an idea of his intentions: "We can choose to imitate Jesus by repeating physically and verbally everything he did, exactly as he did it, or we can imitate him in a deeper sense by exercising that same courage and imagination and coming up with creative new rituals ourselves." This was his endeavour.

186

Elly

He had also brought a guitar. Dara and the three women began singing. I love women's voices. Theirs were so healing and nourishing; indeed, so deeply touching that I cried, hoping no one noticed. I didn't feel comfortable sharing emotions with people I didn't know. We hadn't been invited to open our hearts to each other, arriving separate and remaining so. I didn't experience the flow of energies or feeling of connectedness between members of the group as I did in healing circles or Reiki gatherings.

"Now for some free chanting," Dara announced. "Everyone can do their own thing."

The result, unsurprisingly, was a cacophony. I couldn't work out what his intention was.

Roderic

A passing seagull, equally perplexed, squawked its disdain. I too found this disappointing. Chanting in unison can be immensely powerful, as I had experienced, chanting seven hours a day in a monastery in India for over a year.

After we had participated in reading selected texts from the Bible, Celtic and other sources, and shared our prayer requests, it was time for the Eucharist. While Dara held the homemade bread, Tess held the wine in a chalice. Before breaking the bread, Dara shared his thoughts and gave a blessing, with a focus on Spirit and the Father God aspect. Tess, while holding the chalice, shared her thoughts and gave a blessing, her focus being on Mother Earth and Goddess aspects of the One Spirit. She invited us to reach to the Invisible Realms so they'd become alive for us. Then the bread and wine were passed around, "in the name of the Father and the Mother, the Son and the Maiden, the Spirit and the Wise Old Woman ..." The blessings were made with the Celtic sign of the cross, using both hands to make the sign to the brow, abdomen and shoulders. It felt so balanced to see a man and woman officiating together.

187

Elly

We lunched together afterwards, with salads and seaweed pudding, finishing with fennel tea from the garden. As for Roderic, I was still keeping my distance, watching how he presented himself.

Roderic

We decided to go on another expedition. Elly wanted to walk through the middle of the island, to be immersed in its wildness and see the cliffs on the other side; and I was happy to go with her flow, curious to see where it would lead.

With a primitive map we headed south and, after twenty minutes or so, ended up in a cul de sac and foul-smelling rubbish dump. "Is this Elly's flow?" I wondered, wickedly amused, but choosing not to comment.

Elly

I couldn't stand the fact that when I was leading we ended up in such a ghastly place! We walked, walked and walked, encountering one stone wall after another, in a landscape tightly chequered with these. Then we were lost, which was even more embarrassing as I'd assured Roderic I was a good map-reader.

A mile later, we came to a sunken bushy entrance leading to a small enclosure, carpeted with primroses, surrounding a well. In a harshly male landscape of walled geometry and biting wind, it was a sheltered oasis of warmth and tenderness, indeed the most magical place on the island so far. The only problem was that I had walked straight past it, even though it had beckoned me, while Roderic, behind me, had already entered.

"Didn't you pick up the energies?" he asked.

"Of course I did," I snapped bitchily.

Once again, my focus had been on reaching a goal, the cliffs and other places marked on the map, rather than being fully in the moment and open to whatever presented itself. Often, like this, I miss the magic.

We sat by the well, which radiated peacefulness.

Roderic

As we rose to leave, I wondered what Elly would do next. Turn right and keep on going in direction unknown towards the village she believed to be one mile ahead? Or left and head back home where we were expected for dinner in about an hour? Once again, I decided initially to go with her flow, initially at least. If we were going to be travelling together, our long-term plan, and even from the point of view of living together, we'd have to learn more about flowing harmoniously. This week's holiday appeared to be providing us with the necessary learning!

"Let's go to the village and have a beer," she suggested.

"Okay," I agreed, and we moved off in that direction.

"It may take us half an hour to get there," I pointed out, "and maybe we'll spend half an hour drinking … Then it will take another half an hour to return to this point," I continued, wondering if she was beginning to get the message.

Apparently not! So I persisted: "It has taken one and a half hours to get to where we are. So, in three hours' time, we should be back at Dara's, about two hours late for a dinner that has been prepared for us! What do you think?"

Elly

"Shit! Shit! Shit!" I thought. "I could smash his head in with one of these stones! This is supposed to be a holiday and I'm locked into time-schedules." Evidently, I had no choice. So we turned around and walked briskly home, once more passing the stinking rubbish dump. I wanted to take the first boat off the Island and be free.

"But you've been free all along," Roderic insisted. "You didn't have to be back for dinner. You could have chosen otherwise. All you had to do was be clear what you wanted and speak up your truth. It is only in failing to do so that you lose your freedom. No one takes it from you: You lose it by default."

I could have smashed another stone! Now, we'd certainly be late for dinner.

Roderic

Surprisingly, we weren't. It was in the process of being brought to the table as we entered the house. Once more, an astounding precision in timing. Time was impacting strangely on our holiday. I was still mystified.

Elly

I wasn't! Not, at least, until the following morning:

We had left Dara's at eight-fifteen with plenty of time, so we had been told, to catch the nine o'clock ferry to the mainland. While struggling and sweating along the seashore, carrying our cases, I wondered if I'd made the right decision. Maybe I'd have more freedom if we stayed on the island one more day. I could rent a bike and do my own thing at my own pace.

Half way to the harbour, Roderic put down his baggage and gave me a hug. "What time is it?" he asked casually afterwards.

It was ten to nine. I couldn't believe it. We seemed to have lost at least ten minutes; and in another ten, the boat would be leaving. Had his hug been a time warp? How could we possibly get there on time? We rushed like crazy. After all, I decided, I *was* ready to leave the island. I was too restless and it was too claustrophobic. "Hey, angels! Help us, please," I requested.

As we turned a corner into the harbour, we saw our ferry and sailors getting ready to remove the gangway. Exerting ourselves, puffing and steaming, we reached it before it was raised on deck. The gate closed behind us.

"Split-second timing again!" exclaimed Roderic.

He was still intrigued by these timings as if they hid a great mystery. "I haven't fathomed what they're about yet," he murmured as the harbour disappeared behind us, "but I'm going down to the lower deck to make some notes."

Buzzing with my own dilemmas, greatly dissatisfied with the way I had been behaving over the weekend, I didn't share his fascination. I was more interested in reflecting on how I could stay centred, be more positive, and go with *my* flow.

Roderic

Four times in four days, we had been involved in split-second timings. Why on this occasion, I couldn't figure out. I had to wait for a key piece of information, Elly's thoughts and her change of intention on her way to the ferry, which had switched from 'wanting to stay' to 'deciding to leave', as she shared with me. Then all became clear: *Time is a function of intention.* All the events proved it.

It was a lesson not only about time but about 'going with the flow' *in* time, particularly together. The key is: If you want to flow harmoniously in life with another, you must share the same clear intentions in whatever you do together. Or, as we almost did, you may literally "miss the boat".

Elly

"Free at last!" I thought, with a sigh of relief, as I stepped onto the mainland.

We headed towards the mountains, the Twelve Pins of Connemara, high in their beauty, passing lakes and bogs, listening to a piano concert by Mozart. It was a bright sunny day. I relaxed. Had I learned my lesson? I wondered.

"Which one?" I imagined Roderic asking me in his infuriatingly direct and specific way. "The ones about having clear intentions and speaking one's truth clearly or the ones about being open to the magic, going with the flow, instead of limiting it with programmes, goals, expectations and fixed destinations?"

Unknowingly, I was still hooked on the latter. I had seen picture postcards of the Connemara National Park, which I had been dreaming of for more than a year; and insisted, "We have to go there." So we did. It was far from being the most beautiful area we'd visited. In fact, we had already been driving through the most beautiful area for the past two hours, and the joke was that I had been so stuck on the map, so eager to get to my fixed destination that I had been denying myself the possibility of exploring any of the exciting-looking roads *en route*, going into the hearts of mountains and valleys, hardly noticing what was around me.

After realizing what I'd been doing, I finally got the message. I have to let go of my plans, at least my rigid attachment to them, along with my expectations, which have brought me frustration rather than happiness. At last, I was convinced.

We arrived at the picturesque village of Clifden and sat in the sunshine drinking beer.

"What do you think 'going with the flow' actually is?" I asked Roderic.

"It's not bobbing around like a cork on the ocean, floating, drifting, vulnerable to the whims of wind and waves. That's for sure. Nor is it abandoning oneself to a flow of outer circumstances, as is so often misunderstood. Rather, it's the opposite. It's a function of clear intention. 'Going with the flow' means going with an *inner* flow, which can only be achieved by being centred in one's Self, listening and attuning to whatever comes up, not least from within, your intuitions for example."

Sometimes I really appreciated his mental clarity.

I leaned back, luxuriating in the sun, soaking in the warmth through every pore of my skin, enjoying the laughter of other customers. This was holiday at last! As we headed back to the Connemara wilderness, my head was still buzzing in a chaos of unresolved frustrations, along with new insights not fully digested.

We stopped by a lake, reflective as a mirror, picnicked on a carpet of moss and sheep-dung pellets and lay naked in the sun; after which, returning to the car, we followed a track which wiggled into the mountains. Pure wildness, just what I'd wanted! An expansive space with no trace of civilisation.

While Roderic reposed in the car, I went climbing, over bog, up rocks, towards one of the peaks. The higher I went, the freer I felt, and the more clarity emerged, particularly on my own nature.

I have an inner barometer with which I measure things, I realized, especially power and beauty. When people, animals or landscapes don't meet my standards of perfection, I lose interest and withdraw my love. I had gone to the Aran Islands hoping to meet the ultimate priest with the ultimate wisdom; and when he'd turned out not to be my ideal, wholly unrealisable, wise and lovely as he is, I had withdrawn myself from conversations. How awful! It reminded me of an experience I'd had with Roderic as we passed a dog one afternoon:

"So many ugly dogs in Ireland!" I'd said as it approached, his tail wagging, eager for my affection. I'd ignored him totally, walking straight past.

"Hey! Come back!" Roderic called out to me. "So he doesn't meet your standards of beauty?! So he isn't worthy of your love?!" he mocked.

I was shocked and embarrassed. He was spot on.

"How did *I* ever pass your ruthless tests?" he wondered aloud.

"You almost didn't," I confessed, feeling a bit ashamed.

So I walked back to the dog and squatted down to stroke him affectionately. It was such a lovely experience. He was happy as pie receiving my attentions and turned on his side to be cuddled all over. In fact, he was giving *me* love. So much.

Now, on the mountain, I realized, I'm still doing the same, especially to myself, rejecting myself when I don't meet my own expectations, my ideals of perfection. I wanted to run away from my thoughts and negative feelings, but knew I couldn't. I wished I could shed my skin like a snake. I could only change my attitude. The only way out, through and beyond, was to give loving acceptance to the otherwise unacceptable. I longed to leave behind all the judging and embrace my Being unconditionally, including all of my imperfections.

Roderic

She was gone so long up her mountain I wondered if she'd be coming down with a new version of the Ten Commandments.

Elly

Continuing our journey, we drove through Joyce Country. It was different now. I'd let go of schedules and expectations and relaxed into enjoying wherever I was. Open to the magic and unexpected, we roamed around in a timeless mode, feeling really free. I was in tune with my Self. Only when this is so, can I be in tune with anything else. Finally, I'd found 'It'!

I decided to climb another peak. Inwardly as well as outwardly it was a journey of revelations. Why, for years, I wondered, had I been searching for the ultimate priest? I'd even had them as lovers, a former Roman Catholic and two Mennonites. On the summit, where I remained for an age, the futility of my longing became self-evident. It was, I realized, for nothing on the outside. In a timeless moment, I experienced my oneness with the Universe and sensed something vast that yearned to be expressed through me. The Grace of God fell upon me. I found the Priestess. She was within.

What seemed like an eternity later, I heard a sound, a voice booming across the valley. I turned around. It wasn't God, but Roderic who had climbed up an adjoining hill. Crossing the soggy bogland between us, I flew into his arms.

Chapter 19

Switching on
One's Power

Roderic

Our journey had reminded us of the importance of being 'in tune'. When we were, things flowed magically; when not, we experienced frustrations. Ideally, we should be in tune all of the time, never undertaking anything without ensuring that we are. It should be the first order of the day.

But being in tune with what?

Elly

With our innermost selves or souls, first and foremost.

I was totally convinced after our trip that for a happy journey through life, alone or together, this was my priority. Only when I'm in tune with my innermost being, can I experience peace and harmony. It's my anchor in life. Otherwise, I feel uncentred, disconnected and disorientated, like a leaf in the wind.

Time and again, in my search for security, freedom and power, I have been getting lessons in letting go of my attachment to things on the outside; and I'm still involved in the major transition of shifting my primary point of reference. I fully understood that the more you put your trust in things on the outside, people, jobs or other circumstances, the more fear you create – fear of losing that which gives you the feeling of security which, in truth, is no real security, for deep down you know you're not in control; things on the outside can leave you in an instant.

But can I really put my trust in the inner, in my own inner knowing, feelings and intuitions? Can I always turn to it for guidance, trusting it will lead me to the perfect situations, perfect people and perfect places? – and, of course, in perfect timing? Knowing that it is reliable? That it ever brings forth my highest good? This is what I was exploring, basically a new way of being and operating. The primary conditions were now clear: I had to be centred in my deepest, innermost, essential Self.

Roderic

My computer was a great teacher, flashing its messages 'on' and 'off', showing me wisdom in the utterly obvious. It doesn't work when it's not plugged in; or, for example, when it isn't switched on; or when there's a problem with its inner circuitry. It's the same with us humans. We are bio-computers, sophisticated, multi-dimensional, electromagnetic organisms. But what are *our* power sources? Whatever they are, we should begin each day by connecting with them. Even before this, something more basic: Are our bioelectric systems switched on, or, as can happen, switched incorrectly? We too need to be properly wired up. We should begin each day by checking this out.

Elly had a dozen exercises for achieving this, which took no more than a few minutes. They were all simple, including massaging key points on the meridians of the body. We did these daily and, using kinesiology, we could check the efficacy of them by comparing the before and after responses of our bodies, confirming that our bio-electrical systems were in order. Most importantly, we could check if our bodies had enough water, dehydration being the biggest switch-off.

We were then ready to function optimally in the world. Though, not quite! This was Part I. We also need to attune with the Earth, our own higher selves, and the Cosmos, our primary sources of nourishment, power, and wisdom. Connecting with these on a daily basis is fundamental.

Elly

I conducted our attunements, beginning at eight each morning. I felt blessed being able to set up our own rhythms, free from all outside pressures. Though we followed no set pattern, improvising, ever open to the inspirations of the moment, our various sessions tended to go something like this:

Sit comfortably. Breathe deeply. Bring yourself fully into the now.

Feel your connection, through your feet, with the ground … Be aware of your knees and your hips … Feel the weight of your body on the chair … Feel your spine, from base to top, which gives you uprightness and stability. Go down with your awareness alongside your spine, feeling your muscles … Feel into your belly, your gut. Does it feel light or dark? Is it holding any fears, worries, anxieties? Do you feel at home here? Just be aware. You don't have to change anything … Breathe into your belly … Bring your awareness to your solar plexus. If you feel any tension, just give it loving acceptance … Feel your heart. Is it open to giving and receiving love? … Feel into your throat. Is it open to speaking your truth? … Feel the muscles of your face. Is there tension around your jaws or eyes? … Be aware of any thoughts or emotions? Do not attach yourself to them. Let them go like passing clouds.

Feel your connectedness with the Earth.

Visualize channels of light from the base of your spine, and your feet, going all the way to the centre of the Earth … Allow any tensions, negative thoughts or feelings, any unwanted energy, to be released through these channels into the Earth to be transformed … Now breathe in the love, light, wisdom, power and nurturing energies of the Earth, into your body, up through your spinal column, vitalizing all your chakras, brightening up their colours, as it passes upwards to your crown, onwards to the heavens.

Now bring your awareness to a point a few inches above your head, to your Soul Star, through which you are connected with the One Source of All … Visualize a beam of light moving down from it into your crown chakra. Feel it lighting up the cells of your brain, flowing gently down your neck, through your throat chakra, on its way down your spinal column, energizing your heart, solar plexus, sacral and root chakras, filling your whole body with light … Feel its soothing, tingling sensations as it passes through your neck, spreading out around your shoulders, dissolving any tensions … Feel your heart, chest, lungs, breasts, being filled with light … Let the light from your heart overflow down your arms and into your hands … Let the light spread through all your organs, liver, pancreas, kidneys, spleen and stomach … Let it fill your abdomen and pelvic regions, and move down your thighs to your feet and into the Earth.

Visualize yourself at the centre of a bubble of love and light, radiating out … Expanding outwards, our awareness includes our cottage, the trees, the valley, its birds, animals and people, in a peaceful, harmonious, glowing oneness.

We return to our inner circle.

We invite into this circle our guides, angels, and other Beings of Light. We gratefully acknowledge their input into our lives. We declare ourselves open to working with them, delighting in their presence.

We completed each session with ten to twenty minutes silence, sinking into the Void within, while opening to an awareness of the Living Presence. This was Part II.

Roderic

The important fact was that we had a practice of attunement as a morning ritual. There were exceptions of course, our natures abhorring fixed programmes. While we practised Part I regularly before breakfast, with Part II we were more flexible. There were times when we needed disciplines and structures, others when we needed to feel free to follow the inspiration of the moment. For four consecutive weeks, for example, we began each day by reading Deepak Chopra's *The Seven Spiritual Laws of Success*, discussing and meditating on a chapter at a time, gradually digesting and integrating its insights. He reaffirmed the importance of attuning, particularly with our higher selves. "In aligning with our innermost Selves," he writes, "we align with the power that manifests everything in the Universe."

Elly

I loved our attunements together. The silence was so powerful, much more so than when meditating alone. At times we sank into such a depth of silence that there was no place for any fears or anxieties, just peace. Sometimes the presence of Beings of Light was overwhelming. Once I was actually moved to tears, sensing the presence of one, holding in its hands a sword of Light. It sent me an intense loving smile, a gesture of its unconditional acceptance of my being. Over time, angels became less abstract and more a part of my everyday life.

Attuning together lifts the relationship to new levels. Whenever there is a conflict to resolve, attuning together is more effective than weeks of discussions with battling and blaming. It creates a space in which you can connect together in love and light. It helps the transition of one's sense of self from limited ego to unlimited soul.

It is particularly helpful when making important decisions which serve the highest purposes of both. It is the most essential feature of a soul relationship.

Roderic

One day, I was called to London to sign the contract for the filming of *How to Rob Banks Without Violence*, ready after months of negotiations. Should Elly come too? This was our question. Yes, we thought initially. We could both enjoy some city culture, such a contrast from our life in the countryside. On the other hand, this didn't feel right. While I would be staying with our beloved friends, Tadek and Elizabeth, I wanted to spend some time with them. I had offered to lead them through a Game of Transformation, a three-day engagement. Was Elly interested in this? Perhaps I should go alone? Neither of us was sure.

Elly

Should I support Roderic in focalising the Game? My heart wasn't in it. Deep down I felt I should stay at home and be on my own. Seeking guidance from the Universe, we tuned in. The outcome was clear: We must each honour our own feelings. For further confirmation, we consulted the Oracle, using Ralph H. Blum's *The Book of Runes*. I laid the runes on the carpet for each of us to choose one. "Should I go to England or not?" was my question. One caught my attention, jumping out at me.

"Hey!" exclaimed Roderic as I picked it up. "That's the one I chose."

Obviously it was for both. It was the rune of partnership and had this warning: "In love relationships you are put on notice not to collapse yourself into that union; for true partnership is achieved only by separate beings who retain their separateness even as they unite. Remember to let the winds of Heaven dance between you."

Clear. I would not go to London. This felt perfect, also for our relationship.

Roderic

In Notting Hill I bought a Russian hat to add to my collection from Kasmir and Mongolia. At The Portrait Gallery in Trafalgar Square, I viewed an exhibition of photographs by Lord Snowdon. I admired him greatly. I had even dined with him at Kensington Palace. Along familiar streets around Bond Street and Piccadilly, I wandered through time-fields of personal history. Overexposed to the hustle and bustle, I took tea at the Ritz. I enjoyed the contrast between the sophisticated richness of human civilisation and the raw primal richness of wild nature on the west coast of Ireland.

Elly

On his return, it was time to celebrate the first renewal of our Celtic Marriage. Though there hadn't been the sniff of a doubt that we would commit to another 'year and a day', neither of us had yet made a proposal. Nor did we feel there was anything specific to discuss as we were constantly sharing our innermost thoughts and feelings. And we weren't ready yet for a big celebration.

"Are you expecting *me* to propose?" Roderic asked jokingly.

"Why not?"

We sat at the edge of a sloping meadow under the shade of a hawthorn tree, looking over the Bandon River. Here, surrounded by bluebells and primroses, we had our second marital feast. A herd of cows peering curiously over a fence were our only guests, with the music a springtime chorus of tweets and twitters.

"I've got it!" he exclaimed, in between swigs of elderberry wine. "I'll propose with a riddle. If you get it right, I'm all yours."

"Okay."

"Now, listen very carefully, I will only say this once," he began with slow deliberation and a mischievous grin, with a French accent, mimicking the female resistance agent in the TV comedy *Hallo Hallo*: "If earthly lovers open their legs, what do cosmic lovers do?"

"How ridiculous," I thought, "and the answer is probably even more so."

"You still have two lifelines," he continued, as I was puzzling it out: "You can either phone a friend or ask the audience! The nearest cow!"

"If earthly lovers open their legs," I pondered .... "Cosmic lovers open their wings!" I declared in a flash.

"Spot on! How did you guess? I am now all yours for the next three hundred and sixty-six days!"

"Great!"

Chapter 20

Creating Abundance

Elly

In the darkness, Roderic crept into my room.

"One hot ginger and one hot Roderic!" he announced as he snuggled up beside me for a pre-dawn cuddle. Sometimes he arrived in my bed, sometimes I in his. It was a lovely way to begin the day.

"Did you have sweet dreams?" I whispered, feeling his warm body against mine.

"No. And you?"

"No."

"What!!!" he teased, faking disappointment. "Nothing from the angels?!"

"We need some inspiration for our book!" he'd said jokingly the night before, suggesting that I ask them.

"Well, you've asked," he acknowledged, stroking his fingers around my tummy, "so the inspiration will come. It always does. So do I," he murmured mischievously, going down to my pussy.

Roderic

Another lovely way to begin a day!

Elly

My inspiration for the morning was dancing, my way of connecting body, mind and soul, though lovemaking also assists greatly! Only a few months before, I wouldn't have dared suggest such a thing, rushing to be ready for the day's programme. Now I know that when I take one hour to do what I really feel like doing, I'm much more alive and inspired afterwards. Because Roderic had been so supportive, indeed so insisting that I followed my flow, spoke up my truth and acted on it, I finally felt free to do so.

When he'd left for a walk through the valley, I let loose with Gabrielle Roth's *Endless Waves*, after which I sat in silence on my bed, bathing in the sunlight. That's when I had a flash: "Let's have an *Abundance Week*."

It was a timeless event. In fact, it was both a flash and a flood. In a single moment, a thousand thoughts poured into my head. "We are the creators, more powerful than we imagine," among other key phrases, resounded through it. "What a concept!" I'd thought when I'd heard it first. "Radically life changing," Roderic had commented, "when one decides to accept and work with it." I had finally become convinced.

My concepts had been changing across a broad spectrum, particularly my notions of Divinity and Self. I was no longer the 'poor little me' that I had once been, struggling to survive fearfully in a seemingly hostile world, in a life presided over by a judgemental God 'out there somewhere'. No. The Divine is within me, therefore near and accessible. Indeed, I am a spark of it. I had been waking up, freeing myself from limiting thoughts and negative feelings while going through a major shift in consciousness, *out of* victimhood or relative powerlessness, generally blaming people or circumstances, *into* seeing my self and my life as my own creation. In my flash, I'd realized that all of this had fully sunk in, taken root. Yes, I *am* the creator. While I had thought it conceptually, now I felt it energetically, and was ready to act.

While I had been studying for months, learning of the creative power of thoughts, feelings and every word we utter, and about the Cosmic Laws and principles involved, and though I'd begun applying these, it was in general terms only. I was now eager to do so more specifically, creating, manifesting, drawing into my life, consciously, intentionally, something I or we wanted, thus putting what I'd learned to the test. Hence the inspiration for an *Abundance Week*.

Roderic

It was a delight watching Elly on her path of awakening, transformation and empowerment; like observing a caterpillar becoming a butterfly in a miracle of rebirthing. Our retreat, with its months of intense inner work, was bearing fruits. Out of confusions, questions, fears and resistances, in a slow process of learning, release, re-visioning and re-programming, and, above all, integration, a being of greater self-assurance, peace, joy, clarity and power, was emerging visibly on a daily basis. For me, she was an inspiring example, particularly in the relationship between her knowing of something and the being of it. In this, as I've said, she was far more integrated. While I, in my quest, resemble the hare, she, like the tortoise, moves more slowly. If awakening and transformation were a race, which it isn't, she'd pass the winning post long before me – truth being not in the knowing of anything, but in the *being* of it. We complemented each other perfectly: While I assisted her in coming to mental clarity, she helped me connect more with my feelings and body.

In the spreading and fluttering of her newfound wings, she was also taking more initiatives.

Elly

"Why an *Abundance Week*?" he asked, as I knew he would, curious about the reasons for everything. "Don't you feel abundant?" he joked, sipping his tea, a mixture of horsetail with birch leaves and twigs.

"Yes I do, extremely so," I replied.

While this mightn't have seemed so obvious looking from the outside – as we lived simply in a small rented cottage with barely enough to cover our expenses, and had no car, stereo or DVD – from other perspectives we were immensely rich. Indeed, I'd never felt so rich.

Roderic

"So, is abundance just a feeling?" we wondered. "If not, what is it?"

"If it isn't also a feeling, it isn't worth anything," Elly declared. "If you can't feel rich without money and all it can buy, you'll never feel rich with it, however much you possess. Without the feeling of it, irrespective of what's on the outside, there will always be an emptiness which nothing on the outside can ever fill."

I agreed. While I had felt rich living in the lap of luxury, I had also felt poor living in the lap of luxury; and, while I'd felt poor stripped of everything, destitute and desperate, I had also felt rich stripped of everything, inwardly rich. So, there is an inside and an outside aspect, quite clearly: the *having* of abundance and the *feeling* of it, which are not always synchronous. In *having* or seeking to *have* it, I reflected, one relates primarily to what is on the outside; while in *feeling* it one is dependent on what is on the inside – one's state of being, perspectives and attitudes.

The intimate relationship between the *feeling* of abundance and 'the appreciation of simple things' I had noticed in relation to our meals, for example. We didn't just eat, we feasted. Yet, while the food was wholesome, it was nothing special. So what made it a feast? Simply our appreciation! We delighted in its smells, shapes, tastes and colours, even the way it was laid out on the plate – embellished in season with the bright blue of borage, the yellow gold of dandelions and marigolds, multi-hued pansies, and other edible petals – all in all, the fruits and creativity of an abundant Earth. No, not just a meal, but a visual, aromatic and gourmet spread, fit for princes. Yes, truly, with the same food, one can either eat or banquet. The abundance is the same, a constant in the equation, but is the noticing?

The same may be true of a walk through nature. So immensely rich, fascinating – yet there are some who are moved not a bit by it, who find it boring. Even a desert, which may be seen as an emptiness, is full of life, and for some, like Saint-Exupery, a mystic heaven, over which they wander with a burning passion. Do we not have abundance all around us? Isn't it rather *our* lack – in the dullness of our perceptions, in the absence of awareness, openness and wonderment – than *its* lack which is in question? Abundance is in the ability to see and experience the extraordinary in the ordinary. As the poet Blake observed, "A universe in a grain of sand."

Going further, we can move beyond appreciation into celebration. Abundance may be seen as the art of being able to celebrate each and every moment of life. "Feeling blessed, I feel grateful," said Elly. Abundance and gratitude, these too are intimately linked, even more so, though the demonstration of this would require an essay. Born with many privileges, blessed with many gifts, I have been most ungrateful, though I've been working on this, gratitude being one of my many karmic lessons.

Sometimes, Elly wonders what she teaches me, thinking on occasions it's a one-way process. While I rely heavily on words, she teaches by being who she is. While gratitude is a primary emotion with her, issuing from the heart with a purity, fullness and spontaneity, for me it's firstly and largely a thought, a drier sort of thing, less intense, less flowy. Only once have I wept with gratitude, while Elly, a richly feeling being, is a weeper who sheds tears easily and profusely, with joy, sadness or gratitude. I'd like to be able to do this more often, for the feeling of abundance, I observe, is in the capacity to live life intensely not only bodily or mentally, of which I'm most capable, but with the fullest engagement of my feeling nature.

Maybe our *Abundance Week* is not about me manifesting anything? Maybe it's a week in which I should focus on my relationship with what is around me, being more aware, living more fully in the present, connecting with my feelings? It is clear to me that my sense of abundance is intimately connected with my sense of wellbeing. I *feel* abundant when I *feel* alive, sensually, mentally, cellularly, and vibrationally, fully in my body, grounded and totally present, radiating love, light, power and vitality. This has nothing to do with anything on the outside. Maybe the outside is largely irrelevant? The question seemed worth exploring.

I had felt abundant living in prison. What had made that possible? Nothing on the outside: Rather, on the inside. While it was linked with a feeling of wellbeing, strangely in the circumstances, it was largely a function of my creative imagination. I could explore inner space, envision, give birth to images, conceive and live all manner of dramas, with an abundance of time and, strangely again, an abundance of freedom. So is abundance in the capacity to experience life richly within whatever external limitations? Even when deprived of all outer things?

While abundance is visible in the outer and we observe its fullness, it must exist in the Void too, indeed first and foremost and to a far greater extent, for it is out of the Void that all proceeds. Abundance is in Life's infinite potentiality and unlimited creativity, which is accessible through the Void within. My feeling of abundance comes when I experience my connectedness with this, the One Source of All, in a stillness that is not an emptiness but pregnant.

But is that enough?

The infant yearns for mother's milk; for it, that is abundance. For the worldly man, it is money in the bank and all it can buy. Only for the mystic does it appear to be nothing on the outside. What he seeks is a union with the Divine, the substance and source of all abundance. Another form of milk! Divine Mother's milk! The ecstatic writings of a saint like Hildegard von Bingen may convince us that the ultimate in abundance can be nothing else. Why, therefore, seek anything less? Yet, in the outer world, how abundantly she lived, expressing her love and creativity.

So, perhaps we are moved by these two necessities, one drawing us in, back to Source, the other out, in a ceaseless out-pouring of love and creativity that are the very essence of the Divinity within. Thus, it is not a question of either one or the other.

Jesus, quoted in *The Gospel of Thomas*, states that if we do not learn how to make the inner the outer, and the outer the inner, we will never know heaven. The enlightened see no distinctions. I, not dwelling in this blessed state, appear to have been on a pendulum swing, drawn towards one, while denying the other, then reversing.

Elly

Talking with Roderic about Hildegard, I realised my challenge is to bring out my own love and creativity. While I'm open to the inflow of abundance from Source, my outer expression is still largely blocked. I dare not express myself spontaneously, creatively, crazily or openly. It was a great discovery seeing abundance as both an in-breathing and out-breathing. I had been focusing too much on the in-breath, feeling bloated, waiting for the out-breath that didn't easily come. With my dance and voice work, I have begun working my way out of this. Writing also helps!

I had been pondering on this out in Nature. Meandering through our valley earlier in the year had reminded me of basics. Either spring had never been so rich and vibrant or I had never been so aware and receptive. Flowers, shrubs and trees were bursting out in bud. Horses, cows and birds were preparing for motherhood. The whole valley was trembling with pregnant beings waiting for the celebration of new life. Nothing seemed to block the flow of the life force. Nature was not holding back, but radiating love, beauty and delight, fearlessly, unselfishly, unconditionally, to all who were able to see, hear and rejoice. She was in love with herself, fully present in the now, not bound by the past, nor worried by the future in which she would lose her blooms before dying back into the Earth from which she had come. Maybe that love of self, especially of *Self*, is one of the keys to abundance? Wouldn't it open us to the feeling of abundance as well the receiving of it if we brought Self-love into every moment of our lives?

Roderic

The following day, I remained in bed, my preferred location for in-depth reflections. I had decided to focus on material abundance, specifically my relationship to it. Abundance symbolized by money was a major issue, a karmic one, on which I had been working for many lives. I had explored every possible approach to wealth, it seemed to me, theoretically and experientially, going to extremes. I had renounced it, choosing poverty, believing this to be a spiritual requirement. A great misunderstanding! I had sought money with desperation, ruthlessness and cunning, scheming, manipulating, cheating and stealing, even making these my sport and pleasure. Though profitable temporarily, I had ever been reduced to the state from which I'd come.

My problem, I'd realized, had never been lack of money, but rather my relationship to it, the way I viewed it. With many illusions, I had made numerous false equations. Underlying them all was my inability to grasp the connection between what I needed and the One Source from which all proceeds. Wealth is neither to be earned (said the former slave!) nor seized (said the reformed pirate!), but simply received (said the newly-born enlightened being!). This being so, "The Universe is my banker," I'd declared one day. "All I have to do is call upon it."

I had put this proposition to the test some years ago by going to the top of the Tor in Glastonbury and asking the Archangel Michael for a million dollars for an educational project. While that had proved successful, speedily and dramatically, I had understood only half the picture, as I came to realize. Yes, there is One Source of all we need and all we have to do is ask, but this Source is not *outside* our Selves. We are not separate from it. We are here on this planet as Cosmic Beings to awaken to whom and what we are, Divine in essence, and to use our powers as the creators we are – indeed, as the gods we are – while acknowledging the Source and attuning to It *within* ourselves.

As the 'gods' we are? Is this not a mighty delusion and arrogance? Not at all! "Is it not written in your law," said Jesus, "'I have said, ye are gods'?" – as quoted in the Bible, in *The Gospel of John*, chapter 10, verse 34.

And did he not also say, "Ye shall do greater things than I"?

It is time for us to stop being the dependent child, the wronged and pitifully helpless victim, the resigned fatalist, the apathetic sheep, and *become* the gods we are and are meant to be, fully empowering ourselves as creators, while assuming the responsibility for everything in our lives. *Co*-creator, though, is the word I prefer. While empowering us in our divinity, it keeps us humble.

Elly

Co-creation was an eye-opening concept for me, one I had misunderstood initially. I used to sit in meditation waiting for angels or my guides to tell me what to do, where to go, even what to think, hoping they knew what I needed. It was a passive attitude and not at all helpful in opening up to devic and angelic realms, which a part of me was still resisting. I feared becoming a slave to them as much as I had been to my own demanding and critical 'Christian' voice earlier in life, which had brought me to exhaustion and depression. I didn't want to lose control, giving my power away again. So, how could I open to these realms without doing so?

Caroline Myss, Ph.D., a medical intuitive and teacher, helped me see what I had to do in her book, *Anatomy of the Spirit*, in moving out of the classic dependent child-parent relationship into a mature spiritual one, into what she calls "a co-creative two-adults relationship" with the Divine. In other words, I had to move out of the old religious father-child relationship to God into spiritual adulthood. "Co-creation is in fact the essence of spiritual adulthood," she states, which involves not only "the exercise of choice" but "the acceptance of our responsibility for those choices." So, yes, I can open to the angelic beings and listen to whatever they have to say, but I have to take responsibility and decide for myself. Also, as Roderic declared emphatically: "It is even important for you to learn to say 'no' to them. They never command, only suggest, respecting your freedom totally; and the very last thing they expect you to do is to give your power away, even to them. So, rather than be offended, I'm sure they'll be delighted with any 'No'; and there'll be much wing clapping."

It is also a fact, as he pointed out, that "until you empower yourself you can never be in a co-creative relationship. It will always be one of dependency and subservience." Yes, I understood. This is true in any relationship, whether with angels, family, friends, colleagues or, most importantly, lovers.

Roderic

We had been invited to spend a few days at my mother's, an appropriate location for the continuation of our *Abundance Week*, as mothers symbolically are a source of nourishment. We had been asked to look after her precious cat while she went travelling.

"I don't think I'll survive another bus trip," said Elly. "Isn't it about time we manifested our own vehicle?"

"You're right. Let's do it."

Elly

"Let's tune in and ask the angels to help us find the right one," I suggested, excited to be able to put co-creation to the test.

"No, not yet," Roderic replied. "To work as co-creators, we should first do the ground work. Let's be clear about what we want and then visualize it outside our front door as if it has already manifested."

We weren't too bothered about shape or colour, but did want reliability; and it needed to be large enough, with folding back seats for my Reiki table. Above all, we wanted an honest dealer, who enjoyed giving the best possible service.

Shortly afterwards, we found one in the village, exactly what we'd asked for, and went off to contact the owner. He was a retired farmer and car mechanic, who enjoyed buying and restoring vintage vehicles and proudly showed us his 1950s Sunbeam Alpine. He drove us around in the red Honda which he had for sale and we both felt good about it. As important, we felt good about him. He responded with a smile to our every request and an obliging "No problem, I'll do that for you." This was the service we had requested. We felt we could trust him.

Afterwards, I reflected on our process, which had been so effortless. First we had tuned in to our inner Selves, asking if it was in alignment with our higher purposes to acquire a car at this moment in time. We had done so before and received a negative, as we were to stay where we were in our cottage by the sea. But now we had got a positive response. Then we had clearly visualized what we wanted, asked the Universe, watched the signs and acted on them, proceeding with faith, knowing our request had already been answered. And of course we'd checked if there were any saboteurs, any limiting or negative beliefs or fears, which could block the process; and cleared them.

At first I had had a problem with this process, for it sounded all too simple. I had also found it hard to accept the idea that the Universe provides so unconditionally. But again and again it proved to work. For a lazy sort of person, this was bliss. Had I discovered the Law of Least Effort? We thanked our angels greatly.

Roderic

Packing for our trip to my mother's, I collected material to take for our ongoing workshop, including books on Cosmic Laws and the art or science of manifestation. While doing so, I flipped through a copy of *Money Is My Friend* by Phil Laut and came across a heading, *The Undernourishment Syndrome*. "That could relate to me," I thought.

"If you were not breast fed as an infant," it began, "you may have some of this syndrome. You may have concluded, that "there is not enough milk"." Well, there never had been enough, neither drink nor love-milk. After my birth, I had been passed to a nurse, the beginning of a series of nurses and nannies, the first of whom ran off with the butler, while the second left a few months later, complaining she was sick and tired of lobster and smoked salmon!

– while I had been undernourished nutritionally and emotionally! "Ideas like 'there is not enough milk'," said Laut, "are later translated into 'there's not enough money'." That figured. Either there never was enough or I'd feared there never would be. Deep down, unconsciously, at gut level, I had carried this fear into adulthood; and, being the powerful magnetic force that the unconscious is, it had been creating my realities. Processing all this, I had another busy night.

Elly

"How about some music?" said Roderic as we waited for a ferry to take us across the Cobh estuary, scene of the departing ill-fated Titanic, on our way to his mother in Kilkenny.

"Shall we listen to the tape on *The Laws of Attraction*?" I suggested, enjoying the fact that we had a cassette player in our newly acquired vehicle. "A workshop on wheels!" I added.

The tape reminded us, once again, of what powerful magnets we are, creating all the time whether we're aware of this or not. "You must have had some good thoughts when you attracted me," I smiled, putting an arm on his shoulder and stroking the back of his neck. "Easy," he replied. "I just dreamed of a beautiful angel."

"It is not only your conscious intention but your state of being which attracts things to you," was a key phrase in the tape. "If you want to *be* rich, you must first *feel* rich. You cannot attract abundance from a state of feeling poor. It defies law."

Roderic stopped the tape at this point. "That's one of the most important statements ever," he declared. "I need time to digest it."

"Do *you* feel rich?" I asked him.

"I'm dripping with gold," he replied. "I've a gold medallion around my neck, gold bracelets on my wrists, a golden ball in my belly, and two between my legs. You just can't see it yet! Yes, seriously, I'm beginning to *feel* rich, and open to more abundance on all levels."

"All your anxieties, fears and resentments," the tape continued, "all your negative thoughts and limited belief systems, are attracting to you people and situations with which they resonate."

Roderic

"A horrifying thought, isn't it?" I reflected, "telling us, once again, how important it is to clear out our muck."

Elly

Roderic's mother's place was an ideal base, peaceful, with luxurious décor. I sat in her conservatory, which looked out onto a garden of fruit-trees and flowers, with cat on lap, reading and listening to more abundance tapes, while reflecting on my own blocks and abilities.

I had also once had a problem of lack, I remembered. Though, while Roderic had had an unconscious fear of it, I had seen it around me all the time. Indeed, I had become incredibly focused on it, both in my own life as well as those of others. I would wake up one morning, I feared, and there'd be no water, no food, no money, no energy, no warmth anywhere on the planet. Only lack!

As I had lived with the consciousness of lack, so, as the Law states, I had attracted it. Eventually, I had headed towards becoming what I feared. One day, it was not the planetary eco-system that collapsed in a paralysis around me, but my own body-mind-spirit-system. I found myself with no energy, no inner warmth, no hunger for food, no appetite for life, nor any will to act. And, because of this, I'd ended up with no income. Only at the bottom of this dark tunnel did I realize I had to change my attitudes. This way of relating to life couldn't possibly be God's will.

In moving from a consciousness of lack to one of abundance, I remembered the resistances I'd had due to unresolved guilt. For years, I'd been carrying a huge weight on my shoulders, feeling I was responsible for the whole world, with ever the same thought: How can I be rich and happy while so many others are poor and suffering?

In talks with Roderic, I acquired the understandings which enabled me to release the guilt. "Every soul chooses its own life, its own path, circumstances and experiences, for its own reasons," he reminded me. "You are not responsible for the choices of others. Of course you can help them, but you cannot make them choose. You can help them by honouring and being what you are, uplifting them by your examples, radiating your Love and Light. As the saying goes, 'To heal the world, you must heal yourself.' This is the primary task." Finally, I realized, it was the only thing within my control.

Roderic

When we had identified our negative thought-patterns, resistances and blockages, past and present, we began work on clearing them. My own list astounded me with its vastness. "It's not spiritual to be rich! It's easier for a camel to go through the eye of a needle than for a rich man to go to heaven! Blessed are the poor, for they shall inherit the earth! Money doesn't grow on trees! Money is the root of all evil! It's really hard to make money! Nobody is going to pay me for doing what I like doing! There's not enough for everyone! Artists, writers and creative geniuses, like me of course, are destined to be poor!" ... and so forth and so forth, just to name a few.

Now, after clearing these patterns out of my energy-field, I know and can affirm authentically that it is spiritual to be rich, abundance is my birthright, it's fun being wealthy and I deserve being so. In fact, abundance is my true state of being. I am always fully open to receiving. All my projects are a financial success. Money flows into my life plentifully. The more I prosper, the more I have to share. As for the Universe, it is infinitely abundant, compassionate and generous. It pays me for doing what I really love doing; and there is plenty for everyone. My personal connection with the One Source of All provides me with all I need. For all of this, I am truly grateful.

Elly

After working in the mornings, we went exploring in the afternoons. A mile down the road were the ruins of Jerpoint Abbey, founded in 1160 and colonised twenty years later by Cistercian monks, a wonderful, gentle, peaceful place. It had some beautiful sculpture on its walls. A figure of three, called *The Weepers*, fascinated me.

"Weepers attract weepers," Roderic jibed humourously. "The Law of Attraction in action!"

214

One day, we lunched with friends in their converted mill-house on the edge of a waterfall outside Thomastown. Its spaciousness, beauty and palatial elegance inspired us to envision our own dream house. We used the occasion to collect data for our Creative Visualization Workshop, a novel idea, which one of our many tapes had suggested: "Set aside ten to fifteen minutes each day, for clearly visualizing whatever it is you want to bring into manifestation, using the data you gather from your everyday experiences. Look at other people's houses, cars, qualities, characters, and say "Yes, this is what I'd like", register those elements which please you, own them mentally as your own, and feel into them so you can attract them." This we did. As Florence Scovel-Shinn writes in her *Game of Life and How to Play It*: "What man imagines, sooner or later externalises in his affairs." Our Creative Visualization Workshop gave us a framework in which to practise, using and training the imagining faculty.

Roderic

While the masculine or active way of acquiring something is to go out after it, and the feminine or passive way is to attract it, we need to be able to do both. Most of my life I have been struggling with the former, learning many lessons. Clearly, my focus now was on the latter. No more struggle! Lying back and attracting! Being clear about what I want and open to receiving it. Living, ideally, in a state of Grace. Trusting more fully in Life. Which doesn't mean lying back and doing nothing! Creative visualization combines the active and passive ways perfectly and powerfully.

Elly

After we had lived a year of relative isolation while writing, I was ready to go back into the world and continue with my healing work.

Amazingly, a week after this realization, I was asked to participate in a holistic health fair in Kinsale as a Reiki practitioner and given the opportunity to work as a massage therapist in a luxurious spa near Clonakilty. To me, this was another example of how life responds to clear intentions.

If I was to set up a Reiki practice after the fair, I would need my own place for receiving clients and running courses. To work at home had always been my dream. This meant we needed a bigger house!

Roderic

Our needs for more space were synchronous. While the cottage had been perfect for me on my own, it really didn't work for two anymore. I was beginning to feel restricted, trapped and restless; and, one full moon, simmered explosively. It was clearly time to manifest what we needed.

Elly

"We know what we want," I said, "an office, a room for workshops, a healing room, and a place for guests, close to where we live."

We tuned in and asked the Universe; and also thanked it, for we knew that our request would be answered – indeed, that it had already been answered, since the Universe operates beyond space and time – for which reason it's important to bring everything into the now.

A few days later, our neighbour Dennis knocked on our door with a gift of vegetables, informing us that he was off to paint The Blue House as the tenant had just left. The house was on the edge of the beach, a few hundred yards away and was owned by our landlady. Initially one house, it had been partitioned into two, one for long-term and the other for weekly summer lets. For the moment, we would be happy to have a half.

"Could we look around?" we asked.

"Sure. Come now," he beckoned with his lovely smile.

"Yes, this is ideal," we agreed excitedly, having explored it fully. It even had a courtyard, bordered by a garden, for sitting outside in summer.

Roderic

The following morning, as I opened the door of our cottage intending to walk up hill to our landlady's Georgian mansion to inform her of our interest in the house, she arrived on our doorstep

– such a synchronicity clearly indicating that the Universe was supporting us. We could have it in a month's time, she confirmed.

But where was the money going to come from? We wondered. In terms of our capital, close to zero, and our income, minimal, renting a second house was beyond our current means. The main point on which we both agreed was that we had to continue holding the vision that the house was already ours, with the money for it already flowing in. One cannot manifest while holding limiting thoughts.

"Money comes to me from unexpected sources and in perfect timing," I reminded myself. "No need for panic. Just lie back!"

Immediately, the magic started happening. Though I had signed a contract, an option agreement, for the filming of my book, *How to Rob Banks Without Violence*, with a young producer, Mark Biver, with a generous percentage of the budget to be paid to me on the first day of production (assuming it ever reached that point), there was no cash up front and no likelihood of any for two or three years. But he called during the week to inform me that he was about to make a deal with a company owned by Kate Winslet and her husband Jim Threapleton, who wanted to direct and produce it. They, in turn, had the backing of a major company, Intermedia, who had offered to fund and distribute it. Was I interested and would I agree to assign the contract?

Provided that the terms were the same, I had no objection. But, as he informed me a day or so later, Intermedia, who were evidently calling the shots, wanted to reduce my percentage by a very substantial seventy-five percent, meaning by a couple of hundred thousand dollars.

"Not interested," I declared, "unless they offer some cash in advance."

"They're not prepared to do that," said Mark.

"No deal, then," I replied.

A day or so later, he returned with a paltry offer of £500.

"They must be joking," I exclaimed.

That had seemed to be the end of the matter, with negotiations clearly closed, until he called back a week later to inform me that Intermedia were thinking again. "What would you accept?" he asked.

"I'll get back to you."

Meanwhile, I reflected. What would I consider a fair price? £20,000 in cash, I decided, as a non-refundable advance.

I didn't mention this figure to Mark, only to Elly. "My contract is with the Universe," I informed her. "Intermedia are merely intermediaries!"

Within the week, Mark called again: "Intermedia have agreed to offer you £5,000 immediately on signing, £7,500 in four months' time, and a further £7,500 a year after that. What is your response?" It took me a few seconds to realise that the three figures added up to £20,000, the exact sum for which I had put out to the Universe. How it works is so unfathomably extraordinary, how could one wish for any other partner? Alone, one's own efforts are a mere nothing.

So now we had the money! "Thank you Universe."

Elly

Moving into the Blue House, we cleaned all the rooms, smoking them with sage, and then sat in one after the other, feeling into its special energy. We established our intentions on the energy-field of each, listing the functions and activities we expected to take place there; and invited an angel to preside over the house, our Blue House Angel. My healing room was the most special for me, the first I had ever had, with the silence for which I had always longed.

The very first client I had for Reiki told me, as soon as I put my hands over her eyes, that she could see her angels and guides working on her body. "This treatment also has a gift for you," she declared, a few minutes later. "There is someone standing beside you with a message, but you're not listening." When I moved my hands to the back of her head, I could feel his presence. Then I could see him. He was dressed as a warrior of ancient times and holding a spear. I welcomed him and asked him silently if he could help me in the healing of my client, who urgently wanted to lose weight. This he did, opening her belly with his spear, taking out a black mass of energy and closing it again. Seconds later, the woman sighed and said: "I feel that something black and heavy has just been taken from me. I feel deeply at peace now." I couldn't believe it. I had thought that what I had seen might have been my

218

imagination. Evidently, it wasn't. The Being who had assisted me assured me that from now on he would be present during all my healings. All I had to do was call upon him.

The next morning, while Roderic and I were attuning, I asked for his name. I was given "Arjuna". I had never heard of such a person, nor even such a word.

Later, I shared it with Roderic. "He was the charioteer hero of the Bhagavad-Gita, the Hindu bible, and a disciple of Krishna, the God of Love," he informed me.

In treatments that followed, I could feel his presence and see him at work. This was the co-creativity for which I had been longing. I felt blessed.

My first two workshops were fully booked, which surprised me as I was unknown in the area and we lived so isolated. On the other hand, in view of our *Abundance Week*, it was not so surprising. Applying what I'd learned about manifestation and the Laws of Attraction, I had approached marketing in a new way. The response of people was overwhelming. "It's the best thing that's happened to me in the last fifteen years," said one.

Roderic

We also organised a *Game of Transformation*, giving our first workshop together in a three-day event. What worked so well was the male/female balance as well as the love flowing between us, as participants informed us.

Elly

After a few months of commuting from our cottage residence to our Blue House work spaces, we moved into the whole of the house, which felt more wholesome. That we could now afford to do so was a great gift. Abundance is living in a state of grace in which our needs are always perfectly met. Sometimes even our most frivolous wishes:

I had a bright green sweater which Roderic didn't like. Maybe it would look nicer under a brown coat, I thought. A suede one perhaps. No, better a brown velvet one. I made no mention of this to him. Sometime later, we spent a weekend with his sister, Coral, and before leaving her place, Roderic saw a brown velvet jacket hanging on a door.

"Is that one of mine?" he asked her.

"No," she replied. "It belonged to our father when he was young. It's an old beagling coat, too small for me. You can have it if you like."

He popped his head around the door of our bedroom: "Would you like a brown velvet jacket?" he asked.

I was dumbfounded. It suited me perfectly.

On another occasion we asked the Universe to participate in a joke. We had invited our friends Joyce and Bernard for lunch and wanted to give them crab claws, an idea that had arisen after Roderic had found an empty one on the beach. He had some mischief in mind, wanting to put the empty claw on Joyce's plate; but he needed fresh ones as well. So we said to the Universe flippantly: "Hey, you up there, in here, or wherever you are, we'd like some crab claws for our friends' lunch. Arrange for our fisherman neighbour to bring some. Thank you."

No claws appeared for lunch that day. But the next time they came for a meal, there was a knock on our door in the early morning and our fisherman appeared with a gift of three-dozen claws fresh from the bay. While we'd forgotten our request, the Universe had answered it in its own timing.

We also experienced abundance in the form of magical synchronicities. One morning, as part of our daily attunement with the Earth, Cosmos and our Higher Selves, we practised a breathing technique which we had come across in a book by a woman who used it in Hawaii for calling dolphins to the shore where she awaited them. We had no intention of summoning dolphins but, an hour or so later, we drove to Kinsale and to our astonishment, while crossing the bridge over the estuary, there were around fifty of them leaping around in the waters either side of us. We had never seen a single dolphin so far up river in such shallow waters, let alone fifty. Crowds from the town had come out to see them.

So life went on. We could write a whole book on such magical events.

Roderic

After our *Abundance Week*, which had extended over a couple of months, we had become much richer, inwardly and outwardly. "Let's celebrate," I suggested, "by checking into our local castle. We can romp and play in *ye olde worlde* four-poster bed."

Chapter 21

Cosmic Lovers &
Spiritual Partnership

Roderic

Kilbrittain Castle, originally built in 1035 by the King of Rathleann, a grandson of Brian Boru, High King of Ireland, was four miles away. After centuries of turbulent history, occupation by Irish chieftains, Norman invaders, Cromwellian troops and Anglo-Norman planters, it was back in Irish hands, so its new owners claimed – though the Gaels too were once invaders and Irishness includes all of these races. One afternoon, after a sumptuous meal in gourmet Kinsale's Fishy Fishy Café, we drove up its tree-lined avenue and through its gates.

Elly

I was excited, curious and slightly in awe as I stood before its great oak door. A baron's castle! So much history! And we were going to be staying there! Minutes later, we heard a steel bar slide and the door creak open.

"Delighted you've come," our hostess beamed. "I'm Sylvia. You're most welcome!"

We entered a large and tapestried hall where visitors of old would have left their swords, and followed her up a spiralling stairway to a vast corridor on the first floor, lined with books, antiques and castle paraphenalia.

"Tea and scones?" she enquired, showing us into her elegant drawingroom. "Or perhaps you'd like to see your room first. The castle's empty. You can go upstairs and choose your own."

This we did, selecting the most luxurious, and returned for tea where a fire blazed.

Roderic

Retiring to bed in regal splendour, we read love-poems by Rumi, the thirteenth century Sufi poet. I had gifted Elly an exquisite edition of his work, illustrated with Persian miniatures, along with extracts on thirty-three cards, each a gem, all contained in an equally beautifully illustrated box. The poems were passionate in a subtle way and profoundly spiritual.

"Hey, listen to this, beloved!" I exclaimed. "Rumi writing on the renewal of marriage: "Why get married only once to the same person? We can renew our vows of marriage again and again and it is beneficial to do so to awaken the spirit of our union, to remember that it is the great mystery of love that has led us to each other and that keeps us together ... By renewing our vows we allow spirit to mingle in this marriage." ... Just like our Celtic Marriage! How wise!"

We cuddled and fell into sleep.

Elly

On waking in the morning, I felt my lover's penis hard against my thigh. Turning towards him, I stroked it sensually. Here was the promise of a more tactile passion. Sighing with the pleasure, he too awoke.

"Isn't it about time we had a penis workshop?" he declared forthrightly, some time later. "Now that King Harry finds himself in a castle," King Harry being his name for this part of his anatomy, "he expects to be treated in a kingly fashion! For all the pleasure he gives, he deserves no less. Don't you agree? What would *your* life be without him?"

"Awfully boring!" I exclaimed.

"Then you must honour him in the manner he expects."

"How is that?"

"You could sing him a song and dance around him."

"You want me to perform a striptease?"

"Nothing so mundane," he replied dismissively. "Invent something. How about a five-finger foxtrot? Or a ten-finger smooch, long and lingering? Good King Harry needs pampering and adoring. Devise a ritual. Perform it as an expression of your adoration and deepest gratitude, above all to the Divine who so ingeniously created him – for *your* pleasure; for His own as well, I might add, for He is everything. Anoint him with oils, frankincense and myrrh. Weave garlands around him of daisies or rose petals."

"Anything else for his majesty?"

"Of course. The ultimate. He wants and deserves nothing less. Embrace him firmly with moistened lips, whirling with succulent tongue until he reaches the heights of ecstasy. There's a dance for you! A whirling Dervish tongue dance! Possibly the most ancient of Sufi traditions!"

I enjoyed his saucy flights of imagination as my hands wandered around the courtyard of his kingdom.

"How about the Inner Flute?" I suggested, shifting the focus to a higher level. "You're often telling me how important it is to draw your sexual energies up through your chakras, particularly to your throat centre."

"Yes, I know, and express it outwardly as creativity. I agree, that would be beneficial, but King Harry really isn't interested in such wisdoms. He's not into esoterics; so he hasn't read Mantak Chia or Alice Bailey. A basic, down-to-earth, hands-on sort of fellow, he would much prefer that *you* drew his energies up and out through *your* throat chakra."

Responding to the call with tongue and lips, I gave of my best in juicy caress.

"For flavour enhancement," he murmured in a lull between sighs and gasps, "you can ring downstairs and ask the butler for some *crème de menthe*. Abundance and nothing but abundance! King Harry is greatly in favour of that. And if you're not into the *menthe*, try Bailey's Cream, less sweet and more velvety! 'Become drunk with love!' as our poet commands."

Roderic

As 'God' says, speaking through Walsch, "Play with sex. Play with it! It's just about the most fun you can have with your bodies"!

On one level, the Creator is merely playing with Itself. As Rumi understood, addressing the Divine: "You made this 'we' and 'I' in order that You might play with Yourself." So, behind all that is, there is only One Lover!

Meanwhile, back on Planet Earth! While we had come to the castle to luxuriate in abundance, it was also to reflect on the meaning of the recently proposed title of our book, *Cosmic Lovers*, while clarifying our thoughts on its working sub-title, *Exploring Relationship as a Spiritual Partnership.*

Elly

"So, what is a *cosmic* lover?" I asked Roderic as we sat by a log-fire in the Banqueting Hall, awaiting the arrival of our salmon breakfast.

"One who lies in the arms of his beloved in a castle, sighing to himself, 'I wish we had dwellings like this on Orion'!" he responded flippantly.

Was this going to be one of those occasions when it would take forever to get him in the right mood? I wondered.

"Well, what do *you* think?" he asked, throwing the ball back into my court.

"The most essential recognition I've come to understand is that we're all individuals on a spiritual journey through many lives," I began.

"Yes," he agreed, "the number one basic. The ongoing journey of the soul through many lives on its return to oneness with Source – *that is* the cosmic context, of which the worldly context is merely an aspect."

"And we come into relationship to support each other in this," I added.

"Yes, but in practical terms what does this mean?"

"Awakening, healing, learning and growing, and of course loving," I reflected.

"And don't forget playing, creating, and having lots of fun!" he reminded me. "That's also essential, not only from our perspective but the Divine's."

I still had a tendency to take things too seriously.

"How do cosmic perspectives change the way one views relationships?" he asked, just as our host arrived with a covered silver platter on a trolley, containing, we assumed, our regal breakfast.

"Yummy, yummy!" Roderic enthused as our host removed the lid to reveal our steaming buttered fish.

"There isn't but a one and only love as I used to believe," I continued as soon as our host had departed. "If you see your life on this planet as a one-off event, then you are looking at a closed situation. The conventional view of marriage gives you the false idea that it's forever. It isn't. It's just *one* episode in your ongoing journey through Time in which you've had, and will continue to have, many relationships in many centuries, in many cultures, with many marriages and many lovers."

"Yep!" he murmured, chewing a morsel, before switching into oldie castle mode: "Well spoken! Thy wisdom doth please thy noble companion!"

"A relationship must be dynamic," I resumed. "It's not about freezing a state of togetherness. It must be open to changes. That's why I like our Celtic Marriage for a year and a day!"

"So, are you being kept on your exquisite toes?" he teased.

"Yes, definitely, and I'm happy about that. It reminds me that I'm on my own separate path and encourages me to honour it. If we had a contract for life, I would probably go to sleep."

"No chance of that! Not when I'm around! The last thing I'd want would be a piece of dead mutton around my neck!"

"Our Celtic Marriage recognises and emphasises my essential freedom. Otherwise I'd feel trapped."

"You have been!" he teased. "You've been captured for three hundred and sixty-six days at least! Bonded! Kept in servitude! With not too many precious days left!"

I threw him a kiss.

"The most important thing," I resumed seriously, "is that the relationship serves the individuals, both of them, rather than the individuals seeking to serve it as if it were a sacred unbreakable bond, which it isn't."

Roderic

"How do *you* view cosmic lovers?" she asked, refilling her cup with Earl Grey.

"Shall I pontificate?"

Elly

"What's that?" I enquired, not having come across the word.

"Delivering a treatise with pompous authority, preferably from a high pulpit," he responded.

"You should be good at that!" I replied. "I can imagine you addressing a large crowd and firing them off on a crusade somewhere."

"You must be reading my historical aura!"

The fire crackled. Our host arrived to clear our table. The taste of salmon still lingered in my mouth. I could definitely get used to this kind of abundance.

"Do you have any cognac?" I asked, as we moved closer to the fire, lying back in more comfortable chairs.

He returned with a bottle and a smile. Miserably wet outside, we were now cosily settled in for the morning.

"Cosmic lovers, said the philosopher …" Roderic began.

"Which one?"

"Me, of course!" he chuckled.

"Cosmic lovers, said the philosopher … presupposes cosmic beings. Wouldn't you agree? … Without cosmic beings there are no cosmic lovers! … The greatest philosophers are supremely adept at making the profoundest statements about the obvious! As you can see, I have joined their ranks!

"But, to continue: In one sense, as we are *all* cosmic beings we are *all* cosmic lovers; but in another, since we are *not* all aware of the fact that we *are* cosmic beings, and are *not* all living as the cosmic beings we are, then we have to make some kind of a distinction."

I agreed.

"A cosmic being is one who *knows* that he is one. Or he is waking up to this fact. A cosmic being knows that he hasn't just sprung from Mother Earth – unless She's been stung by the Heavenly Father! – that he's not just a creature of the Earth, though the world may tell him so; and that he hasn't simply evolved from matter, though the form in which he functions may well have done. He knows that he's not simply a body with a brain, which may or may not contain a soul, but that in essence he *is* soul, with body and brain being merely its expressions. He knows that as soul he's eternal; that he's on a journey through Space and Time; and that he has been coming and going on this planet for a long long time. Are these distinctions clear enough?"

"Yes. Very. You are doing well!"

"Dost thou, then, swear before me, as my Celtic wife for a year and a day, that thou art all of these things ... multidimensional ... a soul ... eternal ... unlimited and free?" he enquired, regressing into foolery.

"I do," I declared, bowing with hand on heart.

He was also, of course, being profoundly serious.

"A cosmic being has cosmic awareness and, following from this, cosmic perspectives. Knowing that his current earthly life is but one chapter in an ongoing saga of many lives changes everything. In this enlarged perspective, 'birth' and 'death' are not the moments of his beginning and ending but simply transition points of his 'entry' and 'departure' ...

"Knowing that he has more than one 'life' and that all his 'lives' are intimately related makes him wonder: "How are they related?" ... which leads him to the discovery and understanding of the laws by which they are related ... those governing the life of the soul ... the Cosmic Laws, the Laws of Life, or whatever you want to call them ... such as the laws of Attraction, Cause & Effect, Energy Follows Thought, As Within So Without, and so forth. Knowing how they regulate every aspect of human life changes how he perceives everything. All the seeming injustices of the world and the circumstances in which he finds himself are perceived differently. The more he understands these laws, which are neither religious nor moral, but scientific and universal, the more he perceives that there is no such thing as 'fate' ... nor, even less, 'cruel fate' ... but that all is the working of a perfect justice. The more he understands them, the more he comes to realize the extent to which he is the creator, chooser, causer and/or attractor of the conditions and circumstances in which he finds himself, rather than the seemingly innocent victim. Thus, he, our awakening cosmic being, begins taking full responsibility for every aspect of his life. From being the unconscious creator, he becomes an increasingly conscious one. Growing in awareness, developing his faculties and empowering himself, he becomes his own healer and saviour."

Clearly, Roderic was bent on exploring and expounding on the subject in depth, which I loved.

"He recognises no outside authority telling him what truth is or isn't," he continued. "He has seen through the pomp, the show, the falsities and groundless promises, shot all the popes, rabbis, mullahs and priests, metaphorically, severed all outer allegiances and bonds, and claimed his freedom … The highest authority he knows and acknowledges is within his own being. He seeks it within, as the Master directed …

"Whatever the dramas appearing around him, he perceives them in the context of the larger cosmic picture. He knows that as Man he is an aspect of the Divine on a great adventure, ever unfolding, ever evolving, ever exploring the infinite potentialities of Life and Being. He has a sense of the nature of the Cosmic Game with its cyclical features, emerging from Source, 'falling' into forgetfulness of its own true nature, separation and limitation, *and then* 'ascending', remembering and awaking, returning to the Oneness from which he came."

Our host arrived with logs for the fire. "Does *he* know he's a cosmic being?" I wondered. "He must, with all his books by Rudolf Steiner in the hallway."

"Above all, the primary point of centredness of the cosmic being is within his own soul," Roderic continued. "In this, he's a very different creature from the average worldly individual. It's as if he were a member of another species, though he isn't. Simply, some of us are awaking while others are still sleeping, that is all."

Thus Spoke Roderic!

"What does it mean being centred in soul? Sounds like a great idea, as many might say, but what does it mean in practice?" I asked, having answers but seeking clarity.

"It means being centered in the space of stillness where one's innermost Self is experienced not as a concept but as a living presence. It's going beyond mind. It's being centered in a realm of pure awareness, a state of being of increasing inclusiveness, of potentially infinite expansiveness and, above all, of love, bliss and peace."

Roderic

It was time to go back to the original question, "What is a cosmic lover?"

"Shall we explore it in our four-poster bed?" Elly suggested.

We wound our way up the spiral stairway to our suite beneath the castle turret. "Maybe we've already spoken enough," I wondered aloud as we entered our room.

"Oh! I thought we'd only just begun," she encouraged.

Elly

"When cosmic lovers come together," Roderic resumed as we lay on the bed, "it is with the recognitions just described, who and what we truly are as cosmic beings, where we have come from, where we are going, and the laws governing our earthly existence. Of course it's a love relationship, even a passionate one, but it's imbued with a different set of intentions and purposes ...

"For the cosmic lover, the relationship becomes a spiritual one, a Spiritual Partnership, meaning that it exists to nourish the essential life processes of awakening, healing, learning and growing, which includes the unfolding of the unique potentialities of each, and so forth; and provide mutual support in this. Though this sounds serious, it's much more fun, much more exciting, as well as much more fulfilling, for it is in alignment with one's deepest yearnings and primary intentions in being on Planet Earth."

"How would you say that this affects the way cosmic lovers relate to each other in practice, ideally?" I asked.

"Why don't *you* write down a list of what *you* think and I'll do the same?" he suggested. "Then, we can compare notes."

"Good idea. I'll prepare mine while soaking in a bath," I replied. Water clears my mind and helps the flow of inspiration.

"Give her, O Lord, a Holy Conversion," my beloved muttered as I went to prepare it.

Meanwhile, he picked up my book on Rumi and read aloud: "Sufi masters are those whose spirits existed before the world. Before the body, they lived many lives."

"The greatest poets had these cosmic perspectives," he declared and quoted various lines from memory.

Roderic

"There is only one history and that is the soul's," wrote W.B. Yeats, the first of Ireland's Nobel poets. "Many times man lives and dies."

I once listed all the poets I had encountered who had expressed the same in their own way, indicating their belief in the soul's immortality and its many earthly incarnations. Among the Romans were Pindar, Virgil and Ovid, along with Cicero, statesman and philosopher. There was the Celtic bard Taliesin who remembered his lives in many centuries and cultures; the Elizabethan Edmund Spenser in *The Fairie Queene*; and the romantics, Shelley in *Ariel* and Wordsworth in his *Ode on Intimations of Immortality*, who wrote:

> "Our birth is but a sleep and a forgetting.
> The soul that rises with us, our life's star,
> Hath had elsewhere its setting, and cometh from afar."

Gandhi was familiar with these lines and quoted them in a letter to his close disciple, Madelaine Slade, daughter of Admiral Sir Edward Slade.

There was William Blake, "I cannot think of death as more than the going out of one room into another," and the dramatist, poet and scientist, Goethe, "I am certain I have been here a thousand times before and I hope to return a thousand times more," who concluded appropriately, "What is lacking is Self-Knowledge. After that the rest will come." There was his contemporary, Schiller; and Thomas Traherne who remembered back into his mother's womb and beyond into pre-existence; Alfred Lord Tennyson; and Matthew Arnold in *Empedocles On Etna*; as well as Sir Edwin Arnold, knighted by Queen Victoria; and John Masefield, Poet Laureate, in *A Creed*:

> "I hold that when a person dies
> his soul returns again to earth;
> arrayed in some new flesh disguise.
> Another mother gives him birth ..."

231

There was Dante Gabriel Rosetti, Rainer Maria Rilke, who was convinced he'd been in Moscow in a previous life, and Heinrich Heine who, when asked whether he believed in the immortality of the soul, replied with mocking outrage: "I, should I doubt it? I, whose heart is rooted in the most distant millenniums of the past … I? I should not believe in immortality?"

In *The North Sea*, he wrote amusingly: "Who can understand the divine irony which delights in accentuating the manifold contradictions between body and soul? Who can tell what tailor now inherits the soul of Plato, what dominie is heir to Caesar's spirit? Perchance the soul of a Genghis Khan now animates a reviewer who, without knowing it, daily slashes the souls of his faithful Bashirs and Kalmucks in the pages of a critical journal …" Are our reviewers in *The New York Times*, *Washington Post* or *Sydney Morning Herald*, former warriors of Mongolian hordes, now ready with their scimitars?!

There was Walt Whitman in *Democratic Vistas* and *Leaves of Grass*, "No doubt I have died myself ten thousand times before," and his *Song of Myself*, "I know I am deathless … We have thus far exhausted trillions of winters and summers. There are trillions ahead, and trillions ahead of them." And the Easterners, of course, such as Rabindranath Tagore, Nobel Laureate, and the Lebanese-American, Kahlil Gibran, "A little while, a moment of rest upon the wind, and another woman shall bear me."

Aside from the poets, I made similar lists with extensive quotes of prominent individuals in other professions and walks of life who had held similar beliefs. As the tree outside my window might say, the list is unbeleafable!

Despite the fact that reincarnation, a clear recognition of man's cosmic identity and the immortality of his soul, has been the belief of many of the greatest *western* minds of the last two and a half thousand years, and despite the well-documented scientific evidences of modern times, it remains a truth our culture dares not acknowledge, not officially. Even today, it is treated as a heresy. For establishment orthodoxies, entrenched in their dogmas, the implications of acceptance are far too threatening.

"The ongoing journey of the soul through Time", "Cosmic beings", "Cosmic laws" and "Cosmic lovers", how far from the prevailing dogmas of our times! Yet, *cosmic* rather than *earthly* beings denotes the reality of who and what we truly are. If we are ever going to find the meanings we seek, we need a re-education in the basic facts of life.

Elly

While Roderic's interests are more in the collective and universal, mine are more intimate, relating to my own little drop in the ocean.

How *do* cosmic perspectives make a love-relationship different? I had been reflecting on this for some time, while reading books, listening to tapes, and during our discussions. Now, I wanted to summarise what I considered to be the essentials.

In bringing my thoughts together, I decided to write out ten guidelines for a Spiritual Partnership – my Ten Golden Precepts!

"The sun has come out," Roderic declared over an hour later. "Let's go out."

I had almost finished.

"Bring your list with you," he suggested as I dressed. "We can discuss it under a tree in the castle courtyard. Or you can stand on the balcony and recite it, while I adore you from underneath."

Such a romantic!

"What about *your* list?" I asked.

"I don't have one yet."

"What have you been doing, then?"

"Ruminating! *Rumi*-nating!" he joked, and read another quote:

"My soul is screaming in ecstasy. Every fiber of my being is in love with you."

We found ourselves in a courtyard of gravel and lawns, surrounded by buildings and old stone walls, with many cosy corners.

"What a place for a celebration!" I exclaimed.

"Musicians playing on the balcony, guests dancing around on a Maypole beneath, venison roasting on a spit by the tree," Roderic visualized aloud.

"A cluster of trumpeters, here," he declared, standing by the entrance gate, "to announce the arrival of bride and groom."

233

Roderic

It would soon be the first of May. We'd have been together for another year and a day. We knew we'd be renewing our agreement again. Perhaps this was the place for a Celtic Wedding, for an official celebration, rather than the stone circle at Lough Gur, which we'd originally envisaged.

"Maybe our guests can also stay here," Elly pondered aloud.

"Yes. Why not? They can all romp and play in four-poster beds. I'm sure your mum and dad would like that! It'll make a great *cours d'amour*, most suitable for king, queen, courtiers and troubadours! … Dream on! Dream on! Dreams are the stuff that reality is made of."

Elly

"So what's the first of your guidelines, darling?" Roderic asked as we seated ourselves in a sheltered corner.

"My *Ten Golden Precepts for a Spiritual Partnership*," I replied.

"Oh! Am I sitting at the feet of a prophetess?"

"Yes! So behave yourself!"

"One," I began: "*Agree that you are two souls on a journey through Time, who meet as equals.*"

"Great. Basic. We are all souls first and foremost. Next?" he responded with unusual conciseness.

"Two: *Decide that your priority is spiritual growth. Do so because it's your joy and passion.*

"Yes, growth, inner growth, is at the heart of the matter, the essential core of a cosmic lover relationship. I assume it includes awaking as a soul."

"Of course."

"Next?" he prompted, hastening me on.

"Not yet," I countered. "I want to emphasize that a growth-based relationship is the very opposite of a need-based one. They're fundamentally different."

"Yes," he agreed, "an important recognition."

"In a need-based relationship, you are threatened by growth and change. You're afraid that your partner might grow away from you, become freer, lose his/her neediness, his/her dependency on you, rather than delighting in the fact that he/she is maturing. In a need-based relationship, you look to another to make you feel complete, while in a growth-based one you're feeling complete within yourself, or intentionally working towards this. You are two wholes, or aspiring wholes, rather than two halves, relating with each other."

"Yes. That's clear. But what happens when only one of the partners considers personal healing and growth a priority?"

"Then you can hardly speak of a Spiritual Partnership, can you? It takes two."

"So, what happens when one is and the other isn't? Or one of them starts awaking and changing their perspectives, taking personal growth more seriously?"

"Several possibilities: Either you and your partner grow together, which is wonderful. Or *you* grow while your partner refuses to do so, or to support you in your growth; in which case, you may choose to go on your separate path. Or, you decide to give up your growth, in order to maintain your relationship; in which case, you may end up frustrated, bitter and depressed."

"I think many women in particular find themselves in this situation," said Roderic. "They seem to be waking up and growing much faster."

"Yes! I'm blessed," I said, putting a hand in his.

We paused as a robin hopped towards us with a tweet and a chirrup.

"So, what comes next?" he asked. "I'm sure this little fellow is eager to hear."

"Now that my audience is enlarged, here is number three: *Take full responsibility for all aspects of your life, knowing you're the cause of what you experience rather than the victim.*

"When you take full responsibility," I elaborated, agreeing with what Roderic had once told me, "you cease blaming others. You know you've drawn an experience into your life for a reason and that it's there to show you something about yourself, and/or present you with something *you* have to resolve. The situation and the other person are reminding you of that, or reflecting something to you, triggering something that's already in you. When you take responsibility in a conflict situation, for example, you will ask yourself, "What is it that *I* have to look at *in myself* in this situation?

235

Why does it make *me* so angry, upset or sad? Why have *I* drawn this into my life? To heal what? When you both do that, the relationship changes dramatically."

"Yes," agreed Roderic. "I think it's one of the most important rules in the game. What so often happens is that one partner judges and blames the other, and then, through the process of action-reaction, accusations and counter-accusations, you end up in a giant escalation, with no one really listening, the same old records played over again, and a fiery explosion that doesn't solve anything. Cosmic lovers own the responsibility personally, in all situations, and help each other see and understand the underlying issues ... which may involve peeling a lot of onions! ... and meticulous honesty."

"Maybe I should include this as a separate item."

"A commandment!" he corrected. "Thou shalt move beyond all action-reaction! Or dwell forever in a hell of your own making!"

"Perhaps it *is* all covered in taking personal responsibility."

"Four," I continued: *Don't expect another to meet your needs – whether physical, emotional, mental or spiritual.*"

"Yes, vital," he agreed, "I think this is a key point. At all times, one honours the freedom of the other. How can one do so if one places expectations on him? When *my* freedom is threatened, I run a mile!"

"I know you do. So do I."

"It also re-emphasizes the importance of taking full responsibility for one's own life and happiness."

"At the same time," I added, "it's important to be clear about your needs, along with your dreams and aspirations, and communicate these fully so your partner knows how to support you without your expecting him or her to do so. Expectations lead to disappointments and frustrations, don't they? They are relationship-killer number one, I think."

"Definitely. Next? My adorable prophetess!"

"Five: *Focus on what you have to give rather than on what you'd like to receive.*"

"Is that what you're doing, beloved?" he challenged. "Why is that so important?"

"While it's the nature of the soul to give," I clarified, "the ego focuses on receiving. "What's in it for me?" it asks. It helps shift your focus out of being needy and dependent into giving out of your abundance. It's also linked with the next one, six, which is: *Be as aware of the needs of the other and respond to them as if they were your own.*"

I remembered vividly when Roderic was lying in bed for three days, processing, open and vulnerable, asking him if I could dance in the next-door room. He'd said "yes", assuming I'd be playing the music softly and probably not for very long. Instead, I had it on full blast for an hour, trance-dancing. When I was finished and Roderic came out of the room looking so fragile and exhausted, I realised how selfish I'd been, becoming sick in the stomach, with shaking legs. He'd obviously needed peace and quiet, not an assault on the core of his being. In that moment, I realised how vital it is to be fully aware of the state and needs of another. What you can do to another when you are not aware can be quite criminal. What I like about Roderic is that he is aware of my needs sometimes before I am.

"Yes, essential," he commented. "Relationship gives us an opportunity for expanding our little bubble of ego-awareness into a larger one of increasing inclusiveness."

"I think you should combine four, five and six," he said. "They're all about needs."

After a discussion, I agreed. So, number four was now as follows: *Don't expect another to meet your needs, whether physical, emotional, mental or spiritual. Rather, be aware of the needs of the other and as responsive to them as if they were your own.*

Two horses arrived, as if to listen, their curious faces peering over the fence. I greeted them and continued:

"Five: *Give loving acceptance to all aspects of your partner, including those that would otherwise irritate you.*"

This is the most challenging! I've realized that when I focus on trying to change how my lover is, the process never ends, nor my irritations; but when I give this up and accept him as he is, I can relax and focus on myself. As I've come to understand, as long as I have irritations I am carrying unresolved pains.

"Yes, this is really important," he said: "How you relate to the dislikes which you may have to live with everyday. Of course one can ignore them, but that's not a solution. As we know, holding things in and allowing them to gather energy becomes potentially explosive – or, gnawing away, lethally destructive to your own system. However, while endeavouring to give loving acceptance to what you don't like is a step in the right direction, I like to go further. I want to know the darkest of the dark on the shadow side of my own as well as my partner's nature, to bring it out into the light and embrace it in loving acceptance. While instinctively we may try to present the best part of ourselves, to ourselves and others, hiding and suppressing what we don't like, I'm into reversing this process. In a loving relationship, committed to truth and growth, we can do this in a supportive environment; which requires, of course, that we move beyond judgement and just let things be."

I agreed, but wasn't there yet. Roderic seemed to have mastered the art of giving loving acceptance to everything, at least in the context of our relationship. While a brilliant observer of my weaknesses and errors, he mirrors things back to me in an unattached way, usually with humour. "How many ducks are you expecting today?" he'd ask me, finding water all over the bathroom floor, yet again, after I have been showering.

"There's another point linked with this," said Roderic. "Abuse. No one should accept the abuse of another."

"Yes, I agree; there are limits, particularly violence."

"So, we'll re-phrase five: "*Give loving acceptance to all aspects of your partner, including those that would otherwise irritate you, but excluding abuse.*"

"Okay," I continued, now for number six: "*Speak up your truth and do so with love.*"

If you don't speak up your truth, how does anyone know who you are, what you think, dream or feel? People think they have to withhold their truth to preserve harmony in a relationship, even the relationship itself. They tend to do so out of fear of rejection, of not getting enough love if they show their true selves, which I've done for years. But when you align yourself with your soul and the Universe, there'll always be an abundance of love, and you'll be less dependent on others. And the more you speak your truth, the more you become aligned. Speaking it out of anger may seem easier, but tends to be destructive. That's why I need to remind myself to do so with love. Speaking my truth clearly and fully in the moment, I've found to be one of my greatest challenges. I'm still working on it. Roderic calls me 'the master of the half-finished sentence' – with the other half getting stuck in my throat!

"Speaking up your truth, yes, risky but liberating, and absolutely essential," he said. "Regularly sharing what you think and feel is one of the surest ways of dissolving the causes of potential conflict or becoming strangers and drifting apart. What other gems from your lovely lips?"

I smiled. "Seven: *Direct your love, wisdom and creativity beyond the relationship.*"

"Yes, otherwise it tends to fall in on itself. This includes the notion of service, sharing your gifts with the world."

I've never fully understood why, but I feel it's essential to give service to something larger than the relationship. Roderic quoted Albert Schweitzer, "I don't know what your destiny will be, but one thing I know: The only ones among you who will be really happy are those who have sought and found how to serve." This includes the rearing of children, of course, which we were considering. Meanwhile, we were writing our book, which we hoped would inspire others in their desire to create more fulfilling relationships. We were also giving workshops, separately and together, supporting others on their life journeys; and we had other projects of an educational nature which we were preparing for launching.

"Eight: *Accept that the form of the relationship may change.*"

"What do you mean?" That I can have a second wife?!" he challenged.

"No way! What I want to say is that a relationship may come to an end one day. You may feel it has gone as far and as deep as it can go, that you've explored everything, that you've gifted all you can gift, that you've fully expressed and exhausted your potentials, that you've nothing more to do together in the world, that your growth is no longer served by remaining together. Spiritual partners stay together as long as they grow together."

"Okay," he acknowledged.

"If you have lived with the idea that you have to stay together 'until death do you part', a separation might be traumatic, full of guilt, sense of failure, or rejection; whereas, if you've lived from the perspective of soul, recognising that your relationship is, in the larger context of your existence, always a purely temporary one, you can more easily accept that it has come to an end."

"How's that?" he asked, inviting me to elaborate.

"The key is not to be attached to the outer form. Then the love you share can be forever. You can even separate lovingly, thanking and blessing the other, especially when you know that in honouring your truth you are also serving the truth in another."

"I don't think you can do that fully, sincerely, if you haven't come to the realisation that there's no such thing as a victim, that there is therefore never anyone to blame," he replied. "Only then can you really release the other lovingly, thanking them for everything."

"Now numbers nine and ten are missing," I realised. "So I'd like to add another, to emphasize the importance of one's relationship with one's Self."

"Great."

"So, number nine is: *Acknowledge that your primary obligation is neither to the other nor the relationship, but to your Self.*

"Yes, though that could easily be misunderstood," said Roderic, "and be taken as a recipe for ego-selfishness. But I know what you mean: Your self as a soul or higher self."

"Yes. Your primary responsibility is to your own growth, awakening and healing, to honouring your own truth, uniqueness and creativity."

"It's crucial," he added, "that you don't neglect your own path in favour of another's, or you'll end up disempowering your Self, as often happens in a relationship."

"But also, I want to emphasize, that you can't have a happy, healthy and fulfilling relationship with someone else if the one with your Self isn't right. Love of Self is the essential foundation."

"Absolutely spot on!

"Then I'll add it."

"So now you have nine, instead of ten," he noted, as we strolled out the courtyard to the tree-lined avenue. "Do you have another? Ten is the number of completion and fulfilment."

"No," I replied, after reflection. "Have you any ideas?"

"Yes. Sex. You've made no mention of it. Possibly it's the most confused area of all, around which there's the greatest ignorance."

"So what would you add? What guideline?"

"More an instruction," he countered. "Revolutionize your approach to sex. Accept you know almost nothing about the subject, though you may be full of desire and certainly have a penis or vagina."

I laughed.

"Realize that the way in which you're functioning sexually is extremely limited. Resolve to become educated. Familiarize yourself with some basic concepts. Cease seeking a merely genital orgasm. Go for something better. Stop ejaculating. Know why it depletes you, why it's debilitating. Learn to direct your sexual energy inwards, upwards, and throughout your body. Learn how to transform it. Seek higher orgasm. Know you'll be rewarded, as pleasure becomes joy, joy becomes ecstasy, and ecstasy becomes bliss. Yes, become educated. Study the principles of Tantric sex or the wisdoms of a Taoist master. Buy books on the subjects. Attend a workshop. Seek out your master. Or a lover priestess! Take yourself through a crash course. Make sex an adventure in love and discovery, open-ended, no longer finite. Resolve to intensify your feeling attentions. Expand your awareness. Open the doors to deeper communion, a love communion with Divine Reality. Make your unions truly cosmic."

I was impressed by his flow, which came out in a breath.

"How would you reduce this to one or two sentences?" I asked.

"Revolutionize your approach to sex. Play with it. Engage in it as a sophisticated art. Understand it as a path to enlightenment."

So this became my number ten.

Roderic

We walked back to the castle.

"A great list," I said as I put an arm around her. "When shall we start practising it?!"

241

Elly

I gazed through a trellised window of our castle bedroom at the meadows far below. Cows and horses were grazing peacefully. A mist was sweeping in from the ocean. Irish weather, ever changing!

Roderic opened a bottle of champagne. We returned to bed.

I picked up my book of Rumi. One passage struck me in particular: "True love exists beyond the people we love."

That's interesting, I thought, pausing to reflect.

"Listen to this," I urged Roderic and read the text aloud:

"Our bodies, our minds, and even our souls are the abodes of love, not love itself. Love exists everywhere around us and permeates everything – it is the treasure of this world, and by its very essence it cannot be kept captive inside our own coffers. True love exists beyond the people we love. When we understand this, the expectations we place on others diminish. We are loved by existence itself, and so we don't need to feel rejected or hurt when a partner or friend isn't able to love us the way we wish. When our feelings depend on no one we have attained a high state of realization – our love is our own, our happiness is our own; we are responsible for the way we feel and there is no longer any need to ask others to provide us with these states. Link your spirit to love itself," Rumi says, "open your heart to existence, choose love as your spiritual journey and you will never be disappointed in humans."

"That's it!" I exclaimed: "Bring your self into a state of love, independent of anything or anyone."

"Very wise and beautiful," Roderic commented, snuggling into my arms. "Read it again."

Chapter 22

Cosmic Birthing

Seven Years Later

Elly

I had never expected that a romantic relationship could continue being so loving, joyful, magical and exciting. After our many years together, nine to date, I am amazed by this. Neither of us has lived with anyone for such a length of time. Each day feels likes a new adventure even when little is happening on the outside, possibly because so much is happening on the inside, as our relationship continues to grow, deepen and expand. To share life with a companion and be able to explore and express all aspects of my being, shadow side included, living my truth openly on all levels, and still be loved and adored, is a wonderful experience. I feel greatly blessed.

Roderic

So she is! So am I! To live in love, joy and playfulness on a joint adventure, while being so fully and unconditionally supported – what more could one wish for?

This doesn't mean there haven't been any hick-cups. If any arise, we have our ways of resolving them, which we do in the moment they arise. Thereby mole hills do not become mountains. We also have our Ten Golden Precepts which reduce the likelihood of their arising in the first place.

Elly

The most challenging situation so far, which proved beyond my ability to resolve instantly, related to my desire to have a baby. I had longed for one. Roderic, too, thought this would be great.

Shortly after we had begun translating our passions into seed-sowing ceremonies, I had a dream of the most beautiful, peaceful, wise little being, snuggling up beside me, who introduced herself as Crystal. The following morning, when I went to the beach, descending my usual path through the grass, a glistening stone caught my attention the moment my feet touched the sand. Picking it up, I saw it was a crystal, clustered, pointed and six-sided. In hundreds of days of walks to the beach, I had never come across one. When I was over my initial surprise, I asked myself how it was possible that a young being had appeared to me during the night giving her name as Crystal and I had found one at my feet the following day. Maybe she was our child-to-be? Maybe she was letting us know of her impending arrival? I was thrilled and rushed home to show it to Roderic.

Roderic

I shared her delight and was equally curious about the synchronicity.

The idea that a being may already be in existence even before it is conceived is seldom considered. For me it's a certainty, since, years ago, when I was on business in the Far East, I had the most vivid experience in which I remembered dialoguing with the souls of my parents before I was even conceived. It was more than a memory. In a flash of soul-awakening I re-lived the moment in my awareness with utmost clarity. We were discussing the mutual benefits for the growth of our souls, of their being my parents and I their son. So was Crystal preparing us for her arrival?

Elly

Thereafter she began appearing in my dreams quite often, at different ages. In one, I was pregnant and could see her transparently in my womb. I was overwhelmed by the thought of a soul coming into my body in the creation of new life; as well as by the prospect of becoming a mother. Her presence became so real I began buying little items for her. But months passed and there was still no sign of her arrival. I became increasingly disappointed and began blaming Roderic. While welcoming the idea of a child, I didn't feel he was cooperating as much as he could be, and should be, sowing his seeds frequently enough during my times of maximum fertility. Dragging him into bed with a now or never approach turned him off completely. "It's all too planned," he would say. Demands and expectations closed his doors, as I knew so well. More than frustrated, I became desperate and angry; which is not the best state in which to invite a child. Would it ever happen? I wondered.

"Trust," Roderic would say, "and allow the magic."

I realized I was still trying to control life, effectively planning the magic out of it. What a challenge to trust and let go of something you desire so much, particularly when your biological clock is ticking. While his view was that if things weren't happening magically we were not working in attunement with the Universe, mine was, "Fuck the magic, just fuck me!"

"Obligatory love-making is not much fun!" he commented, responding to my increasingly less subtle pressures. "And a bed is so commonplace! Let Crystal be conceived in nature under the sun or moon and stars! Not under a light bulb!"

So, one day, we decided to go on a trip.

"Let us be guided to the right place," we requested as we headed west along the Kerry coast.

"Shall we stop and explore this beach?" Roderic suggested as we drove along a winding road on the Iveragh Peninsula. It was deserted and seemed like an ideal spot.

Shiny pearly oyster-shells lay scattered on sand and seaweed. While collecting the most beautiful of these, I found another crystal. My heart jumped for joy. Surely it was telling us we had found the right place?

Clouds were packing and racing. A storm was brewing. A dark rain-belt was moving towards us across the ocean, closing the gaps where the sun's rays beamed their light. The setting was spectacular. This was the moment it seemed to both of us. There was no time for beach mats; soon we'd be drenched. We found a large rock flat and rounded. As we embraced against it, an otter scurried out of the water across the sand. Otter was my female totem, symbolizing motherhood and playfulness. While Roderic poured his seeds into me, the heavens poured its drops onto us. As we rushed to the car to avoid the deluge, a large double rainbow appeared. Altogether a dramatic and auspicious event, certainly more romantic than a bed, and most assuring, for the Universe had given us signs in abundance. Crystal must definitely be on her way now, we thought.

Roderic

But several more months passed and there was still no sign of her. We were mystified. Had we misread the signs?

Elly

Her non-arrival was particularly perplexing since many of my Reiki students, clients, therapists and friends were picking up 'baby' unprompted in my energy-field. Was this simply because my mind was so focused on the subject or was the soul of Crystal actually around me?

"There is definitely a soul around you," a professional psychic friend assured me.

When I consulted the runes, I was given a picture of myself standing before a gate, waiting, because I had to learn the art of waiting. "That's a bit stiff," I thought, "I've been waiting for months. How much longer?"

I also had to do some inner work before I could pass through the gate, they suggested. Reflecting on this, I realized I had to effect a change of consciousness. From being mummy's little girl, as I still was to some extent, I had to become the mummy of a little girl. A five-rhythms dance-workshop I attended in Dublin helped me make this transition energetically. Leaving the consciousness of little girl behind, I danced myself into motherhood.

Some time later, we went on a holiday in France. We spent six weeks in a campervan following pilgrim routes and visiting ancient sites linked with Mary Magdalene, the Cathars and Templars, going with the flow, following our guidance. Far from light bulbs and well out in nature, we made love in the most wonderful places, in Merlin's Forest of Broceliande, on an open-air altar beside a holy well at La Chapelle de la Madelaine near the megalithic stones of Carnac, in a meadow at Vézelay beneath the towering Cross of Saint Bernard of Clairvaux, on a perfumed bed of wild thyme as we clambered up a mountain to Magdalene's Cave, on the banks of a river in the marshes of the Camargue, by a stream at the Fountain of Lovers at Rennes-les-Bains, in a pasture of wild narcissus high up in the Pyrenees, even under the eyes and sword of the Archangel Michael at Mont Saint-Michel … but still no baby!

Along the way, we had paid our respects to various Black Madonnas, most memorably at Le Puy, where I felt her presence powerfully, at Les Saint-Maries de la Mer in Provence, and at the magnificent mountain retreat of Montserrat in Spain; and whenever I asked for insights on the arrival of Crystal, I got the same simple sentence, "All is well." Was this another message to trust, not to force events or be attached to any outcome? Very challenging!

Roderic

Eventually, after our return to Ireland, we decided to have medical tests. From my own point of view I would not have bothered, believing that if Crystal was on her way, she would arrive; that it was a soul matter which didn't need forcing. But, as Elly wanted clarity on the physical aspects, I was happy to go along with this.

Elly

After Roderic was found to be fertile, the next steps were up to me.

I consulted my doctor, who asked me discouragingly, though realistically no doubt, "Do you really want to go through all of this?"

Mustering up the courage, I decided yes.

It is not necessary to go into the details here, but simply to say that every time I took the practical steps in going down this road obstacles appeared, blocking the way, as if my guidance was telling me that this was not for me. Finally, after months of waiting, miscommunications and lost letters, I was invited for a check-up in a maternity hospital in Cork. But the date was fixed during the two weeks we had booked to go camel-riding in the Sahara Desert, the only time we had planned being away during the year. Clearly a coincidence; but was it also a sign? In any event, it was the final straw – the one that broke the camel's back! – which led us to seriously consider the possibility that having a child was not to be.

It was the beginning of a process of gradual acceptance. At times, I cried my eyes out, feeling a deep pain in my heart for not having my own little baby and family. The longing to hold a tiny bundle of joy in my arms was overwhelming. It would be so lovely to go through the process of pregnancy and birth together with my beloved; and to love and nurture a precious soul while guiding it through its first steps in life. I was exhausted by the whole process. Not to mention Roderic! The continuing monthly cycles of rising hopes and expectations followed by their subsequent crashing every time I got my period had been unsettling, physically and emotionally. It had also put a strain on our relationship. At the same time, strangely, somewhere deep down inside, I felt that the non-arrival of a child was the right outcome, that my soul had not chosen to have a primary focus on a personal family this time around. The more I tuned into this feeling, the more I sensed I would be involved with a more extended family; and I was at peace with this, though I had no idea what form it might take. Here again I realized what a vast difference there was between an emotional response to a situation from a limited personality perspective and that of one's soul coming from a higher level of awareness. It was peace or turmoil. I oscillated between both. I knew I could be at peace at all times when I succeeded in bringing the two together; but I had not found a way yet. How do you do it when the desire to give birth and experience motherhood is so much a part of your feminine make-up? Not giving expression to it feels like denying an essential part of your self. No doubt, if we hadn't received so many signs I could have accepted the situation much earlier. We wondered about these and the insights and feedback we had received from others. Maybe there was a meaning to them we hadn't grasped yet? Maybe there is a soul waiting to incarnate and be with me but she doesn't necessarily have to be birthed through me?

"Maybe it's your own soul, seeking to come more fully into incarnation?" Roderic suggested.

"Could be." I had often had the feeling that a large part of me was hovering above my head waiting to come in. A couple of days later, my osteopath, who had been helping me become pregnant, suggested the same thing.

Roderic

One day on our way to Sneem, we stopped at our traditional watering hole, the Strawberry Field Cottage, with its irresistible

248

tongue-curling pancakes. While I ordered our usual, Elly went to the toilet. On emerging, she said, "I've got my period."

"Maybe, after all, it's a blessing," I suggested, the idea coming to me in a flash.

"Amazing you say that," she replied, "as it's just what I got."

Independently we had both got the word 'blessing'. "Maybe it's a sign, signalling a completion and telling us it's time to move on."

"I wonder what the urge to give birth is really all about?" I pondered aloud, wanting to go deep in understanding the phenomenon. "Is it just a basic animal instinct, a programming by life to ensure the continuity of the species?"

"With billions of people already on our planet, propagation of the human species is surely a minor concern at this time," said Elly.

"That's true. Perhaps it's for personal reasons, then? Maybe having a child gives life a sense of meaning and purpose."

"That's for sure. So maybe it's to fill a hole in oneself?"

"Or in one's relationship?"

"They could both be major reasons."

"They are both out of neediness," Elly observed.

"It could also be to make sure one is taken care of in later life, as in underdeveloped countries without social services," I suggested.

"Again out of neediness."

"There could be so many reasons! Even the ego's desire, illusionary of course, for the perpetuation of its mortal self."

Elly

That struck a note. Once, during a ritual on a beach in Holland at a woman's dance workshop we were asked to visualize our ancestral line of mothers, grandmothers, great grandmothers and so forth standing behind us; and then to see the line extending onwards into the future through our daughters and daughter's daughters; and I realized that my line would stop with me. It was an awful feeling seeing myself as the dead end of a millennia-long sequence which could be traced back to stardust and the beginning of Time. "Was this my ego?" I'd wondered. But happily my soul lineage goes on for ever, I realized later.

"Maybe, more positively, the longing to give birth is a natural expression of one's love for each other?" I suggested before drawing in a sniff of the scintillating scent of lemon basil which had just arrived on my yummy pancake.

"To bring into being an offspring that is half you and half me is such a miracle of creation," I added.

"Absolutely."

"I wonder what it would have looked like?"

"Stunningly beautiful!"

"A mischievous angel! ..."

"On the other hand," I pointed out, "I know several women who have had no desire for a partner but a desperate desire for a child."

"So do I," said Roderic. "This shows that the desire to give birth may be looked at on its own. In fact, nature illustrates just how irrelevant a partner can be. Think of those unfortunate males who get eaten by their mates immediately after they've sown their seeds."

"How cruel!"

"Typically ruthless females, I'd say!"

"Maybe the underlying motive in giving birth is to experience unconditional love? Love for your child seems so limitless and selfless."

"In nature we also see examples of this, extreme ones, with mothers of a species who, in an act of ultimate self-sacrifice, even allow themselves to be devoured by their offspring," said Roderic.

"Yet unconditional love can be expressed at anytime towards anyone," I proposed tentatively. I remembered the time I found a goldfinch lying injured on the side of a road. When I picked it up, it snuggled up in the warmth of my hand, and surrendered so trustfully, to die peacefully. The flow of love through me was so overwhelming I couldn't imagine anything greater even towards my own offspring. It's the same when I connect with the essence of a flower or a tree. So it's not only a child which offers opportunities for unconditional loving. It can be anyone or anything when one's heart is open.

Roderic

"Maybe the urge to give birth *is* more than just an animal instinct? Maybe we have to go deeper?" I proposed later, as we sped on through the rugged now-treeless landscape. "Maybe it's part of our divine nature?"

"What do you mean by that?"

"Well, we're more than just animals. We have a dual nature, being both body *and* soul, as you know. Though we've emerged from the Earth, we are also sparks of the Divine, whose origins are elsewhere. So there must also be a cosmic dimension to the impulses which arise from our innermost depths. Wouldn't you say?"

"Yep. Never thought of it like that."

"So, being expressions of the Divine, the impulses which move *us* must have something in common with those which gave birth to the universe in the first place."

Elly

That was a stunning realization.

But it left the question, "What is the nature of these impulses?"

I had already acquired insights on this while reading Roderic's recent book, *Pre-Creation*, which I had been editing and in which he puts the question to the Creator, "What were the reasons, needs, urges or impulses which moved You into creating?" and receives the reply:

> *"My nature being Love, My need is to express that Love.*
> *"My nature being Joy, My need is to express that Joy.*
> *"My nature being Infinite Potentiality, My need is to explore and give expression to Infinite Potentiality: Infinite Potentiality seeking Infinite Actualisation!*
> *"My nature being Infinite Creativity, My need is to explore and give expression to this.*
> *"My need is to express and experience My Self and in doing so to explore all possibilities.*
> *"Any creator, any lover, any child, any Being with Life in it, understands this. To love, to create, to play, to know and enjoy the fullness of Being – it is all very simple."*

251

It really did seem all that simple!

So, being sparks of the One Divine in our innermost nature, *our* desire to give birth must also be the desire to love, create, play, explore and enjoy the fullness of being. What a realization! I'd found the passage so clarifying and inspiring that I'd read it over and over again.

Later it dawned on me that the birthing impulse relates not only to babies but to conceiving and bringing into being anything from a work of art to a new civilization, for it is the very same impulse that gave birth to the universe.

Roderic

It's amazing the insights we acquire when we shift from the idea that the Divine is exclusively "out there somewhere" to the fact that "It" also resides within our own beings; that there is no separation.

Elly

So, if a child was not meant to be, what had my recent experiences been about? I wondered.

One morning I woke up with the understanding of why I had to go through such a prolonged physical and emotional process of yearning for one and being disappointed by not becoming pregnant. Every time this happened it intensified my desire to create, love and nurture; and also, thereby, my feelings of motherhood and parenting, drawing forth an increasing willingness for selfless service.

Selfless service?! What a challenging subject! At least, that's how I found it. That we are here to serve life and do so joyfully was not something I would have embraced so fully if my desire for a child had not arisen, serving being such a mega-quality of motherhood. I'd had such a huge resistance to the idea; and the expectation of motherhood had opened my heart and soul and dissolved it.

The shift from demanding that life serves you to accepting the idea that you are here to serve it is a major one. It's an initiation, a moving to another level of being, one more in harmony with one's divine nature. In other words, a movement from ego to soul. Now, in honouring my divine nature, I can give expression to motherhood and parenting in a more extended way. My natural female impulses can be directed into the nurturing, empowering and awakening of anybody, not just my own biological offspring.

Roderic

With these realizations and having built a strong foundation of love, common aspirations and mutual understanding, it was time to expand our bubble of love to include more of the world. It was time to go beyond the idea of a personal family unit to embrace the larger concepts of "One Family of Humanity living on One Planet" – or, better still "One Family of All Living Creatures" – and serving this. Outward-pointing, as we state in our Ten Golden Precepts, is essential for the health of a relationship, while a love turned inwards consumes itself, burning out eventually. To thrive and grow, it needs to be directed towards something larger than itself. Maybe the primary reason soul mates come together *is* for the purpose of serving life?

Elly

Yes, I'm convinced. Everyone should have a dream, – preferably a big dream – one that presents a challenge in which one can express one's creativity and potentials to the fullest, taking one beyond one's comfort zones, stretching one to one's limits – a dream that makes a difference in the world. Ideally, in a Spiritual Partnership, you have a shared dream in which your love, energies, talents and other resources are joined and pointing in the same direction …

Roderic

… thereby creating a Power of Two, a mighty force!

Elly

We have a big dream. Sometimes, I've wondered if it was too big. Life would be so much easier, it seemed, if I could just cultivate my garden, do my "reduce, re-use, re-cycle" bit, give the occasional workshop, play some tennis, and sun myself in exotic places once in a while, living happily ever afterwards. But it didn't take long for me to realize that that would not bring me the fulfilment I sought. So I knew I had to go for it whatever it would take.

The importance of doing so was brought home to me one evening as we were watching the golden-oldie movie *Flash Dance* when the lover says to his beloved, a young aspiring dancer, who was thinking of quitting because entrance to the city's elitist dance-school seemed so difficult: "Give up your dream and you'll die." It was so dramatically illustrated, it really hit me. Yes, it's so true: Give up your dream and you die.

Roderic

Our big dream is to set up a new type of university.

That may seem ridiculously ambitious, since neither of us has been anywhere near one. But that's how it is! It's called *University of Earth & Spirit* and is based on the Four Pillars, Earth, Spirit, Soul, and Cosmos, with Co-Creativity as a primary feature.

One of the main reasons for the mess in which we find ourselves, whether as individuals or as a civilisation, is our disconnectedness from these core features in all spheres of life. Indeed, it may be considered the root cause of all our problems.

In our disconnectedness from the Earth, we have lost our awareness of the processes of Nature and the recognition of its sacredness. We have also become disconnected from the Intelligences at work within Nature to such an extent that we not only ignore but deny their existence.

In our disconnection from the Cosmos, a multidimensional phenomenon of both inner and outer realms, we have done the same.

In our disconnection from Others, we live in fear, hate, conflict, or indifference, thus lovelessly and often painfully.

In the disconnection within Our Selves lies the primary cause of all our disconnectedness. While our minds, hearts and bodies are substantially disconnected from each other, even more seriously we have become disconnected from Our Innermost Selves, our Souls or Higher Selves.

In our disconnectedness from Spirit *within our own beings* we have cut ourselves off from the Primary Source of nourishment, love, wisdom, joy, inspiration, guidance, power, healing and creativity. As a result, we experience existential *angst*, sense of futility, depression, despair, all manner of confusion, insecurities, aimlessness, helplessness, hopelessness, aloneness and resignation. And, to whatever extent we are disconnected, we remain undernourished, disempowered, and out of alignment with our unique potentialities and higher purposes, the recognition and honouring of which would make our lives vastly more meaningful and fulfilling.

With all these disconnections we have become thoroughly dysfunctional, a danger to ourselves as well as to others, a danger indeed to the whole of life on this planet.

It is therefore vital, as we see it, to bring these core features to the forefront of education, enabling us to operate from a state of optimum connectedness.

While Co-Creativity involves working consciously with one's Soul or Higher Self, it also includes the recognition that we are not alone as humans on this planet and can open lines of communication leading to collaborations with other Intelligences within Nature and the Cosmos, enabling us to function in a vastly more effective and enlightened way.

Elly

While Roderic had been working on preparations for the setting up of the university over the last fifteen years – "on and off", as he'd say – evolving its concepts and producing its foundation documents, we had been working together on it for the past few years. We had already held our first year-long Mastership Training Programme as a pilot project on behalf of the *Faculty of Soul Science & The Laws of Life* and been developing modules for Teacher Training Intensives as well as On-line Courses.

Now that I had released the idea of a child, I could fully engage with the University in its birthing and grounding processes. It was a huge relief that the period of uncertainty was finally over, that I was at peace with the outcome, and could move on passionately.

At the same time, with Roderic being so clear on his role, I had to find what was uniquely my own. I had spent much time, initially, assisting him with books relating to the launching of various Faculties. I had been editing his two works, *Pre-Creation* and *The Story of Creation*, both subtitled *From the Creator's Perspective*, on behalf of the *Faculty of Philosophy & the Cosmology of Human*

Evolution. I had been doing the same with his trilogy on the theme, *Going Way Beyond Darwin*, including its three titles, *Kiss Goodbye to Darwin*, *Dawkins & The Great Delusions of Blind Evolution*, followed by *The Theory of Involution* and *Intelligent Evolution*, which he was preparing for publication to coincide with the bicentenary of Darwin's birth and the hundred and fiftieth anniversary of his *Origin of Species*, also on behalf of the same Faculty.

I had also been assisting him in the editing of *Gospel of the Living Tree*, subtitled *For Mystics, Lovers, Poets & Warriors*, a beautiful, poetic and profound work on the role of trees in human consciousness and culture, with an introduction to our *Faculty of the Living Tree*.

While I loved doing all this, exercising my critical faculties, I also needed to be sounding my own notes in well-defined ways.

While Roderic's focus was on articulating the concepts of the University, writing its foundation documents, and making practical preparations for its grounding in the world, mine related more to its inner foundations. My specialty, I feel, is in bridging inner and outer realms, visible and invisible, material and spiritual, which I see as part of the archetypal role of the Priestess. I like to do this by leading people through actual experiences, as I have been doing for years with Reiki initiations and guided meditations, but now wished to do in more extensive ways. I feel able to do so because I have been deepening my connection with my soul and the Divine, assisted by various simple but powerful practices, over recent years. These include the Soul Mantram given by the Tibetan Master Djwhal Khul and the Antakarana or "Rainbow Bridge" meditation techniques developed by two of his disciples, which, together, invoke the soul and promote its fusion with the personality – practices which I have found fascinating and very effective. They should be taught in every school around the globe; and will certainly be included in our courses.

Others in which I continue to be engaged involve cultivation of the awareness of "The Living Presence", otherwise known as the "I AM Presence", within my own being. I had been kick-started in this during our campervan pilgrimage around France after visiting a Brazilian wisdom-teacher-alchemist in the Pyrenees. She had lent us two of her most precious books on the subject of the "I AM",

Unveiled Mysteries and *The Magic Presence*, written by Guy Ballard (under the name Godfré Ray King) who had received his information from the Ascended Master Saint Germain on Mount Shasta in California in the 1930s. We had been riveted by their contents and, in the year which followed, had devoured all eighteen volumes. Then, out of the blue, I was invited by one of my students to accompany her on an all-expenses-paid journey to Mount Shasta where she wanted to be initiated into Reiki Mastership. It was a great gift which enabled me to visit locations connected with Guy Ballard's experiences where, by acts of Grace, I too had revelations and divine encounters.

Back home, Roderic and I had our own communications with Saint Germain; and, after several of these, we invited him to work with us.

Roderic

With Co-Creativity being one of the primary features of the University, we had begun setting up what we call our Cosmic Team, consisting of various Beings of Light, including Ascended Masters, Angels, Archangels, Nature Spirits, along with representatives from Alcyone in the star system of the Pleiades.

This may sound strange but we spent days "interviewing" them – tuning in vibrationally, clarifying their specific input and tasks in relation to the unfolding of the University and the everyday functioning of its various Faculties. Who had actually invited whom onto the Team was not always clear, since some of its members had already presented themselves wholly unexpectedly, as Arjuna to Elly, as she has already related.

One of the first to pop in to my own life was Thoth:

One day, a decade or so ago, when I was sitting in my office in Somerset, England, I had stopped for a few minutes of relaxation and was lazily meditating with my eyes closed when suddenly the words "I am Thoth" resounded in my head. At the same time, the image of a man presented itself, one with a face from which a snipe-like beak protruded. Three times the words "I am Thoth" were uttered, with a pause in between each. "Who the hell are you?" I wondered, astonished. I had never heard such a peculiarly sounding name nor read of such a mythic figure.

257

Immediately afterwards, I went next door to consult a historian and literary scholar. "Thoth was an Egyptian god," she informed me, "generally featured with the beak of an ibis. He was known as a Master of Wisdom and The Lord of the Word of the Gods."

Since then, I learned a great deal about him. Before he was an Egyptian, he was an Atlantean. He had brought knowledge from this highly advanced civilisation to the early primitive Egyptians before it disappeared into the ocean. He had initiated the building of the Pyramids, so it is believed. He is also acknowledged as the inventor of hieroglyphics and as the author of *The Emerald Tablets*, more often attributed to Hermes, one of his later incarnations.

I had no idea why such a mighty being had presented himself and it took a few years and more encounters before I came to any clarity on the subject, during which time the beginnings of a working relationship had developed. From an inspiring influence he has become my personal mentor as well as a member of our Initiating Core Group.

This, other than Elly and I, consists of three members of our Cosmic Team: Thoth for his energetic commitment to the promotion of Wisdom and Higher Knowledge and the flow of "the Word into the world"; Sophia, representing the Cosmic Feminine; and Saint Germain for his intimate knowledge of the Laws of Life as well as his alchemical wizardry in manifesting.

Elly
It is priceless being able to ask for and receive assistance by way of inspiration, insights and clarity from Other Intelligences, knowing that we are acting in the realization of a joint project. While working intuitively with our Team, which includes a wide range of inner processes, we also use kinesiology in checking the feedback we receive.

Roderic
In working co-creatively in this way, we know that we are involved like many others in a new way of working for humanity – new in our time at least, for such a way has always existed, though long forgotten. We were merely *re*-discovering and *re*-introducing it. We

were excited by the possibilities and resolved to exploring it as fully as possible in everyday practical contexts.

Elly

I was also excited as we began moving into an outer worldly process.

One of the first events on the ground was a gift of four acres of wild nature, hillside and woodlands in County Kerry, by Roderic's sister Coral. It was here where we'd spent our first days together; and we visited it often. It took us several months before we realized that it could have anything to do with the University. I loved this plot of land with its stunning views of bays, islands, mountains and ocean, woodlands, and intimate womb-like valleys. The charming grass-roofed Round House was still standing, though a little wobbly on its legs. The woodlands were overgrown, throttled by rhododendrons and needed clearing. It would be ideal as a location for our *Faculty of Forest Gardening*, we thought, and imagined it being developed as a demonstration edible landscape rich in crop-bearing trees and shrubs.

Roderic

Thinking about the site prompted us to come to clarity on where the University and its various faculties *would* actually be located. The first thing we were clear about was that there wasn't going to be one purpose-built mega site where everything was situated. We didn't want to impose our visions on the Earth with massive building projects and the concreting over of yet more land, the traditional male-dominated approach to what is called "development", which has resulted in so much damage to Nature and communities around the world. We planned on using existing facilities as much as possible, building eco-friendly dwellings, and even using temporary ones such as yurts, allowing more intimacy of connectedness with Nature.

We had thought that the ideal location for an initial base would be a country estate with a hundred or so acres of woods and fields and a large Georgian house perhaps, with a walled garden. When we tuned into our Team, we received no confirmation of this. Maybe there was a step before it? We also received the insight that how we went about setting up the University was as important as the University itself. Rather than working from the top down, the intention was to work organically from the ground up, following the Path of the Seed. While more in harmony with Nature it is also a more balanced male-female approach, beginning with the fertilization, followed by the sowing and germinating, continuing with the sprouting, nourishing, unfolding and blossoming.

Elly

When we asked our Team for clarity on the seeding process, I received the image of an Oak, which I recognized as being one that stood in a glade on our land. I had a great love for this particular tree. It had always impressed me with its regal presence, though I wondered whether this was kingly or queenly. While it has a strong male quality which stands out noticeably against the delicately shimmering, obviously feminine Silver Birch, it also has distinctly motherly qualities which it demonstrates in providing shelter and sustenance for hundreds of species. For me it's the guardian of its grove.

So was this the site for the seeding of the University?

When I shared the idea with Roderic he smiled, remembering his own experiences under the same tree years earlier. "I had always imagined a centre of learning that would spread out from under it," he declared. "I had a vision of sitting under it, spouting wisdoms to earnest seekers assembled on the woodland floor. Actually, it has already happened like this. It has already been a seeding-ground where, over seven years, while giving birth and expression to KOAD, our Centre for Nature Research and Education, the larger concepts of a University of Earth and Spirit have been germinating. Yes, the Oak is a really appropriate symbol," he enthused. "The University is like an acorn, small yet embodying the blueprint of a mature tree in its complexity and vastness, with the potential to grow into a mighty organism."

"So, is this also where it is to be founded?" we asked our Team, as it seemed unlikely for so many reasons, being so small, having no facilities other than the Round House, a shed, an overgrown ruined stone cottage, and woodlands of almost impenetrable undergrowth.

260

We received a hesitant confirmation which needed further clarification. Questioning further we came to understand that its primary functions would be on an inner level, in which it would continue being a place of germination and initiation.

We spent days exploring the site, feeling into its different energies and opening dialogues with members of the Devic Kingdom overlighting it, including Pan, personification of the Spirit of Nature. We declared our intentions, including our willingness to work in harmony with them, asked their permissions, invited their cooperation, indeed their creative input, and listened for their responses. I delighted in the feeling of being a custodian of such a beautiful patch of Planet Earth.

"It needs a name," said Roderic, who later came up with the Grove of Akademus, which I liked, and the Team agreed.

One drizzling St Patrick's Day, we began clearing the choked up area around the Oak to let it breathe and shine forth its beauty. It was such a happy feeling, so much fun, and so rewarding. All the cells of my body jubilantly informed me that I was doing the right thing. I felt so at home.

We spent a whole week immersed in the woods clearing the rhododendrons whose growth is otherwise unstoppable and all-devouring. We sawed their branches, stripped away their twigs and leaves, preserving long straight poles for future use; and made spectacular bonfires from the residue mixed with gorse and brambles. I enjoyed watching the smoke wafting up through the dangling leaves of Silver Birch mingling with the sun's rays in a dazzling dance of light.

Roderic

Back at the Blue House, though we still lived like hermits, we found ourselves being connected up with people from various parts of the world with whom it was clear we would have working relationships. Some had specialized skills. Others ran or were linked with centres in Spain, France, Egypt, Brazil, Canada and Australia. We even had three ladies from an esoteric school in Moscow arriving on our doorstep, who were really keen to work with us. Who was organizing this? We seemed to be involved in a process in which we were as much the observers as the doers.

While *we* held the clear intentions, others, our Team, weaved the network and worked the magic. It was a cosmic process.

Elly

One afternoon, I planted three young Myrtle trees on our land. As I was welcoming them a robin arrived. It then proceeded to hop around the trees, making a full circle around each as if performing a ritual. At the same time, the sweetest sound of a flute echoed through the woods, which I had never heard before and have never heard since. When the robin had completed its rounds, the music stopped. Where had it come from? I had no idea.

"Maybe it was Pan playing his pipes," Roderic suggested, his eyes lighting up with a sparkle. "He is famous for it."

I did think it remarkable that there was such a synchronicity and precision of timing in the robin's little ritual, the melody starting with its first hop and ending with its last. If there had been anyone else piping in the woods, surely he or she would have gone on playing? Maybe it was Nature's way of letting us know that we were welcome? Maybe in the lifting of her veils she was signalling her willingness to work with us?

Roderic

Once we had accepted that the Grove of Akademus had a continuing role to play in the unfolding of the University, we started to visualize what forms this might take. One of the first things we recognized was the special character of the land as an area of wild nature which would not be compatible with hordes of people streaming through it. Rather than a campus, it was more of a retreat. When we asked our Team for further clarity and inspiration, we came to understand that its primary function was as a womb for birthing, a Nature-based Inner Sanctum out of which various aspects of the University would unfold. There was also plenty of land around us for this. It was clear that the unfolding was to be a step-by-step process. So all we had to do at this moment in time was focus on the immediate next steps, trusting that all would unfold in perfect timing.

Elly

We felt that one of the next steps was re-creating the Round House. Apart from its romantic associations it was a place with a very special energy. A friend of a friend of ours who had never visited the site had seen it in a vision with a column of light rising through it and radiating all around. It would be ideal as a sanctuary, a "Holy of Holies", a place for in-depth connecting with Earth, Spirit, Soul and Cosmos.

Staying in it one night, I had another dream of being pregnant. The following day, Roderic found a crystal in the earth nearby. This time, we knew it was not about the birthing of a child, but our university. After nine years of pregnancy, the waters were breaking!

It would of course be a home birth!

Ten Golden Precepts
For a Spiritual Partnership

1. Agree that you are two souls on a journey through Time who meet as equals.

2. Acknowledge that your primary obligation is neither to the other nor to the relationship, but to your Self. Love of Self is paramount.

3. Decide that your priority is spiritual growth. Do so because it is your joy and passion.

4. Take full responsibility for all aspects of your life, knowing that you are the cause of what you experience rather than the victim.

5. Don't expect another to meet your needs – whether physical, emotional, mental or spiritual. Rather, be as aware of the needs of the other and respond to them as if they were your own.

6. Give loving acceptance to all aspects of your partner, including those that would otherwise irritate you, but excluding what is clearly abuse.

7. Speak up your truth and do so with love.

8. Direct your love, wisdom and creativity beyond the relationship.

9. Accept that the form of the relationship may change.

10. Revolutionize your approach to sex. Play with it. Engage in it as a sophisticated art. Understand it as a path to enlightenment.

Invitations to Readers

♥
How do I Find My Soul Mate?

After reading our story, you may like to find your own soul mate! The first thing you'll probably do is write down the qualities of your ideal partner on all four levels (physical, emotional, mental, spiritual). While that's a great way to start, there's more to the process. To support you we offer workshops and a free online course on how to find your soul mate, through our website.

At **www.cosmic-lovers.org**, you'll find:
- Free downloads
- How to find your soul mate, a free online course
- Preview our other books, including *Wisdoms on Love.*
- Soup and Soul Club: A forum of kindred spirits

♥
Spread the Word and get a Free Poster!

If you have been inspired by this book, please spread the word! Email 5 friends and get a beautiful poster of the **Ten Golden Precepts for a Spiritual Partnership**, free!

Spread the word at: www.cosmic-lovers.org/tell-a-friend.html

♥
What are Your Alternative Approaches to Marriage?

Have you been exploring alternatives to traditional marriage, creating their own agreements, vows and rituals of remembrance and celebration? If so, we'd love to hear from you, as we have been approached by filmmakers wishing to produce a TV documentary on the subject, who are looking for material.

Email us at: stories@cosmic-lovers.org or
submit your story online at: www.cosmic-lovers.org/stories.html

♥
University of Earth & Spirit

Would you like to learn more about University of Earth & Spirit and how you can participate?:

Visit us at: www.UniversityofEarthandSpirit.org

Acknowledgements

We would like to express our heart-felt gratitude to our beloved friends, to Roger Foxall for his inspired sword-wielding editing, while reading so meticulously and caringly through the first draft of our book, as well as for his many invaluable suggestions; to Ann Clare McCarthy for her in-depth reading of the subsequent draft, her sparkling response and beautifully written comments which inspired us greatly; to Charlotte Cargin, our wise, loving and radiantly beautiful soul-sister, who undertook a major final editing providing us with many a profound insight, and who has been firing us with her conviction that the world is waiting for a book like this ever since; to Paula McLinchey, Afric Hamilton, Bernard Bossonet, Sheila Kern and Susan Allen for their time in reading earlier drafts, sharing their unique perspectives and encouraging us along the way; and to our poet-friend Seamus Cashman for giving us the benefit of his life-time experiences as an editor and publisher, along with sound practical advice. We extend special hugs to our dearest friends Joyce Bossonet and Kristin Bonney who played pivotal roles in bringing us together; and a big thank you to our wonderful neighbours who make our seaside valley such a happy, nourishing and inspiring place. We are also immensely grateful to our currently resident wizard, Harper Stone, sent by the Heavens, for his delightful company, artistic flair, and way-beyond-our-grasp computer skills. Elly would like to thank her Dad for being a lovable rock throughout her life. Last but not least, we send a troupe of angels laden with blessings to Roderic's sister Coral for her continuing love, generosity and support over many years.

About the Authors

Elly van Veen, born in Holland, has been active in the healing profession for over twenty years, working as a physiotherapist with children, treating physical and emotional disorders and a variety of learning disabilities, combining conventional and holistic approaches, including edu-kinesiology, Australian Bush Flower Essences and Reiki, for which she received training in Holland, Australia and the USA. On moving to Ireland in 1999, she set up her own practice as a Reiki Master, giving treatments, workshops and courses.

A life-changing experience at the age of thirteen became her wake-up call, which set her on a quest for the truth and meaning of life. Ever since, her journey has been an intense and exciting step-by-step process of inner healing, adventure, discovery, and soul-awakening.

Her heartfelt mission is in 'sounding the note of soul' in all areas of life and in connecting others with their innermost selves. In relation to this, she is actively engaged with her beloved partner, Roderic, in preparations for the setting up of a new type of university, *University of Earth and Spirit*, based on the Four Pillars of Earth, Spirit, Soul and Cosmos. She is also active as a co-founder of *The Soup & Soul Club*, being set up to serve as a local forum for kindred spirits, and simultaneously as a planetary network.

In Cosmic Lovers, her first book, jointly written with Roderic, they explore how a romantic relationship is fundamentally changed and enriched when soul dimensions are at its heart.

Roderic Knowles, brought up in the wilds of the west coast of Ireland and educated at Eton, is a poet, philosopher and passionate tree-lover. After "the best education that money can buy", he felt a deep dissatisfaction, with none of life's fundamental questions addressed. A circuitous path led him through various explorations and adventures around the world, latterly as an international business consultant, running a unique private network which gave him direct access to Prime Ministers, Finance and other Ministers of over a dozen countries; thereafter, after bringing his business to an abrupt halt, he went in search of Masters of Wisdom, with whom he spent several years, seeking to fathom the mysteries of life, while studying Cosmic Laws and undergoing deep transformational processes.

He is the author of several books, *Contemporary Irish Art, How to Rob Banks Without Violence, What the Hell Am I Doing on Planet Earth?, Pre-Creation, The Story of Creation from the Creator's Perspective* (2009), and *Gospel of the Living Tree for Mystics, Lovers, Poets & Warriors* (2009). He is also initiator and co-founder of the *Living Tree Educational Foundation* and the *Earth-Spirit Educational Foundation* whose primary aim is bringing into being a new type of university, *University of Earth & Spirit*.

Celtic Marriage for a Year and a Day?

Readers' Responses

Having both experienced traditional marriage, we decided to have a Celtic Marriage after Elly and Roderic had introduced us to the concept. We both think it is a wonderful way of relating to each other. The concept of a Celtic Marriage allows for **enhanced personal freedom, self-development** and **expression**. The onus is on both parties to keep the relationship working well. If not, it dissolves the next year. For us it has resulted in a **fantastic relationship** that is **based on equality**, **honesty**, **trust** and **respect**; and has **allowed more intimacy** than anything we have experienced before. A Celtic marriage is **a brilliant recipe for a successful marriage in the 21st Century!** Everyone should know about it.

Thank you Elly and Roderic for introducing us to a wonderful way of sharing our lives together.

– Anke & Stewart, Australia

A Celtic Marriage with its annual optional renewal emphasizes that **a commitment between partners is never taken for granted**; but is a **dynamic process**. The ritual of renewal after 'a year and a day' **increases our awareness** of the 'here and now' and at the same time invites us to evaluate our relationship.

Prior to the upcoming renewal date we look for a stone in Nature, one that symbolizes our relationship in this moment in time. We put the stone somewhere where it can function as a receiver, an antenna, to collect and bring to our attention aspects we wish to develop in our relationship.

On the day of renewal and celebration, we paint the stone in a colour that resonates with the feelings at that moment and decorate it with symbols or images which express our desires. And we commit ourselves for another year and a day.

271

This form of relationship allows us much more breathing space than the traditional one with its daunting promise, "Till death do us part."

– Maria & Yvo, Holland

For me, a Celtic Marriage is closely related to the rhythms of Nature. During the time the Earth moves around the Sun, you and your beloved go through all the natural cycles – **withdrawing inwardly, emerging, blossoming** and **releasing**, followed once more by **renewal**. For me, the symbolic day of looking back and looking forward is a beautiful ritualistic framework.

– Pieter van Leeuwen, Holland

The idea of a commitment for life, as in a traditional marriage, made me panic, while no commitment led me to hopping from one relationship to another and an endless repetition of complicated patterns. When Elly told me, ten years ago, about the possibility of a Celtic Marriage, I had the immediate feeling, "Yes, this must be it!"

Now, after eight years of sharing the sweets and bitters of life with Pieter and being a mother of our two sons, seven and three years old, I can say from my own experience, "Yes, **a commitment for a year and a day is the ideal arrangement that allows love and awakening to dance hand in hand.**"

This weekend we renewed our Celtic Marriage once again. We both felt clearly that, in spite of various obstacles, along with occasional thorns and lack of roses, we wanted to prolong our partnership for another year and a day – realizing that there was also work to be done!

Evaluating the year that has passed, we asked ourselves:

- What promises and intentions had we made?
- What had inspired us and nourished us?
- What had been fruitless, frustrating and stagnating?
- Where had our path, our mission lead us?

Out of this came a list of resolutions or "working-items" which would **prevent the same frustrations from happening, unblock the stagnations**, and **support the love and nourishment** we have for each other and our shared mission, while **remaining true to ourselves and our personal paths**.

We concluded with a ritual of confirmation and celebration, and a 'YES' spoken with more conviction than ever for the "year and a day" to come.

– Joyce de Rozario, Holland

About Cosmic Lovers

While *Cosmic Lovers* is first and foremost a **love story**, permeating it are the following themes or core features which give much to the book's originality, power and relevance:

The Soul Factor

In *Cosmic Lovers* soul is at the heart of relationship. **Even in a partnership, the primary relationship is with one's own soul**. Then it is a relationship between two souls who meet as equals. For a relationship to be experienced as deeply fulfilling, our innermost needs, those of soul, must be acknowledged and addressed – **soul, rather than our ego-personality**, being our True Identity. But what are its needs? And even before this: What *is* a soul? While 'soul mate' has become a buzz phrase, what does it mean? **What does it mean to be a soul and to live and love as one?** *Cosmic Lovers* goes to the core of these questions in the context of everyday experiences. When soul perspectives are consciously at the heart of relationships everything changes fundamentally. This lifts the relationshiop to a new level; it becomes a **soul mate relationship** and **spiritual partnership**.

Cosmic Dimensions

Cosmic Lovers gives a **simple yet profound** overview of the whys and hows of Creation and Man's place in it, with Man as Soul, as a Being of Light, arising from the One Source of All and, after billions of years, returning to It.

With this perspective it is clear that we, as souls, are first and foremost *Cosmic Beings* – the whole picture being that **we have a dual nature, consisting of both body *and* soul**. And dual origins: While our bodies have evolved from the Earth, our souls have involved from Spirit – our evolving physicality arisen out of the Earth and our involving spiritual nature descended from Higher Realms. But, while our bodies are purely temporary, our souls are immortal.

The Cosmic Context of our Earthly Lives

While our lives appear to have begun at 'birth' and seem doomed to end at so-called 'death', **our souls are on an ongoing journey through Time** – a journey which involves many comings and goings, many 'lives', on this planet and other realms within the multi-dimensional cosmic framework of existence.

An essential feature of this underlying cosmic context of our lives are the Laws, the universal **Cosmic Laws of Life**, which govern every aspect of the life and journeying of our souls, especially while here on Earth – such as the **Law of Attraction, Energy Follows Thought, Cause and Effect, As Within So Without,** to name but a few – which are the rules of what may be called the **Game of Life**, and give consequence to every thought, feeling, attitude, intention, gesture and action we express. Their workings in the lives of individuals and also in the context of a relationship are an integral feature of this book. **Awareness of these Laws also changes the way we relate fundamentally**. It marks **the end of blaming** circumstances and others, **the end of helpless victimhood**, and the dawning of the realization of the extent to which **we are the attractors and creators of what we experience in our lives**.

So what do love and relationships have to do with cosmology? Clearly, everything! As Father Matthew Fox puts it, "**Love is always about a cosmology. Lovers exist in a universe, not just in a personal relationship." For the meaning and fulfilment we seek, we need to see the larger picture**. We are not simply earthly beings having occasional spiritual experiences but Cosmic Beings having life-times of earthly experiences. Even as lovers.

Other Significant Cosmic Dimensions

We are gradually awakening to the fact that we are living in a multi-dimensional universe. We are also gradually awakening to the fact that we ourselves are multi-dimensional. Further, we are awaking to the fact that we are not the only intelligences in the Cosmos. Intelligences are at work throughout the Cosmos, both externally and in multi-dimensional realms within it, as well as in Nature all around us. **We are also awakening to our own higher intelligence, that of our Soul or Higher Self**. In our awakening, we are learning to connect, open lines of communication, and even enter into co-creative working relationships with these intelligences, to our great benefit. In *Cosmic Lovers*, all this is featured. These co-creative working relationshiops are the given realities, potentialities and perspectives. For example: The story begins with Elly and Roderic meeting through what they have playfully called a **Cosmic Dating Service**. Unknown to each other, Elly in Holland and Roderic in Ireland each put out **a request to 'the Universe' for their ideal soul mate**, specifying their requirements. They are brought together cosmically in an encounter marked by inexplicable synchronicities.

Elly and Roderic share their experiences of *Angels*, *Archangels*, *Ascended Masters* and other *Beings of Light* who presented themselves. In the chapter, *Cosmic Birthing*, in **going for their Big Dream**, they set up their *Cosmic Team*, consisting of various Beings of Light; and begin the process of working co-creatively, **bringing their dream into reality**.

Relationship as a Spiritual Partnership

Cosmic Lovers explores the concept of '**Relationship as a Spiritual Partnership**' which, while **based on love**, includes **clear intentions of mutual support** on each individual's soul-path of **awakening**, **healing** and **creative unfolding. This gives to a relationship a clear focus, rock-solid foundation and meaningful purpose**.

While there have been occasional treatises on the subject, these have been by psychologists, counsellors or philosophers - in other words, academic and theoretical. While the concept has begun to enter popular imagination (discussed on the Oprah Winfrey Show, for example), *Cosmic Lovers* **is the first book which explores the subject experientially and dramatically**. Gary Zukav writes in his bestseller, *The Seat of the Soul*: "**As the archetype of spiritual partnership is new to the human experience, there are neither codes, conventions, nor guidelines for it.**" Thus, society has been without its dramatic representations to serve as inspirational models. As Meg Ryan lamented recently, "**While there is much mythology about getting together, there is none about staying together.**" *Cosmic Lovers* **provides a much-needed response in the literary birthing of a new myth.**

While luxuriating in an ex-king's castle, Elly expounds on her **Ten Golden Precepts for a Spiritual Partnership,** a summary of insights acquired on her quest.

A Celtic Marriage 'For a Year & a Day'

'A Celtic Marriage for a Year and a Day, **Renewable Annually'** is **an alternative to** the choice of **either 'a traditional marriage** with a commitment for life' **or 'an open-ended relationship** with no commitment'. In rapidly changing times, the promise of a life-long commitment seems unrealistic to many. Besides, the soul being essentially free, it cannot nor should not be bound in perpetuity by any form of agreement which limits it. The moment it feels trapped, it rebels and seeks its freedom. *Cosmic Lovers* proposes and demonstrates a format for couples which **balances the paradoxical needs of both freedom and commitment**: a Celtic Marriage 'for a year and a day', renewable annually. It has many advantages and **can be just as sacred**.

Enlightened Sex

Many women are fed up with mens' limited approach to sex, ruled by his emphasis on orgasm and his rush to achieve it. Entertainingly and informatively, *Cosmic Lovers* features the art of the non-ejaculatory approach, along with other practices, which lead to **prolonged enjoyment, deeper communion** and **greater ecstasy for both**.

A Woman's Journey of Self-Empowerment

While *Cosmic Lovers* is a woman's **quest for her dream lover** and an **ideal relationship**, it is also about her transformational journey. It is about a **woman reclaiming her power** in the profoundest sense, moving out of victimhood and assuming full responsibility as a creator in how she lives and experiences her life. It is also illustrative of a **man's supportive role** in this.

Shattered Dreams of Motherhood & their Creative Transformation

Infertility resulting in childless marriages is a widespread phenomenon, causing great distress to couples. In its concluding chapter, *Cosmic Birthing*, *Cosmic Lovers* shows how **the impulses to**

give birth, mothering and parenting, **can be given joyful and fulfilling expression** in other **powerfully creative and life-enhancing ways**.

Cosmic Birthing: Everyone Should Have a Big Dream
Ideally in a **soul mate relationship** you have a **shared dream**, one which serves something **beyond the relationship**. With a **power-base of love** you can direct it, along with your wisdom, creativity and other resources, outwards into serving the Earth, humanity, or life in general. Elly and Roderic's big dream is to set up a new type of university, *University of Earth & Spirit*, in which they are both passionately engaged, working in a Co-Creative process with Angels, Ascended Masters and other Beings of Light.
Website: www.UniversityofEarthandSpirit.org

General Context
Cosmic Lovers was completed 7 years ago, long before publications such as *The Secret*, *Cosmic Ordering* and *The Laws of Attraction* came sweeping across the planet. It is only in the last few years that soul factors, spiritual dimensions, Cosmic Laws, once considered too far out, even unbelievable, have been entering mass consciousness at such an accelerated rate. What *Cosmic Lovers* does uniquely is illustrate these **vitally relevant spiritual and cosmic concepts** dramatically, doing so **in the context of a romantic relationship in everyday life**.

♥

Love is always about a cosmology.
Lovers exist in a universe, not just in a personal relationship.
– Father Matthew Fox.

278

Ordering Information

Earth Cosmos Press is an independent publishing company linked with University of Earth & Spirit. It has been set up to publish, produce and promote books and other media in attunement with the aims of the University and its various Faculties. To learn more and get involved, visit www.UniversityofEarthandSpirit.org

You can order Cosmic Lovers:
♥ At any good bookshop by quoting the ISBN number.
  ISBN: 978-0-9561042-0-5

Online:
♥ At www.EarthCosmosPress.org

Earth Cosmos Press